D1558987

PAUL AND SENECA

SUPPLEMENTS

TO

NOVUM TESTAMENTUM

VOLUME IV

LEIDEN
E. J. BRILL
1961

PAUL AND SENECA

BY

J. N. SEVENSTER

Professor of New Testament Exegesis and Ancient Christian Literature
in the University of Amsterdam

LEIDEN
E. J. BRILL
1961

PRINTED IN THE NETHERLANDS

CONTENTS

PREFACE

When comparing Paul with Seneca it is possible to include in that comparison all that is known concerning their persons, their lives and their ideas from other writings than their own. Regarding Paul one could use the data in Acts, especially Acts 17. In the case of Seneca the data could be drawn from works of those ancient writers who have written about him more or less fully. In the present work this has been done very little. In writing about the comparison between Paul and Seneca I have almost exclusively drawn from their own writings. I have left aside questions of authenticity but on grounds of the consideration of such questions I have quoted very little from the Pastoral Epistles. Further for the purpose of comparing Paul with Seneca it does not, in my opinion, make much difference if even one or two of Paul's other letters are taken for unauthentic.

The quotations from Paul's letters are taken from the Revised Standard Version of the New Testament, New York 1946; those from Seneca's writings are from the text and translation in the Loeb Classical Library, from the Epistulae Morales (1953 edition), from the Moral Essays I (1958), II (1951) and III (1958).

I am greatly indebted to Mrs H. Meyer for all the work she has given to the translation. She has devoted herself with great accuracy to finding the exact english equivalents of the dutch; a task that was anything but easy.

My assistant, Mr. A. Reisig, has taken great pains in compiling the registers and verifying the quotations from the works of Seneca, for which I am extremely grateful.

May this book contribute to the solution of problems which have really been important from the beginning of our era to the present day.

J. N. SEVENSTER

INTRODUCTION

The subject of this study and even its title are by no means new. During the last hundred years this theme has been dealt with repeatedly, both in books and articles devoted solely to it and within the framework of more ambitious works, or in articles comparing one particular aspect of the writings of Paul and Seneca. Among the former may be mentioned the following in chronological order: A. Fleury, *Saint Paul et Sénèque, Recherches sur les rapports du philosophe avec l'apôtre et sur l'infiltration du christianisme naissant à travers le paganisme*, Paris, 1853, 2 vols.; Charles Aubertin, *Sénèque et Saint Paul. Étude sur les rapports entre le philosophe et l'apôtre*, 1857, ³ 1872; F. C. Baur's lengthy article 'Seneca und Paulus, Das Verhältnis des Stoicismus zum Christentum nach den Schriften Seneca's', *Zeitschrift für wissenschaftliche Theologie*, Vol. I, 1858, p. 161 ff. and p. 441 ff.; Johannes Kreyher, *L. Annaeus Seneca und seine Beziehungen zum Urchristentum*, 1887; J. B. Lightfoot, 'St. Paul and Seneca' in his: *Saint Paul's Epistle to the Philippians*, 1890, ² 1956, pp. 270-333; Kurt Deissner, *Paulus und Seneca*, 1917; H. Preller, *Paulus oder Seneca*, 1929; Th. Schreiner, *Seneca im Gegensatz zu Paulus*, 1936; Pierre Benoit O.P., 'Sénèque et Saint Paul', *Revue biblique*, 1946, pp. 7-35.

Some works in which the theme of the relationship between Paul and Seneca is discussed, either within a wider framework or with reference to some detail or other, are: Bruno Bauer, *Christus und die Cäsaren, Der Ursprung des Christentums aus dem römischen Griechentum*, 1877; J. Leipoldt, 'Christentum und Stoizismus', *Zeitschrift für Kirchengeschichte*, 1906, pp. 129-65; G. A. van den Bergh van Eysinga, *De wereld van het Nieuwe Testament*, 1929; J. de Zwaan, *Jezus, Paulus, Rome*, 1927; E. Stauffer, *Christus und die Caesaren*, 1948; Max Pohlenz, 'Paulus und die Stoa', *Zeitschrift für Neutestamentliche Wissenschaft*, 1949, p. 69 ff. (with special reference to Acts 17); H. Böhlig, 'Das Gewissen bei Seneca und Paulus', *Studien und Kritiken*, 1914, p. 1 ff.; Heinrich Greeven, *Das Hauptproblem der Sozialethik in der neueren Stoa und im Urchristentum*, 1935; G. Boissier, 'Le Christianisme de Sénèque' in *Revue des deux mondes*, 1871, pp. 40-71.

Study of these and other books on this subject reveals the wide

range of opinions existing concerning the relationship between Paul
and Seneca. Even with regard to the question whether they ever met
each other there is a great divergence of opinion. Frequently the
question is answered in the negative, or at the most the possibility
of contact between them is deemed to be slight; however, sometimes
it is thought that they met repeatedly and were even on very intimate
terms. The writer to go furthest in this respect is perhaps Fleury.
He is for instance of the opinion that Paul owed the favourable conclusion of his trial at Rome to the intervention of Seneca. When,
according to Fleury, Paul arrived in Rome he was worried about the
outcome of the trial. And so it must have been a matter of great
importance to him to find as influential a protector for himself as
the empress Poppaea was for the Jews. He could wish for no better
patron than Seneca who then still exercised a great deal of influence
on Nero. Paul's best recommendation to Seneca was the kindness
shown towards him by Gallio in Corinth. Or maybe Seneca sent
for Paul. In any case it was owing to Seneca that Paul's trial went off
so satisfactorily and that the Apostle enjoyed comparative freedom in
Rome. Hence for Fleury it is completely understandable that Paul
should first travel to Spain after his release: what was more natural
than that Seneca should desire to have the Gospel carried to his home-
land (he was, as is known, born at Corduba) by the same eloquent
speaker who had imprinted it upon him; and how easy it must have
been for Seneca to give Paul the necessary support for the journey.
Accordingly Fleury is one of those scholars, who are quite convinced
that there must have been many meetings between Paul and Seneca,
and who are so confident of their ability to reconstruct all sorts of
details concerning this, that they repeatedly overstep the line between
fact and romantic fantasy. Kreyher, too, displays great ingenuity in
finding all sorts of indications of the important part Seneca must
have played in Paul's life. Hence it is to be expected that in the
familiar pericope 2 Thess. 2 : 1-12, for which the number of expla-
nations are legion on account of its obscurity, he sees Nero as the
Antichrist and Seneca as ὁ κατέχων, he who restrains (v. 7).

It goes without saying that if one deems the personal contact to
have been so close, one will readily accept considerable conformity
in their ideas as well. Seneca's ethics and theology are, according to
Fleury, of a decidedly Christian nature, sometimes even with regard
to particular dogmas; Fleury for instance believes that the dogma of
the Trinity is clearly expressed in Seneca. And when Seneca speaks

of the perfect wise man, this would refer to Jesus Christ. In Kreyher the section on 'Biblische Anklänge in Seneca's Schriften' likewise contains a long and impressive list of apparent points of agreement between texts from the Pauline epistles and Seneca's writings.

Quite a different light is thrown on the problem when the historicity of Jesus and Paul is denied, as is done by Bruno Bauer and van den Bergh van Eysinga. In his work *Christus und die Cäsaren* the former already indicates his line of argument in the sub-title: *Der Ursprung des Christentums aus dem römischen Griechentum.* He attempts to prove in this book that Greek thought, as it developed in the Roman empire and in Rome in particular, is one of the most important sources — if not the most important — from which Christianity has arisen. Chronologically, too, it precedes the New Testament, so that, according to Bauer, Seneca was instrumental in shaping the nascent Christianity of the gospels and the epistles of 'Paul'. Van den Bergh van Eysinga also considers the primitive Christian religion as the culmination of a development, as the end of the religious history of antiquity, as the sum total and result obtained by antiquity from all its spiritual labours. Within this framework he, too, describes Seneca's notions as one of the sources behind this development, and he discovers in him many ideas that display a striking similarity to the New Testament, and therefore greatly helped to clear the way for the writings concerning 'Jesus' and 'Paul'. It is of course far easier to believe this if one considers, as these writers do, the epistles of 'Paul' to be a fictitious work written after the death of Seneca. Then any influence of Paul on Seneca is out of the question. In an essay, 'Christelijke denkbeelden bij Seneca', in one of his last books van den Bergh van Eysinga concludes by declaring, 'that the nascent Catholic Church at Rome drew from a wealth of late Stoic traditions which are strongly voiced in Seneca's conception of the world and philosophy of life.' [1] Accordingly when members of the so-called 'Radical School' compare Paul and Seneca, only the latter is looked upon as a historical figure, while 'Paul' is considered as the fictitious centre of a particular pattern of ideas belonging to the second century A.D., and therefore chronologically late enough to have been partly shaped by the writings of Seneca.

Many writers are, however, less rash in drawing parallels between

---

[1] G. A. van den Bergh van Eysinga, *Godsdienstwetenschappelijke Studiën* XX, 1956, pp. 35-64.

Paul and Seneca, especially those who are, to say the least, uncertain whether there was ever any personal contact between them, and who therefore restrict themselves to a comparison of their ideas. F. C. Baur for instance appears here and there to be convinced that the points of agreement between Paul and Seneca are very striking, and sometimes also that the Stoic prepared the soil for Christianity, but he nevertheless considers the difference between them to be very great and accordingly devotes the final chapter of his lengthy article to 'the principal distinction between Stoicism and the Christian philosophy of life', After describing Seneca's thought on the life after death, Baur comments:

> 'Dieses ganze Bild des Zustandes der künftigen Welt hat so viele Berührungspunkte mit der christlichen Anschauungsweise und trifft auch im Ausdruck und in einzelnen Zügen so vielfach mit ihr zusammen, dass die sittlich-religiöse, ächt menschliche Gestalt aller dieser Vorstellungen, nicht wesentlich geschwächt werden kann. Es gibt wenigstens in dem ganzen Gebiet des klassischen Altertums nichts, worin die durch Philosophie geläuterte Ansicht von dem künftigen Leben zu einer reinern und ebendamit dem Christentum verwandteren Form ausgebildet worden wäre.' [1]

Nevertheless it is obvious that he realizes that one of the differences between Stoicism and the Christian eschatology is that the Jewish-Christian notion of the last judgment and all that goes with it is lacking in the writings of the Stoics, even if, as he thinks, some analogies are to be found. And when he writes about the principal difference between the Stoic and Christian conceptions of life, he is quick to note that it is characteristic of the former that man, that is to say the self-satisfied ego of the Stoic philosopher, is the be all and end all; hence man alone, the wise man perfected by virtue, is the absolute subject of this conception of life. [2]

Lightfoot also discovers various similarities between Paul and Seneca, but he treats them very critically and repeatedly points out the difference in background, even when at first glance the texts from both writers seem to display great conformity. There are, indeed, writers who constantly emphasize the contrast between Paul and Seneca, underlining at every opportunity the difference between their points of departure. To this category belong for instance Deissner, de Zwaan, Preller, Greeven and Schreiner, of the aforementioned. When comparing Se-

---

[1] *Zeitschrift für wissenschaftliche Theologie*, 1858, p. 230 f.
[2] Op. cit., pp. 234, 242.

neca's writings with the gospels and Pauline texts, they continually stress what is peculiar to the latter. On matters concerning theology, anthropology and ethics there are according to them profound differences between Paul and Seneca.

May not all these differences of opinion concerning the relationship between Paul and Seneca that have apparently existed for so long, and for that matter still exist, be in themselves sufficient reason to take up this subject again? Moreover, the fact that comparisons, particularly between their ways of thinking, have not always been made on a truly broad basis, has encouraged me to examine this problem afresh. I have thereby taken advantage of the opportunity to consult many new works on both Paul and Seneca. Furthermore, although the present work is primarily intended as a historical study, it will frequently be obvious to the reader that many modern problems are being discussed by implication.

CHAPTER I

THE PERSONAL RELATIONSHIP BETWEEN THE APOSTLE AND THE PHILOSOPHER

In order to arrive at an estimation of the relationship between Paul and Seneca it would be of the greatest value if it were known with certainty — as some scholars quite adamantly maintain — whether they ever met each other personally. Indeed it might almost be expected that they did, or at all events that they were at least aware of each other's existence. Paul was, after all, one of the most outstanding figures in the early Christian Church, the rise of which did not remain a secret in the ancient world. He travelled throughout a great part of the then known world and was most certainly in Rome for a while. Seneca was for a time a very influential man in the Roman empire, both on account of his prominent position in the state and society, and on account of his writings which are among the most important documents for this particular period of Stoic philosophy.

Paul and Seneca lived at approximately the same time. Seneca was born at Corduba in Spain in 4 or 5 B.C., his suicide as a consequence of the conspiracy of Piso took place in A.D. 65. The dates of Paul's birth and death are not known with accuracy, but are bound to have been at about the same time. It is for instance striking that Tacitus records the torturing of the Christians under Nero in *Ann*. 15. 44, and begins 15. 48 with an account of the conspiracy of Piso, to which Seneca whose death is then described in 15. 60 ff. fell victim. Even if Paul were not killed during the persecution, it certainly seems most improbable that Seneca would not have known of the existence of the Christians in general, and of Paul in particular.

They both lived in the same world of the Roman empire. When reading Seneca's writings anyone at home in the epistles of Paul and Acts constantly encounters names also familiar from the New Testament, names which are of course mentioned in passing and in a completely different connection, but which by their presence go to show that both men were living under the same empire at the same time.

A few examples are sufficient to illustrate this. In one of his letters to Lucilius Seneca contemplates, as he does so often, the numerous ways in which man's life is threatened. On earthquakes he writes: 'How often have cities in Asia, how often in Achaia, been laid low by a single shock of earthquake! How many towns in Syria, how many in Macedonia, have been swallowed up! How often has this kind of devastation laid Cyprus in ruins! How often has Paphos collapsed." [1] With this we are in the world of Paul, not only of Acts but also of his epistles: Asia Rom. 16 : 5; 1 Cor. 16 : 19; 2 Cor. 1 : 8; Achaia Rom. 15 : 26; 1 Cor. 16 : 15; 2 Cor. 1 : 1; 9 : 2; 11 : 10; 1 Thess. 1 : 7, 8; Syria Gal. 1 : 21; Macedonia Rom. 15 : 26; 1 Cor. 16 : 5; 2 Cor. 1 : 16; 2 : 13; 7 : 5; 8 : 1; 11 : 9; Phil. 4 : 15; 1 Thess. 1 : 7, 8; 4 : 10; 1 Tim. 1 : 3; Cyprus absent in the epistles but frequently mentioned in Acts: Acts 11 : 19; 13 : 4; 15 : 39; 21 : 3; 27 : 4; Paphos Acts 13 : 6, 13, the earthquake at Philippi in Macedonia Acts 16 : 26 ff. Hence names are frequently encountered in Seneca, which are more or less familiar to us from the Pauline epistles or Acts. [2]

In another letter Seneca gives a lively description of the arrival of an Alexandrian ship at Puteoli. All the townspeople of Puteoli go down to the docks and know exactly which fleet is entering the harbour. Seneca records, not without Stoic complacency, how, while others were hurrying to the water-front, he basked in his own indolence, and although he had important business interests in Egypt, he made absolutely no haste to find out from his agents how his affairs were progressing. [3] That Alexandrian ship which Seneca was watching might well have been the one on which Paul went to Italy, and from which he disembarked at Puteoli (Acts 28 : 11, 13).

Or to take an example from quite a different sphere: both Seneca and Paul were apparently quite familiar with the concept of the *paedagogus*, who was such a well known figure in the Roman world of their time. [4]

Consequently it is evident that Paul and Seneca lived at the same time in the same world. One of the most striking proofs of this is the

---

[1] *Ep.* 91. 9.

[2] E.g. *N.Q.* iii. 25. 4: Macedonia, Galatia, Cappadocia; ib. 25. 5: Sicily, Syria; ib. 25. 11: Lycia; ib. vi. 26. 4: Paphos, Nicopolis, Cyprus, Tyrus; ib. vii. 28. 3: Achaia, Macedonia; *Apocolocyntosis* 1: Appia via.

[3] *Ep.* 77. 1-3.

[4] Seneca: *Ep.* 11. 8-10; 25. 6; 27. 5; 60. 1; 89. 13; 94. 9; *Ira* ii. 21. 6, 9; Paul: 1 Cor. 4 : 15; Gal. 3 : 24, 25; cf. R. Boulogne, *De plaats van de paedagogus in de Romeinse cultuur,* 1951. Boulogne frequently mentions Seneca, but never Paul H. J. Marrou, *Histoire de l'éducation dans l'antiquité,* p. 202, 207, 355, 351.

fact that a number of the same people played a role in both their lives, at least, as far as Paul is concerned, according to Acts. Claudius to whom, after his death Seneca devoted his work *De morte Claudii,* the *Divi Claudii Apocolocyntosis,* is mentioned in Acts 11 : 27-30; 18 : 1-3. Of greater importance is the name of Gallio, Seneca's brother, whose real name was M. Annaeus Novatus, but who had been adopted by his father's friend, the well known rhetorician, Junius Gallio, whose name he assumed. Seneca dedicated several of his essays to his elder brother: *De Ira* (still addressed to Novatus), *De Vita Beata* (addressed to Gallio, hence later than the *De Ira*), and *De Remediis Fortuitorum.* Seneca frequently mentions Gallio. [1] The remark he makes about Gallio's illness in *Ep.* 104.1 is not without significance for the chronology of Paul's life. There Seneca tells how he suddenly had an attack of fever, and immediately decided to leave the city, ordered his carriage and did not even allow his wife Paulina to stop him. He continues: 'for I remembered my master Gallio's words, when he began to develop a fever in Achaia and took ship at once, insisting that the disease was not of the body but of the place.' This comment of Seneca's makes it seem probable that Gallio did not stay in Achaia any longer than was absolutely necessary. Since A.D. 44 Achaia had been a senatorial province. In A.D. 15 Tiberius had changed the senatorial provinces of Macedonia and Achaia into imperial provinces, thus complying with a request from these provinces themselves. But in 44 Claudius had returned them to the senate. So if Gallio did not remain in Achaia for more than the one year that he was obliged to spend there as proconsul of a senatorial province, then one may be fairly confident of giving an accurate date to the well known inscription in Delphi, in which Gallio's name occurs: his year of office then extended from May A.D. 51 until the same month in A.D. 52. [2] With this the date of Acts 18 : 12-17 is also determined.

But now the question arises whether the pericope in Acts concerning Gallio creates the impression of a meeting having taken place between Gallio and Paul. If so, it would, according to some scholars, considerably strengthen the likelihood of a subsequent meeting between Seneca and Paul. It is, however, not very plausible. For Acts 18 : 12-17 seems rather to suggest that Gallio dismissed the matter as rapidly as pos-

---

[1] *N.Q.* iv A, Praef. 9-13; v. 11. 1, *Ep.* 104. 1.

[2] Cf. D. Plooy, *De chronologie van het leven van Paulus,* 1918, pp. 27-48; A. Deissmann, *Paulus,* 1911, p. 159 ff.; A. Sizoo, *Uit de wereld van het Nieuwe Testament,* [2] 1948, pp. 38-42; Kreyher, p. 131 ff., de Zwaan, p. 94 ff.

sible. [1] Hence this pericope certainly does nothing to reinforce the supposition of a personal relationship between Seneca and Paul.

Although no name is mentioned, a text-variant of Acts 28 : 16: 'the *hecatontarch* passed the prisoners over to the *stratopedarch*', has sometimes been taken to refer to a particular person. In this connection conclusions have sometimes been drawn from the use of the singular; for Burrus was the last to be *stratopedarch* or *praefectus praetorio* alone. After his death in A.D. 62 two *praefecti praetorio* were appointed, Faenius Rufus and Ofonius Tigellinus. [2] Now if Paul really were passed on to Burrus, a great friend of Seneca's, whose star rose and fell with that of Burrus, is it not probable that he would have come into contact with Seneca through Burrus? On the other hand it must be admitted that the textual evidence for this addition to Acts 28 : 16 is not strong. None of the old Greek manuscripts give it, and the motive for its insertion is not directly obvious. Perhaps it was an attempt to indicate the official sequence of events, namely that Julius transferred the prisoner to he proper authorities. At all events, if the insertion were original, it is difficult to imagine why it should have been omitted later. Moreover, it is not very likely that Burrus discussed every prisoner who was passed on to him with Seneca. They will have had more important things to talk about. Hence this text-variant is by no means strong enough to serve as a foundation on which to construct a theory concerning close personal contact between Paul and Seneca. [3]

Allusions to Seneca which some scholars have been anxious to point out in other texts from Acts and the Pauline epistles rest purely on hypothesis: Acts 25 : 11; [4] Phil. 1 : 12-17; [5] 4 : 22; [6] 2 Thess. 2 : 1-12; [7] Luke 1 : 3, Acts 1 : 1. [8]

Neither is there anything in Seneca's writings to indicate that he was in any way connected with the Christians. It is in itself remarkable that he never mentions them. Nevertheless some students of the sub-

---

[1] Cf. however Kreyher, p. 131 ff.

[2] Tacitus, *Ann.* 14. 51.

[3] On Acts 28 : 16 cf. Plooy, op. cit., pp. 80-83; Fr. Pierre Benoit O.P., 'Sénèque et Saint Paul', *Revue biblique* 1946 p. 9.

[4] Kreyher, p. 133 ff.: 'Sollte hier keine Hoffnung auf den Bruder Gallio's mitgesprochen haben?'

[5] Kreyher, p. 135 f.

[6] Kreyher, p. 136 f.

[7] Kreyher, p. 139 ff.: ὁ κατέχων = Seneca, p. 144.

[8] Kreyher, p. 150 ff.: Theophilus = Seneca.

ject believe they can demonstrate that he alludes to personal acquaintanceship with Christians. But this, too, is based on only the vaguest of information. When in one of his epistles Seneca speaks of dying and whether it is to be feared or not he refers to death as one, 'whom only yesterday a manservant of mine and a maid-servant did despise!' [1] This has sometimes been taken to mean that Seneca had not long before seen some of his slaves die a gruesome death during the persecution of the Christians under Nero. [2] It goes without saying, however, that such a conclusion is based purely on guess-work.

Accordingly in the writings of the New Testament and in those of Seneca there is nothing to prove that the Apostle and the philosopher ever met each other. Neither is there any historically trustworthy evidence that they were familiar with each other's writings. It is understandable that not everyone has found it easy to resign himself to this, so that various traditions have sprung up concerning meetings said to have taken place between them and a correspondence they are supposed to have carried on with each other. Among the oldest sources of such a tradition may be mentioned the *Passio Petri et Pauli* written by Bishop Linus. In the second book the Passion of Paul is described. We are told of his stay in Rome, his many conflicts with various important people, in particular with Nero, the numerous miracles he performed and finally of his decapitation. Of significance for the present study is what is said here about the emperor Nero's tutor:

> From the house of the emperor all those who believed in the Lord Jesus went out to listen to him [Paul] and the great joy and jubilation of the believers grew daily. But the emperor's tutor also felt such bonds of friendship for him, since he saw in him divine knowledge, that he could scarcely desist from associating with him, so that when he was unable to converse with him personally he availed himself of his sweet and friendly colloquy and of his counsel by means of letters, frequently directed to him and received from him. And so with the succour of the Holy Spirit his doctrine spread and was so appreciated that he had full permission to teach and was most gladly heard by many. For he disputed with the philosophers of the heathens and refuted them, so that many of them too declared themselves persuaded by his teaching, for a certain tutor of the emperor read his writings aloud in the latter's presence and described him to be admirable in every way. [3]

---

[1] *Ep.* 24. 14.

[2] Kreyher, p. 55 f.

[3] The fragments of this text which bear most directly upon our subject read in Latin: 'Sed et institutor imperatoris adeo fuit illi amicitia copulatus, videns in eo divinam scientiam, ut se a colloquio illius temperare vix posset, quominus, si ore ad

It is generally recognized that this is a late work, at least in the form in which it has been passed down to us. A work in which reference is made to the Trinity, to the Holy Sacrament, to formulas from the Nicene Creed, in which the numerous Bible passages correspond at least in part word for word with the text of the Vulgate can only be of a late date. The only question is whether such attributes stem from an ecclesiastical adaptation, and whether the work in its original form is not much older, and of Gnostic origin. There is little that can be said about this with certainty. In any case the indications in this direction are by no means sufficient for us to conclude with Kreyher that this work is evidence of a tradition concerning the relations between Paul and Seneca dating from a time only about fifty years removed from the events recorded. [1] It so obviously bears traces of having been put together with considerable recourse to the imagination and here and there clearly in imitation of other writings that it must be denied all historical value.

The same may be said of the correspondence between Seneca and Paul which has been passed down to us. In the aforementioned work a reference is made to the frequency with which they exchanged letters, while in addition to this two of the fathers of the Church allude to such a correspondence. Augustine who records the reason why Seneca never mentions the Christians, either favourably or otherwise, [2] was evidently familiar with letters from Seneca to the Apostle Paul. In *Ep.* 153. 4 *ad Macedonium* he writes:

> Seneca who lived at the same time as the Apostles and from whom there are a number of letters to the Apostle Paul justly says: "Whosoever hates the wicked, hates all men". [3]

Jerome who commits himself even more openly on this subject refers to a mutual correspondence. In *De viris illustribus* 12 he writes:

> L. Annaeus Seneca from Corduba, disciple of the Stoic Sotion and uncle of the poet Lucan, led a particularly sober life. I should not in-

---

os illum alloqui non valeret, frequentibus datis et acceptis epistolis ipsius dulcedine et amicabili colloquio atque consilio uteretur .... nam et scripta illius quidam magister Caesaris coram illo relegit et in cunctis admirabilem reddidit.'

[1] Kreyher, p. 169.

[2] *De Civ. Dei* 6. 10, 11: 'Christianos tamen, jam tunc Judaeis inimicissimos in neutram partem commemorare ausus est, ne vel laudaret contra suae patriae veterem consuetudinem, vel reprehenderet contra propriam forsitan voluntatem.'

[3] 'Merito ait Seneca, qui temporibus apostolorum fuit, cuius etiam quaedam ad Paulum Apostolum leguntur epistolae: omnes odit, qui malos odit.'

clude him in the list of the Saints, if Paul's letters to Seneca and Seneca's to Paul, which are read by many, did not give me just cause. Although he was Nero's tutor and very powerful in his day, he says in these that he would like to occupy that place among his own people that Paul occupied among the Christians. He was put to death by Nero two years before Peter and Paul received the crown of martyrdom. [1]

This comment of Jerome's pleads for the existence of a correspondence between Paul and Seneca which was very well known in his time — it was read by many —, while he himself was apparently so impressed by the contents that he could number Seneca among the Saints. It is debatable whether we still possess this correspondence to which Augustine and Jerome refer. A correspondence of this sort, containing fourteen letters, has been passed down to us. To be sure, the oldest manuscripts only date from the ninth century, while many are as late as from the twelfth to the fifteenth century. But it is of course possible that these are the same letters to which Jerome refers. Part of the eleventh letter would seem to support this, since it contains a statement of Seneca's which is reminiscent of the only information Jerome gives us concerning the contents of the correspondence. In order to give an impression of the style and subject-matter of these letters the eleventh letter is quoted here in its entirety:

> Seneca to Paul greeting. Greetings, my dearly beloved Paul. If such a great man as you and one who is beloved of God is to be, I do not say joined, but rather closely associated in all respects with me and my name, then your Seneca will be wholly satisfied. Since, therefore, you are the peak and crest of all the most lofty mountains, do you not, then, wish me to rejoice if I am so close to you as to be considered a second like unto you? Therefore do not think that you are unworthy of having your name in the first place in your letters, or else you may seem to be making a test of me rather than praising me, especially since you know that you are a Roman citizen. For I wish that my position were yours in your writings, and that yours were as mine. Farewell, my dearly beloved Paul. Written March 23 in the consulship of Apronianus and Capito. [2]

---

[1] 'Lucius Annaeus Seneca, Cordubensis, Sotionis stoici discipulus, ac patruus Lucani poetae, continentissimae vitae fuit. Quem non ponerem in catalogo sanctorum, nisi me illae epistolae provocaverint, quae leguntur a pluribus, Pauli ad Senecam et Senecae ad Paulum, in quibus, cum esset Neronis magister et illius temporis potentissimus, optare se dicit esse loci apud suos cuius sit Paulus apud christianos. Hic ante biennium quam Petrus et Paulus coronarentur, a Nerone interfectus est.'

[2] The English text of the entire correspondence in M. R. James, *The Apocryphal New Testament*, 1926, pp. 480-4, and in Cl. W. Barlow, *Epistolae Senecae ad Paulum et Pauli ad Senecam <quae vocantur>*, Rome, 1938, pp. 139-49. The text of the eleventh letter is quoted according to Barlow, p. 147 f. See also on this correspondence

One of the fourteen letters is quite sufficient to display this correspondence in all its empty phraseology, its meaningless insignificance and insipid, exaggerated flattery. Indeed, with respect to this aspect of the correspondence there is virtually no difference of opinion, [1] while the language, style and construction are also unanimously considered to be very clumsy. Even Kreyher refuses to attach the slightest historical value to these letters. [2] He denies, however, that this is the correspondence alluded to by Linus, Augustine and Jerome. He is therefore of the opinion that a correspondence between Paul and Seneca, with which both Fathers of the Church were familiar, really has existed, but that this has been lost, while a completely spurious one has been preserved, which he explains as an attempt to reconstruct the letters, the existence of which was known from the writings of the Fathers of the Church. But it can be argued that what Jerome has to say about the contents of the letters is very reminiscent of the end of the eleventh letter from the correspondence known to us: 'For I wish that my position were yours in your writings, and that yours were as mine.' The readings of the Latin text sometimes differ con-

---

Lightfoot, pp. 329-33; Baur, pp. 463-70; Aubertin, pp. 357-444, together with Latin and French text; Kreyher, p. 173 ff.; Alfons Kurfesz, Zum apokryphen Briefwechsel zwischen Seneca und Paulus, *Zeitschrift für Religions- und Geistesgeschichte*, 1949/50, pp. 67-70; the Latin text of the eleventh letter according to Barlow, op. cit., p. 134 f.: 'Seneca Paulo salutem. Ave, mi Paule carissime. Si mihi nominique meo vir tantus et a Deo dilectus omnibus modis, non dico fueris iunctus, sed necessario mixtus, *optime* actum erit de Seneca tuo. Cum sis igitur vertex et altissimorum omnium montium cacumen, non ergo vis laeter, si ita sim tibi proximus ut alter similis tui deputer? Haut itaque te indignum prima facie epistolarum nominandum censeas, ne temptare me quam laudare videaris, quippe cum scias te civem esse Romanum. Nam qui meus tuus apud te locus, qui tuus velim ut meus. Vale mi Paule carissime. Data X Kal. Apr., Aproniano et Capitone consulibus.'

[1] Devastating criticism is, for example, to be found in G. Boissier, 'Le Christianisme de Sénèque' in *Revue des deux mondes*, 1871, pp. 40-71; p. 43: 'Nous possédons encore ces lettres, et l'on s'étonne beaucoup en les lisant qu'elles aient suffi à saint Jérôme pour placer Sénèque „dans la liste des saints". Jamais plus maladroit faussaire n'a fait plus sottement parler d'aussi grands esprits. Dans cette correspondance ridicule, le philosophe et l'apôtre ne font guère qu'échanger des compliments, et, comme les gens qui n'ont rien à se dire, ils sont empressés surtout à se demander l'un à l'autre des nouvelles de leur santé.' Cf. on the other hand, P. Faider, *Études sur Sénèque*, 1921, p. 89 ff.; see also Fr. Pierre Benoit O.P., 'Sénèque et Saint Paul', *Revue biblique*, 1946, pp. 7-35; p. 8: 'Il a fallu toute l'ignorante candeur du Moyen Age pour faire grand cas d'une telle production.' Neither is James particularly enthusiastic in his introduction to the letters: 'The composition is of the poorest kind: only its celebrity induces me to translate it once again.'

[2] Kreyher, p. 178 ff.

siderably. [1] But nevertheless the meaning always more or less concurs with what Jerome says. Kreyher, however, is of the opinion that Jerome's quotation, from the letters known to him, in any case meant something quite different from the somewhat similar passage in the eleventh letter, and that it is more likely that the Church Father has preserved the original text. Accordingly Kreyher, who is completely convinced of the spuriousness of the correspondence we know, clings to the theory that a number of letters have existed which were still known to Augustine and Jerome. Their contents are, however, unknown to us.

Nevertheless it still seems most likely to me that Jerome is here drawing on his imperfect, probably second-hand knowledge of the contents of the correspondence known to us. This would mean that the latter existed in 392. In view of the fact that Lactantius was obviously ignorant of such a correspondance, when in 325 he wrote that Seneca would have been a true Christian if he had had someone to guide him, it is probable that these letters date from between 325 and 392. [2]

Hence it must finally be admitted that there is absolutely no historically reliable information pointing either to personal intimacy or to a correspondence between Paul and Seneca. Of course it cannot be proved with complete certainty that there was never any contact between them, [3] but so long as there is no more substantial evidence than at present, Barker's view remains the only valid one:

> There is of course not the slightest direct evidence in or out of Seneca that the philosopher was a Christian, had any relations with St. Paul, or any dealings with Christians whatever. But the most improbable ideas die hardest .... [4]

And so when comparing the lives and writings of Paul and Seneca with each other, we must look upon them as being those of two people from the same time and the same world, who have had no personal contact with each other and do not consciously discuss each other's

---

[1] See Barlow, op. cit., p. 135.

[2] Lactantius, *Inst. Div.* vi. 24. 13-14: 'Potuit esse verus Dei cultor si quis illi monstrasset.' The tradition relating to the correspondence, its language and style, its date and origins, are dealt with extensively in Barlow, op. cit., pp. 1-112; cf. P. Faider, op. cit., pp. 89-104.

[3] Cf. G. Boissier, op. cit., p. 50 f.: 'Ainsi sur cette première question, qui consiste à se demander si Sénèque a connu saint Paul, on doit dire qu'on ne sait rien de positif, que les arguments donnés des deux côtés ne suffisent pas pour qu'on se prononce, et que, quoiqu'il soit plus probable qu'ils sont demeurés étrangers l'un à l'autre, on ne peut jusqu'à présent rien affirmer avec une entière certitude.'

[4] E. P. Barker, *Seneca's Letters to Lucilius,* Vol. I, 1932, p. xxiii.

ideas in their writings. If they seem to approach each other closely here and there or have ideas in common, this happens unbeknown to both of them.

Before comparing the contents of their writings it may be of value to examine the differences in their characters. Even in antiquity opinions of Seneca's character differed considerably. Dio Cassius had for instance a far less favourable opinion of him than Tacitus. [1] Neither have such differences of opinion disappeared in modern times, although it may be said that he is seldom any longer regarded exclusively as the noblest representative of classical humanism among the Romans, as some classicists of the past have done. [2] Generally speaking more attention is paid to the less pleasant aspects of his character. This, too, can lead to very varied conclusions, since some scholars are inclined to condemn him strongly for his faults, while others do their best to excuse him. The opinion given by Stauffer, when he describes how Seneca became Nero's tutor, is by no means favourable. He writes:

> Der vielerfahrene Meister hat seinen gelehrigen Zögling gewissenhaft in alle Laster eingeweiht und bald sah der junge Prinz ebenso feist und selbstgefällig aus wie der alte Lebemann und Amateurphilosoph. [3]

The implication that it was not Nero who lead Seneca astray but vice versa is worth noting. One's attitude towards this depends on whether one sees Nero, after the first five years of his reign, as a diabolical criminal whom Seneca and Burrus did their utmost to restrain in the face of the pernicious influence of a malevolent court-clique, or whether one sees Seneca as a member of this clique. Kreyher also acknowledges that Seneca was no hero, that he lacked the courage required for martyrdom, the heroic bravery which he himself extolled so highly. However, according to Kreyher this may be excused since:

> diese Tugend ist überhaupt nicht gewöhnlich und pflegt insbesondere mit einer hervorragenden Ausbildung der reflektierenden Intelligenz selten gepaart zu sein. Ein *grosser* Charakter ist Seneca allerdings nicht gewesen, aber ein respektabler, im Grunde seines Herzens gewiss aufrichtig frommer Mensch.

He goes on to draw a parallel with Thomas Cranmer and concludes that despite everything Seneca passed the test which he had imposed

---

[1] Cf. P. Faider, op. cit., p. 19 ff., 74 ff.

[2] J. Stelzenberger also quite naturally refers to Seneca as 'eine edle Persönlichkeit', *Die Beziehungen der frühchristlichen Sittenlehre zur Ethik der Stoa*, 1933, p. 44.

[3] E. Stauffer, *Christus und die Caesaren*, 1948, p. 150.

upon himself in *Ep.* 26. 5 ff. with flying colours. [1] Indeed, according to Tacitus, *Annales* 15. 60 ff., he was in death heroic, even though he did not accept it, until there was no alternative.

Without doubt a great deal of criticism may be levelled at Seneca's character and behaviour. He seems to have had no difficulty in adapting himself to the life ot tne imperial court. And what is even worse, he was shamefully blind to all his pupil Nero's atrocious crimes. He certainly displayed no inclination towards martyrdom in this respect. When Nero indulged in the most unrestrained debauchery and had his adoptive brother Britannicus, his mother Agrippina and his first wife Octavia put to death, Seneca in no way censured this, and probably even partly condoned it, lending himself as he did after the death of Agrippina to writing a justification of this matricide to be presented to the senate. Such behaviour cannot be explained away by the statement, perhaps not entirely incorrect in itself that 'Gesinningstüchtigkeit und Überzeugungstreue von der antiken Denkweise überhaupt wenig begriffen wurde.' [2]

Seneca's whole career displays a certain duplicity which gives rise to grave doubts about his strength of character. The fact that he praises and glorifies firmness of character so highly and in such lyrical terms makes this all the more disconcerting. He extols a sober and ascetic life but nevertheless participates in the dissipated gormandizing of the imperial court. He says that wealth does not make for happiness but he does not refuse the millions bestowed upon him by Nero's favour. He attempts to get rid of them only when he discovers that people of great wealth are not usually long-lived under Nero. Equally repugnant is his attitude towards Claudius whom he indirectly flatters quite blatantly in the *Consolatio ad Polybium,* in the hope of being recalled from banishment on Corsica, whom he eulogizes in a funeral oration, but ridicules mercilessly in his *Apocolocyntosis.* In this satire he gives free rein to his personal hatred.

With respect to literary style he condemns the quibbling of Stoic dialectic but if it suits his purpose he indulges in it himself. He recognizes the artificiality of the rhetoric of his day, but is nevertheless

---

[1] Kreyher, p. 42 f.; cf. P. Faider, op. cit., p. 210, 215 f., 217 f., 263.

[2] Kreyher, p. 42, who justly refers in this connection to Marcus Aurelius's opinion of the Christians. He might well have recalled Epictetus's opinion of the Galileans; cf. however H. Wagenvoort, *L. Annaei Senecae Divi Claudii Apocolocyntosis,* 1936, p. 6; Max Pohlenz, *Die Stoa,* 1948, p. 304; Gérard Walter, *Néron,* 1955, pp. 150-157.

one of the most eminent exponents of it. He frankly acknowledges that the contents of a philosophical work are more important than the form, yet he never lets the opportunity slip by to make a rather weak pun or to drive home a point wittily or supposedly wittily. He sometimes allows what he considers to be a good find to lead him off on to a by-path which does not bring him back to his main line of argument for a considerable time. All this gives much of his work a flashy and capricious quality, while the argumentation is here and there difficult to follow and sometimes pronouncedly weak. [1]

It is precisely this duplicity that makes it possible to lay the emphasis on one particular aspect of his character and conduct. In our day, too, he has no lack of champions, even among those who have an eye for his failings. It is easy, says one of these, to find fault with Seneca and to call him a shilly-shally or even a hypocrite. But it is harder to do him justice in accordance with the conflicting tendencies within him, tendencies which were rooted in his time. For Seneca Nero's favour was a danger. But in any case he used the time when he was at the height of his power to achieve great things for the benefit of mankind. The honesty of his intentions may not be denied him. He derived his inner strength from his Stoic philosophy. Despite the fact that he did not always succeed in reconciling his conduct with Stoic doctrine, he nevertheless died a Stoic death. And his death entitled him to say to his friends that the finest inheritance that he was leaving them was his life. [2] Another writer does not wish to deny him, despite all his duplicity, praise for having seriously wrestled with the problems of life as it is lived, for having endeavoured to lead a noble and pious life and having made every effort to make his conduct and philosophy one. [3] Attempts to dig deeper claim to reveal that all that is detestable in Seneca stems from a particular type of neurosis. Then there is not much left that may be charged against him. Who would blame him for being ill? It is after all a fact:

> that most neurotics are superficially detestable either to a small or a large audience, but that the causes are preponderously beyond their control, the problem more clinical than moral and detestation irrelevant ... Ab-

---

[1] Seneca's style was criticized early, cf. E. Vernon Arnold, *Roman Stoicism*, ²1958, p. 114 f.: Alfred Gercke, *Seneca-Studien*, 1895, p. 138, 151; at the end of his book *Leib und Seele in der Sprache Senecas*, 1924, p. 150 f. Fritz Husner defends Seneca's style, although he understands the objections made to it.

[2] M. Pohlenz, op. cit., p. 327; cf. E. Vernon Arnold, op. cit., p. 113.

[3] H. Preisker, *Neutestamentliche Zeitgeschichte*, 1937, p. 54.

normal his character is; not devoid of a disfigured greatness in its
mutilation, and one which it is more profitable to understand than to
condemn unconditionally. [1]

A psychological approach of this kind virtually precludes moral judgment, whether favourable or not, and the only course open is to
understand the diseased condition which inevitably gives rise to a
certain pattern of behaviour. Even if we do not go so far in relieving
Seneca of all moral responsibility, it is still not necessary to condemn
him unconditionally. For it must be admitted that he was in many
ways in no easy position, that his circumstances in life made things
particularly difficult for such an unheroic nature as his, and that he
most certainly was not lacking in good intentions. But it is impossible
to condone various aspects of his character; his cowardice, his servile
and self-interested flattery of Claudius and Polybius, his acquiescence,
to say the least, to outrages he saw being committed around him, are
all inexcusable, even if we consider them to be understandable in
view of the complexity of his character.

If, side by side with this, we attempt to form a clear picture of
Paul's character, it soon becomes obvious that it is difficult to make
a comparison. The sources at our disposal for describing the characters
of these two men are entirely different from each other. We do not,
it is true, possess a first-hand, detailed character description of Seneca,
but Roman historians have nevertheless given so much more or less
first-hand information that it is possible to draw valuable conclusions
from this. Moreover Seneca's own writings, which are far more numerous than Paul's, display, on account of the nature of their contents,
very much more of their writer's character than Paul's letters which
after all deal with matters of importance to churches or persons with
whom he had very specific ties. Their relationship has its roots in
their common purpose. Likewise in the Acts of the Apostles not the
slightest attempt is made to describe Paul as a personality; no interest
is shown here in his character as such. Naturally this does not mean
that it is impossible to make any inferences concerning Paul's character
from such writings. It may perhaps be concluded from Acts 15 : 36-41
that Paul was rather excitable and domineering. Acts 16 : 1-3 and
21 : 17-26 could testify to his willingness to compromise, which might
also be said to lie beneath his own words in 1 Cor. 9 : 19-23. Was
Paul rather timid by nature and therefore reticent in the presence of

---

[1] E. P. Barker in *The Oxford Classical Dictionary*, 1950, p. 828.

the Corinthians, only daring to speak boldly at a distance? His opponents seem to have accused him of this (1 Cor. 2 : 1-5; 2 Cor. 10 : 1,
2). Was he someone who was quick to feel that his own position was
being undermined and who therefore sought compensation in an exaggerated sense of his own importance (Gal. 1 : 8, 9), in violent abuse,
not shunning strong language (Phil. 3 : 2 ff., 18, 19; 1 Thess. 2 : 14 f.;
2 Cor. 10 ff.), and making use of cutting irony and virulent word-play
against adversaries who would not recognize his authority (Gal. 5 : 12;
Phil. 3 : 2)?

Indeed, conclusions concerning Paul's character have frequently been
drawn from numerous texts in Acts and the Pauline epistles. Klausner
for instance is of the opinion that Paul struggled with his overweening
arrogance and his desire for the highest authority and absolute spiritual
power among the Apostles and the Christian churches, 'aber er wird
nicht immer Herr über sich.' A quotation from Gal. 1 : 8, 9 is introduced by Klausner as follows: 'Mit schäumender Wut ohne Zurück-
haltung und Hemmung, bricht er in den Ruf aus: ...' [1] By making
Paul's words reflect his character thus, we are neglecting to take them
seriously in the way the Apostle intended them and to do justice to the
purport of such words. According to Paul himself there is no question
of personal arrogance or authoritarian conduct in Gal. 1 : 8, 9. It is in
no way his purpose to assert his personal authority; what he is endeavouring to do is to establish a place for himself as an Apostle and hence
a place for the Gospel which he preaches. In 1 Cor. 9 : 22 f. this
apparently authoritarian conduct is made understandable. With this behind him he can both write ruthlessly sharp and violent words and use
phrases and images with which he fervently endeavours to come close to
his churches (Gal. 4 : 19, 20; 1 Cor. 4 : 14, 15; 2 Cor. 6 : 11-13).
Therefore anything he says about himself can only be considered within
the framework of what he feels himself called upon to write to the
churches by reason of his apostolic mission and the Gospel. We sometimes tend to read Gal. 1 and 2, 2 Cor. 11 : 23 ff. primarily from
biographical interest, but Paul certainly does not offer these chronological data and his account of his experiences as a contribution to an autobiography, still less did he write it down because he found himself of
absorbing interest. He only brings himself to record something about
himself and his experiences — and this with great reluctance in 2 Cor.

---

[1] Joseph Klausner, *Von Jesus zu Paulus*, 1950, p. 540; cf. A. Chorus, *De vier evan-
gelisten als menselijke typen*, n.d., p. 95 f.

11 : 23 ff. — because the legitimacy and independence of his apostolate are at stake. Therefore by drawing biographical and psychological conclusions from such passages in his letters, we are transposing them into quite a new key.

The difference between Paul and Seneca in this respect may well be illustrated by the way in which they write about their bodily disorders. Since youth Seneca was evidently ill a great deal and, if we may believe him, suffered from various complaints: chronic catarrh, frequently very violent, [1] fevers, [2] asthma, which troubled him all his life, [3] fainting-fiths, [4] and gout. [5] He often refers to his health, and not without an air of importance, firmly convinced as he is that his readers will appreciate both his lengthy speculations on this topic and the moral exhortations which he brings to bear upon it. When questioned about the nature of his illness he feels himself called to answer:

> ... no kind is unknown to me .... I have passed through all the ills and dangers of the flesh; but nothing seems to me more troublesome than this [asthma] .... Yet in the midst of my difficult breathing I never ceased to rest secure in cheerful and brave thoughts.

And this is a reason for him to hold one of his many discourses on death and to assert that it should not be feared. [6]

A letter entirely devoted to the endurance of illness is *Ep.* 78. Seneca starts by commenting on what Lucilius has apparently written to him about suffering from continual catarrh and fevers. He has read this with regret, particularly since he knows all too well what it is like, 'because I have experienced this sort of illness myself'. At first his youth enabled him to make light of these complaints, 'but I finally succumbed, and arrived at such a state that I could do nothing but snuffle, reduced as I was to the extremity of thinness.' Then he felt so miserable that he often wished to make an end to his life. Only the thought of the suffering that he would cause his old father restrained him. 'And so I commanded myself to live. For sometimes it is an act of bravery even to live.' [7] And then he sets down a detailed account of the thoughts

---

[1] *Ep.* 78. 1; *N.Q.* vi. 2. 5.

[2] *Ep.* 78. 1; 104. 1.

[3] *Ep.* 54. 1; cf. *Helv.* 19. 2: *per longum tempus aeger.*

[4] *Ep.* 77. 9; cf. G. Boissier in his article 'Le Christianisme de Sénèque' in the *Revue des deux mondes,* 1871, p. 65: 'Ce jeune homme pâle et maladif, qui fut mourant dès sa naissance....'

[5] *V.B.* 17. 4.

[6] *Ep.* 54; cf. *Ep.* 55. 2; 65. 1.

[7] *Ep.* 78. 1, 2.

that had strengthened him at that time, and takes the opportunity to
give Luculius advice as to how can endure illness:

> One can endure the suffering which disease entails, if one has come
> to regard its results with scorn .... Everything depends on opinion ....
> It is according to opinion that we suffer. A man is as wretched as he
> has convinced himself that he is. 1

If a man is in pain, it can help him:

> to turn the mind aside to thoughts of other things and thus to depart
> from pain. Call to mind what honourable or brave deeds you have done;
> consider the good side of your own life. Run over in your memory
> those things which you have particularly admired. Then think of all
> the brave men who have conquered pain ... 2

Hence it is not only in times of war that a man can show his courage:

> There is, I assure you, a place for virtue even upon a bed of sickness ....
> You have something to do: wrestle bravely with disease. If it shall
> compel you to nothing, beguile you to nothing, it is a notable example
> that you display. 3

And then he proceeds to argue that there is no need to fear death,
so long as one has thoroughly and heroically attuned one's mind to it.
'That which has been long expected comes more gently.' 4

Hence sickness leads Seneca to focus his attention on the sick man
and his heroic endurance of pain, and to use this as a basis for moral
exhortations. He probably closely studied the symptoms of his troubles
and ailments in the medical works of his day, 5 and his thoughts
repeatedly move towards his illnesses. Although he does not conspi-
cuously make himself the centre of interest, he is sometimes not without
a sense of his own importance as a man greatly versed in suffering, and
it is on this basis that he lays down a Stoic line of conduct for the courageous man.

It is in quite a different way and in quite a different connection that
Paul writes about his ill-health in Gal. 4 : 13-15 and 2 Cor. 12 : 7-10.

The first thing that strikes us is that there is really so little definite
information on the nature of Paul's complaint. Rather widely divergent
suppositions are all we have to go on. It is still even doubted by some

---

1 *Ep.* 78. 12, 13.
2 *Ep.* 78. 18.
3 *Ep.* 78. 21; cf. *Ep.* 67. 4: 'Nor am I so mad as to crave illness; but if I must
suffer illness, I shall desire that I may do nothing which shows lack of restraint, and
nothing that is unmanly. The conclusion is, not that hardships are desirable, but that
virtue is desirable, which enables us patiently to endure hardships.'
4 *Ep.* 78. 29.
5 *Ira* iii. 10. 4: *prodest morbum suum nosse...*

scholars whether Paul is in fact writing about an illness. Many early
Christian commentators, in whose footsteps some modern scholars follow, are of the belief that in Gal. 4 : 13 Paul is alluding to bodily
injuries received in the mission field. Likewise 2 Cor. 12 : 7-10 is
sometimes taken to refer to suffering undergone as a result of persecution. The σκόλοψ τῇ σαρκί has also been interpreted as something
in the nature of temptations to impurity, partly perhaps as a consequence of the translation *stimulus carnis*. While in quite recent years one
commentator has advocated an entirely different solution: by the thorn
in the flesh Paul means his failure to win the Jews over to the
Gospel. [1] Without entering into a detailed discussion of the many studies, both theological and medical , that have been devoted to this
subject, I nevertheless wish to say that I do not find these solutions
very satisfactory and consider it plausible that Paul is alluding to some
complaint in both pericopes. The nature of the complaint will never be
determined with absolute certainty; neither can a conclusive answer be
given to the question whether the complaint of 2 Cor. 12 is the same
as that of Gal. 4. [2] But in connection with the present subject it is unnecessary to wait for definite answers; what is of significance here is the
fact that uncertainty exists. For this indicates how little weight the
Apostle attached to his complaints as such and of what slight interest
he deemed them to be to his readers. He only mentions them when
they have some bearing on a subject entirely unrelated to autobiography
or morals. In Gal. 4 he wishes to remind his readers that the relationship between them as Christian communities and him as an Apostle
was once better and much closer than it is now. What were they
not glad to put up with from him then! What would they not have
done for him in those days of sickness! They received him as a mes-
senger of God, as Christ Jesus. In 2 Cor. 12 he is indirectly provoked
into referring to his sickness by his opponents' violent and contemp-

---

[1] This theory is to be found in an article by Ph. H. Menoud, 'L'écharde et l'ange
satanique (2 Cor. 12, 7)' in *Studia Paulina in honorem Johannis de Zwaan septuage-
narii*, 1953, pp. 163-71.

[2] For the study of these exegetical problems the works devoted to this subject by
Windisch and Allo are still of great value: H. Windisch, *Der zweite Korintherbrief*,
1924, pp. 385-8; E. B. Allo, *Seconde Épître aux Corinthiens*, 1937, pp. 313-23.
This also includes an extensive reference list of both theological and medical works.
Among the articles since published may be mentioned alongside the above-cited
article by Menoud in the same volume: H. Clavier, 'La santé de l'apôtre Paul', pp.
66-82. Further: *Th. W.* III, p. 820 f., p. 204, and iv, p. 1090. From the medical
angle: J. E. Schulte, 'De apostel Paulus en zijn „ziekte(n)"' in *Ned. T.T.* xi,
1956-7, pp. 110-18; H. W. M. de Jong, *Demonische ziekten in Babylon en bijbel*,
1959, p. 124 ff.

tuous remarks about his apostolate and consequently about him personally. With great reluctance Paul shows that he, too, can boast. The attitude of his opponents forces him to take this step. Boasting serves no purpose, but if it is unavoidable, then he will go on to visions and revelations of the Lord. If he wishes to boast, he shall not do so as a fool, for he will speak the truth. But in order that he might not become too elated, he has been given a thorn in the flesh. Hence it may be seen that it is only within the framework of the impassioned discussion pertaining to his apostolate that his sickness is alluded to. Without dwelling on the complaint itself, or trying to make himself important and interesting he records that he thrice prayed to God that the thorn in his flesh, that angel of Satan, might leave him. This complaint is only significant in connection with the prayers and answers to which it gives rise. Consequently it may well be said that if Paul had not had troublesome opponents in Galatia and Corinth we would never have heard of his ill-health.

This automatically brings us to the difference in character between the sources upon which we have to rely when comparing Seneca and Paul. For the fact that they wrote for widely divergent purposes must constantly be borne in mind. Seneca's writings are those of a conscious artist, they are intentionally literary. This not only applies to those writings which are obviously presented as literary works, such as his tragedies, but also to the letters which for form's sake are addressed to one particular person. His letters to Lucilius, too, are 'really nothing but short philosophical treatises'. [1] It is not only in his incorrectly named twelve dialogues that certain subjects are discussed from the point of view of Stoic doctrine and philosophy of life, but in his letters, too, a variety of moral reflections are offered, even though sometimes under the guise of personal and practical problems. The letters to Lucilius are obviously literary and intended for a wider circle of readers. They contain for example an extensive discourse on drunkenness (*Ep.* 83. 9-27), on the simplicity of olden days (*Ep.* 86. 1 ff.), on liberal studies (*Ep.* 88), on content and style in writing (*Ep.* 100), on the relationship between the philosopher and his pupils (*Ep.* 108), on degenerate literary style (*Ep.* 114), on those who turn the night into day (*Ep.* 122).

Accordingly Seneca's writings are all typically literary products.

---

[1] H. Wagenvoort, *Varia Vita*, 1927, p. 112, cf. W. von Loewenich, *Paulus, Sein Leben und Werk*, 1949, p. 13; B. A. van Proosdij, *Seneca als moralist*, ii, [5]1961, p. 2.

This definitely does not hold for Paul's letters which have quite a distinctive character of their own. Firstly it must be remembered that these are letters written by the Apostle to particular churches and particular persons on particular occasions. They never set out to be systematically coherent reflections on particular subjects. They were written in consequence of quite definite situations and specific relationships. And we, who read these letters, are like curious people eavesdropping on a telephone-conversation, who by listening very carefully to what is said at one end of the line can guess some, but certainly not all, that is said at the other end. The churches ask Paul all sorts of questions and do not wait in vain for an answer. Or Paul himself takes the initiative because of various difficulties and abuses that have reached his ears. Naturally we are doing an injustice to such letters if we simply regard them as a series of theological or moral treatises, from which disconnected utterances may be collected arbitrarily, for the purpose of constructing with them a theological or ethical system. In order to do Paul justice close attention must often be paid to the context in which he writes certain words, to whom they are addressed, why he writes them, which front he is facing, and the aim he has in mind in a particular passage of a letter.

Hence when assembling from Paul's writings all his thoughts on a particular 'subject' we must never forget that we are dealing with letters written under the stress of certain circumstances, while it must also be borne in mind that they are letters written by an *Apostle* to *churches* or to persons to whom he gives certain directions to be followed in the life of the churches. Consequently Paul's letters are never 'personal', in the everyday sense of the word, not even when they deal with specific situations and relationships. Any personal information that they may happen to contain, is mentioned not because it is important in itself, but because it is functional to the message which Paul, 'a servant of Jesus Christ called to be an apostle, set apart for the gospel of God' (Rom. 1 :: 1) is elected to preach to a church.

To sum up: when drawing on the Pauline epistles in order to form a picture of Paul's thoughts on a particular subject it must first be remembered that they are not works of literature, not doctrinal or ethical discourses, but *letters* written to certain churches and dealing with topical situations; secondly, that they are letters from an Apostle of Jesus Christ to churches which he knows to be called into fellowship with the Lord (1 Cor. 1 : 9), and which it is his task at all times and in all situations to bring to decisions concerning the Lord.

Despite the fact that it is not feasible to derive any sort of water-tight system from these letters, it is nevertheless remarkable how successful Paul is in casting the light of his message of the Gospel upon the various concrete problems of the churches, so that we are lucidly, but imperceptibly as it were, informed of the burden of his preachings, while his thoughts on certain 'subjects' by no means remain a secret to us. However, these thoughts must not be removed from their context but be seen against the background of the Gospel, the preaching of which is the Apostle's first, and even sole purpose.

It goes without saying that when comparing these writers the fact that their works are quite different in nature must constantly be borne in mind. Even their motives for writing are different: the philosopher wants his writings to be wise lessons in living for everyone; the Apostle of Jesus Christ is full of the Gospel which he wishes to preach, both by word of mouth and in writing, to the churches which have been called to be saints in te world.

When making comparisons, we are nearly always in danger of being unjust to one or both parties. The mind involuntarily concentrates most on those aspects which are or seem comparable, either by virtue of their similarity or their dissimilarity. This can sometimes lead to an idea or notion being unwittingly given a meaning which it did not have within the framework of the author's complete works. Isolation can easily result in distortion. If the writers with whom we are concerned were able to study a detailed comparison of their writings, they might well feel wronged, and consider that justice had not been done to them, because all their individual ideas, divorced from their context, no longer form a whole that corresponds with their intentions. For if the parts do not occupy their original position in a particular writer's pattern of ideas, then it is no longer possible to see the whole in the sum of the parts. Even if, when reading a writer's works first and foremost with a view to comparing them with those of another writer, we cannot wholly prevent ourselves from concentrating too much on this comparison, nevertheless we can at the same time bear in mind the danger of losing sight of both writers' intentions as a whole. A comparison between Paul and Seneca will only do justice to both of them, and consequently will only be meaningful, if it not only clearly reveals the various separate aspects of their relationship to each other, but also defines what is characteristic of each of them.

CHAPTER TWO

GOD

It has been maintained that the Pauline epistles are dominated by antithetic rhythm. [1] Even on cursory reading it is indeed striking how often Paul uses contrast as a device, when he wants to bring home the essential truths of the Gospel of Jesus Christ to his churches. Such writing in antitheses is in Paul's case not based on a desire to be a literary stylist. He did not consciously submit himself to a rigid form; on the contrary his style is the consequence of his complete and utter involvement in the message of the Gospel. Accordingly the surge of antithetic rhythm on the surface is a sign of turbulent depths. Pauline antithesis occurs again and again in a wealth of variations. [2] All these antitheses may eventually be traced back to that one great one which entered the world and man's life, when God, when the time had fully come, sent forth his Son (Gal. 4 : 4). This was the turning-point in history, because of this there will always be a contrast between 'before' and 'after'. That 'after' is full of peace, mercy, forgiveness, redemption, because God 'was in Christ reconciling the world to himself' (2 Cor. 5 : 19). That salvation is now preached to the whole world. And where it is offered, man may accept it in faith. Therefore in his letters Paul never speaks of life, mankind, the world, and the relationship between people in general, but always of the fundamental contrast between the life without Christ and the life in Christ. For this is the only really significant contrast. It determines between peace and discord, light and dark, being with or without hope (Eph. 2 : 12; 1 Thess. 4 : 13), life and death. Paul not only sees a sharp contrast between 'before' and 'after' in his own life, but, according to him, everyone who believes in God's salvation, which appeared in history once and for always, a church which is convinced, as is the Apostle himself, that God who began a good work in them, will bring it to completion at the day of Jesus Christ (Phil. 1 : 6), will recognize this contrast. This is why Paul could take it for granted that an al-

---

[1] Joh. Weiss, *Das Urchristentum,* 1917, p. 312.
[2] Examples may be found in e.g. Rom. 14 : 7-9; 1 Cor. 12 : 3; 1 Cor. 15 : 42 f.; 2 Cor. 4 : 16-18; Gal. 6 : 7, 8.

lusion to the radical change which had taken place in the lives of the churches would be fully comprehended. [1] The borderline between old and new is wholly determined by the history of salvation in Christ. It is in history that God decisively revealed His salvation and will at one time bring it to completion. God is the holy, majestic God who reigns over mankind and the world according to His will for salvation in history, the centre of which is the revelation in Christ. The only really important turning-points are to be found in the sequence of God's great deeds within the framework of His previously concealed plan of salvation, which He has begun, which has been revealed in Christ, and which moves on towards its completion.

If this is the basic assumption it goes without saying that all terms referring to time such as πότε, νυνί, ἐγγύς, ἡμέρα, νύξ ὥρα, χρόνοι, καιροί acquire deep eschatological significance, that time and history assume a central position in Paul's mind. [2] This is one of the underlying differences in approach between him and Seneca. For Seneca history is never of decisive importance to his philosophical reflections or moral exhortations. Such a refusal to attribute any essential meaning to history is indeed no exception in the ancient world. It forms one of the basic differences not only between Paul and Seneca, but also between the whole of the New Testament and the unevangelized world, with the exception of course of Judaism. In that world philosophical deliberations are not centred on history or the transitoriness of things, but on the permanent aspect of things. The sequence of events in time is considered of secondary importance. It has no metaphysical significance. Even in the study of history there is a desire to pursue the unchanging, the immutable; the search is for laws which always remain themselves in the constantly recurring chain of world events. There is no question of seeing in that unique historic occurrence something that could be decisive for the whole world and every human being. Such a unique and special event cannot acquire significance until it is absorbed into the universality and totality of the cosmos.

Many scholars, both theologians and classicists, have recognized the contrast between Christianity and the view of history taken by the

---

[1] Cf. e.g. Eph. 2 : 11-13; 5 : 8; Rom. 5 : 10 f.; 11 : 30 f.

[2] Floyd V. Filson, *The New Testament Against Its Environment*, 1950, p. 51: 'The fact that God has revealed himself in a definite thread of history and that the Gospel is therefore a story carries with it the essential point that time is real to the New Testament mind.'

ancient world. [1] There is only a difference of opinion concerning
the question whether or not philosophy of history was practised in
antiquity. Bultmann, for example, is able to say that it is characteristic of the Greek mind, 'dass die Geschichte nicht als eigenständige
Sphäre neben der Welt als Natur zum Gegenstand der Reflexion
geworden ist, dass keine Geschichtsphilosophie entstand.' [2] According
to him the only time it might be said that an attempt is made to
contemplate history in this way is when Herodotus observes that in
history God's punishment always follows upon human *hubris*. But in
Thucydides, for instance,

> wird die Geschichte der gleichen rationalen Betrachtung unterworfen,
> wie sie für die griechische Weltbetrachtung charakteristisch ist .... so
> ist die geschichtliche Bewegung nicht anders als die Bewegung des
> kosmischen Geschehens verstanden worden, in dem in allem Wechsel
> immer das Gleiche geschieht. Geschichtliche Erkenntnis bemüht sich in
> der Geschichte das Gleiche, das ewig Gültige, das Exemplarische zu
> sehen. [3]

On the other hand the classicist Wilhelm Nestle, in one of his books,
devotes an entire essay to Greek philosophy of history. [4] In this he
begins by opposing those who deny the existence of anything in the
nature of Greek philosophy of history. He himself is quite sure of
its existence. He says that although of course the Greeks had not
built up a compact system of philosophy of history as for example
Hegel, nevertheless they produced a considerable number of valuable

---

[1] E.g. E. Stauffer, *Die Theologie des Neuen Testaments,* 1945, p. 60: 'Dem
Griechentum ist die Geschichte nur eine Erscheinung innerhalb des Kosmos. Dem
Urchristentum dagegen ist der Kosmos nur eine Erscheinung innerhalb der Geschichte.
Der Grieche lauscht auf die Harmonie der Sphären. Die Männer des N.T. horchen
auf den Schritt der Allgeschichte'; W. Nestle, *Griechische Weltanschauung in ihrer
Bedeutung für die Gegenwart,* 1946, p. 356, where he describes the Stoic view of
history: '... auch der Mensch und die Menschheit ist ein Stück Natur, das mit
seinem Leben, seinem Werden und Vergehen dem Kosmos eingegliedert ist. Ist
dieses im Verhältnis zum Ganzen auch noch so winzig und mag auch jedes Einzel-
wesen mit allen seinen Erlebnissen in dem ewigen Kreislauf der Weltperioden schon
unendlich oft dagewesen sein und ebenso oft wiederkehren: alles das verläuft doch
gesetzmässig, d.h. auch die Geschichte ist ein Stück Naturverlauf gemäss der Schick-
salsnotwendigkeit (Heimarmene)'; Liechtenhan refers to the 'Geschichtslosigkeit des
stoischen Denkens', R. Liechtenhan, 'Die Überwindung des Leides bei Paulus und in
der zeitgenössischen Stoa'. *Zeitschrift für Theologie und Kirche,* N.F. Vol. 3, 1922,
p. 397; cf. also W. Windelband, *Lehrbuch der Geschichte der Philosophie,* [8]1919,
pp. 212-14; R. Bultmann, *Glauben und Verstehen,* Vol. III, 1960, p. 59.
[2] R. Bultmann, *Das Urchristentum im Rahmen der antiken Religionen,* 1949, p. 146.
[3] Ib., p. 147; cf. id., *Glauben und Verstehen,* Vol. III, 1960, p. 155 f.
[4] W. Nestle, op. cit., pp. 334-72.

ideas on the philosophy of history. Nestle wishes to use the term in its widest sense: 'Wir fassen also hier Geschichtsphilosophie im weitesten Sinne als das Nachdenken über geschichtliche Vorgänge und über eignes geschichtliches Erleben.' [1] He then goes on to give a long list of examples. And on the strength of these he is able to conclude that all the great Greek historians, whose example was followed by many lesser ones, 'die Geschichte denkend betrachtet haben.' [2] The problem is, however, whether the mere consideration of historical events, the thoughtful contemplation of history, may be called a philosophy of history. In my opinion such thought is too greatly restricted to a number of disconnected, often only casually recorded ideas to warrant this. Certain ancient historians do sometimes recognize a number of fixed laws. They are then always clearly bent on incorporating all that is historically unique into the universal, by dint of which their view of history is indeed constantly being more or less adjusted to a rational view of the world, so that what Nestle calls 'die geschichtsphilosophischen Gedanken' [3] is precisely what alienates the ancient historians from, rather than drawing them closer to, the New Testament conception of the centrality of history. A survey such as Nestle gives of Greek historical thought only accentuates the fact that there is not the slightest trace of the notion of a continuous, unbroken history of salvation to be found in any of the ancient writers on history. The theme of history in this sense is indeed foreign to all Greek philosophers in whose works otherwise almost all the themes of later philosophy are stated. [4]

What has here been said of the Greek and Roman view of history in general, applies also to Seneca. He, too, has no notion of the essential part played by history in salvation. This does not mean that he knows no history or shows no interest in it. On the contrary, many historical events and persons are mentioned in his writings. He fre-

---

[1] Ib., p. 335.
[2] Ib., p. 372.
[3] Ib., p. 335.
[4] E. Brunner, *Dogmatik* II, 1950, p. 233; cf. O. Cullmann, *Christus und die Zeit*, 1946, p.45; a most important article on this subject has been written by the Dutch classicist, W. den Boer, 'Grieks-Romeinse geschiedschrijving (in haar verhouding tot het bijbelse en moderne historische denken)' in *Ned. T.T.* iv, 1949-50, pp. 305-27; p. 319: 'For them too [the historians of antiquity] history was in the first place a repetition of the same; therefore it may be said with equal justification: history repeats itself'; p. 326: 'The term "God of history" is absolutely un-Greek.' This article is also to be found in: W. den Boer, *Tussen kade en schip*, 1957, pp. 98-130.

quently refers to Cato for example. But he does this, as Bultmann points out, with the purpose of illustrating the invariability, the eternal validity, the exemplariness to be found in history. Tacitus expresses this as follows:

> I shall not deem it beneath my dignity to record these and similar stories from olden times, whenever place and circumstances demand an example of noble conduct or solace for present disasters. [1]

Time and again Seneca, too, makes use of history in this way: he holds up historical figures to his contemporaries as examples of noble conduct, of courageously borne suffering, of how to live and die heroically, of the imperturbability of wise men, who refuse to allow their inner equilibrium to be shaken by any events whatsoever. By means of history he demonstrates that human life is for ever subject to certain fixed laws. History becomes a moral reference book, which can of course be compiled by making an arbitrary choice from historical events. The sequence of happenings is of no importance. The unique events of history are of no interest to Seneca. [2]

This, however, does not mean that Seneca has nothing to say about time; he often alludes to the continual passing of time, but for the most part in reflections of a general nature, resigned and consolatory in tone. How ephemeral is a human life, how insignificant is everything human, when seen in the light of the rapid passing of time. This is his subject in his consolatory treatise for Marcia who lost a son still in the prime of life. Certainly, Seneca admits, he died, humanly speaking, prematurely and before his time. But is that really such a great disaster? Suppose he had lived to the greatest age that man can attain here on earth, what difference would that make? We are all short-lived and we all soon have to relinquish our places to others. We are nothing but guests at an inn:

> "Our" life do I say, when Time hurries it on with such incredible swiftness? Count the centuries of cities; you will see how even those that boast of their great age have not existed long. All things human are short-lived and perishable, and fill no part at all of infinite time. The earth with its cities and peoples, its rivers and the girdle of the sea, if measured by the universe, we may count a mere dot; our life, if compared with all time, is relatively even less than a dot; for the com-

---

[1] Tacitus, *Hist.* iii. 51. 2; cf. E. Vernon Arnold, op cit., p. 297.

[2] Cf. Jean Laloup, *Bible et Classicisme*, 1958, p. 116: 'dans la tradition classique, l'homme et sa condition éternelle sont représentés par des histoires; dans la Bible, une véritable histoire progresse'; see also Georges Pire, *Stoïcisme et Pédagogie*, 1958, p. 120, 124 f.

pass of eternity is greater than that of the world, since the world renews itself over and over within the bounds of time . . . . when you turn your thought upon eternal time, if you compare the space that you discover a man has lived with the space that he has not lived, not a whit of difference will you find between the shortest and the longest life. 1

Elsewhere he makes another similar statement about those who die young:

> Place before your mind's eye the vast spread of time's abyss, and consider the universe; and then contrast our so-called human life with infinity: you will then see how scant is that for which we pray and which we seek to lengthen. 2

In short: why should we mourn the brevity of one individual human life, when even the longest lifetime is as nothing, when seen within the fabric of time, and consequently all things human are of no importance. Hence human life and everything human is seen in the light of the continual march of time, in which particular points in time have no relevancy, in which nothing decisive occurs, no changes take place that would give new meaning to human life, no divine plan in history is perceived, and there is no question of especially significant 'times and seasons' (1 Thess. 5 : 1).

The conclusion of the *Consolatio ad Helviam*, in which Seneca comforts his mother from his place of exile in Corsica, is striking in this respect. She must not worry about him. He is as happy and cheerful in exile as in the best of circumstances. For now his mind is free from all burdens, free for its own task. It is seeking knowledge of the various countries, of the sea, of the terrors that lie between heaven and earth, thunder, lightning, storms, rain, snow and hail:

> Finally, having traversed the lower spaces, it bursts through to the heights above, and there enjoys the noblest spectacle of things divine, and, mindful of its own immortality, it proceeds to all that has been and will ever be throughout the ages of all time. 3

The highest form of enjoyment of the divine is given to the individual when all earthly and human cares have finally faded away, and the mind, independent of place and time, has left behind it everything connected with earthly history.

Hence in Seneca reflections on time are to be found in many variations, but not included among them is the notion that certain events in

---

1 *Marc.* 21. 1-3.
2 *Ep.* 99. 10.
3 *Helv.* 21. 1, 2.

time are of decisive importance. If we look back on the past, all things
are equal:

> All past time is in the same place; it all presents the same aspect to us,
> it lies together. Everything slips into the same abyss. [1]
> Our bodies are hurried along like flowing waters; every visible object
> accompanies time in its flight; of the things which we see, nothing is
> fixed. Even I myself, as I comment on this change, am changed myself.
> This is just what Heraclitus says: "We go down twice into the same
> river, and yet into a different river." For the stream still keeps the
> same name, but the water has already flowed past. [2]

Time is among the many interesting subjects worthy of philosophical
inquiry:

> One must learn about things divine and human, the past and the future,
> the ephemeral and the eternal; and one must learn about Time. See
> how many questions arise concerning time alone: in the first place,
> whether it is anything in and by itself; in the second place, whether
> anything exists prior to time and without time; and again, did time
> begin along with the universe, or, because there was something even
> before the universe began, did time also exist then? [3]

It is noteworthy that such problems concerning time are never
touched upon by Paul, not even in those places where it might be considered to be almost inevitable, as for instance when he describes the
end of the salvation-occurrence (*Heilsgeschichte*) in the words:

> When all things are subjected to him, then the Son himself will also
> be subjected to him who put all things under him, that God may be
> everything to every one (1 Cor. 15 : 28).

Such a statement immediately makes us wonder how we should en-
visage the time that is to come after the end of time, when God will
be everything to every one. It is all the more significant that Paul gives
no hint of his own conception of time, that he does not even indicate
whether he has ever thought about the problem. What Seneca says is
true: numerous questions concerning time spring to mind, if we stop
to think about it. But none of them are consciously brought up by Paul
in the way Seneca does in his melancholy philosophic reflections. On
the other hand Seneca never suggests, as Paul does, that there are to
be seen in time certain turning-points which are of exceptional importance for the salvation of mankind and the world.

When Seneca offers an 'eschatological' prospect, it is in the form of

---

[1] *Ep.* 49. 3.
[2] *Ep.* 58. 22, 23.
[3] *Ep.* 88. 33.

a cyclic recurrence of great epochs. Time and again this world and
everything in it is destroyed, so that a new age may be embarked upon.
In the *Consolatio ad Marciam* he describes how Marcia's dead father
looks out over the centuries to come. Earthly kingdoms and great cities
will fall. Nothing will remain where it is now. Not only men, but
also places, countries and great parts of the universe will be Fate's
playthings. Mountains will be levelled, in other places rocks will rise;
seas will disappear, rivers will be turned from their courses; com-
munications between nations, between the human race will be broken;
cities will be swallowed up, there will be earthquakes; a pestilent
vapour will rise; great floods will cover the earth's surface and de-
luge the earth, kill every living creature, and in huge conflagrations
all mortal things will be consumed:

> And when the time shall come for the world to be blotted out in order
> that it may begin its life anew, these things will destroy themselves by
> their own power, and stars will clash with stars, and all the fiery matter
> of the world that now shines in orderly array will blaze up in a common
> conflagration. Then also the souls of the blest, who have partaken of
> immortality, when it shall seem best to God to create the universe anew
> — we, too, amid the falling universe, shall be added as a tiny fraction
> to this mighty destruction, and shall be changed again into our former
> elements. [1]

Like many other Stoics, Seneca repeatedly expounds the destruction
of the world by fire and floods, and its subsequent renewal, particularly
in his *Naturales Quaestiones* which deals with a wide variety of natural
phenomena. [2] He is convinced that all things human will come to an
end. The earth will then pass away, will either partly or wholly be
destroyed in order that it may be born anew and innocent, without a
trace of any creature who will bring back evil. [3] Then the world will
be dissolved into its elements, the gods will be united into one, and
nature will lie fallow for a short time. [4] 'All things move in accord with
their appointed times; they are destined to be born, to grow and to
be destroyed.' [5] To us, who see everything from too near at hand,
such a dissolution seems destruction. In reality, life and death, composition and decomposition, succeed one another. [6] Constant movement

---

[1] *Marc.* 26. 5, 6, 7.
[2] *N.Q.* iii. 13. 1; 27; 28.
[3] *N.Q.* iii. 29. 5.
[4] *Ep.* 9. 16.
[5] *Ep.* 71. 13.
[6] *Ep.* 71. 14.

and periodic change are inviolable laws of nature. [1] We only have
to observe the constant cyclic motion of nature to discover that there
is an eternally recurring rise and fall. [2]

This belief that everything is for ever recurring in cycles is radically
different from Paul's message concerning the *eschata*. The word ἡμέρα
for instance is often used by him to indicate the day of the Lord Jesus
Christ (1 Cor. 1 : 8; cf. 2 Cor. 1 : 14; Phil. 1 : 6, 10; 2 : 16). That
special day of judgment will come as a thief in the night (1 Thess.
5 : 2; 2 Thess. 2 : 2), it is the day of the complete revelation of the
glory of Christ. Hence it is a day, which is not part of a smoothly
flowing stream of ordinary days. It is a day qualified by the unbroken
chain of salvation-history in time. Against the background of the
coming of that day, often simply referred to as 'the day' (1 Thess. 5 : 4;
1 Cor. 3 : 13; Rom. 13 : 12) or 'that day' (2 Thess. 1 : 10), the life
and the communal life, work, and suffering of the Church are placed
in a special light. That day imposes a limit on all human endeavour,
which will not go on indefinitely, but will come to an end. God, Christ
will pass a last judgment on man's life and work. Neither does human
endeavour go on with constant regularity, but is inexorably bound up
with time, and obtains its deepest significance and meaning from the
salvation-occurrence. That salvation-occurrence does not repeat itself
as part of an ever recurring cycle of all things but its sequence is unique
in time. It leads to that ἡμέρα. In this way 'the day' becomes the notion
in which the coming judgment and the coming salvation are crystal-
lized, because it is the day of Jesus Christ.

And so, roughly speaking, Seneca discusses history and time in three
ways: first, he derives his examples from history; secondly, he reflects
on time in general in a variety of manners; thirdly he believes in the
cyclic return of all things. It is plain that this is vastly different from
Paul's conception of a history of salvation which runs its decisive course
once and once alone.

Behind Paul's central kerygma there is of course also a very particular proclamation concerning God: God acts according to His will for
salvation. Paul does not speculate on God, but it is apparent time and
again that in all his gospel preaching he has in mind the personal,
living, sovereign God, who from the creation of the world until the

---

[1] *Helv.* 6. 8.
[2] *Ep.* 36. 11.

day of Jesus Christ is constantly working for the salvation of mankind and the world. God had His own reason for sending Christ into the world. It was His way of demonstrating what He ultimately wishes to do with mankind and the world. He, the holy God, consciously set out on the path of reconciliation. 1 The whole history of salvation is an expression of the *will* of God. 2

God is the Father, but as 'the God and Father of our Lord Jesus Christ' (2 Cor. 1 : 3). Even the set phrases of salutation at the beginning of the Pauline epistles make it plain that Paul does not take God's Fatherhood for granted, but believes that God has become our Father, because He has embarked upon His work of salvation, because He has accepted us as children (Gal. 4 : 4-6). God has sent forth the Spirit who is of the end of time, and who as the first fruits, the pledge, points to the close of the age. *Now* we may invoke God as Father, abba. *Now* we are children, no longer slaves (Rom. 8 : 15-17). *Now* we may call upon Him in prayer. *Now* God is a God to whom man may say Thou in prayer.

Is Seneca's conception of God so very different? Naturally he does not know the particular proclamation of the Pauline letters concerning God's salvation, but is his notion of God in itself quite a different one from Paul's? Does he, for example, think of God as a being who governs mankind and the world according to a particular purpose? As in many later Stoics, statements are sometimes encountered in Seneca which seem to point towards this, which apparently allude to a God who personally intervenes. The pantheism of the early Stoics seems to have acquired a theistic flavour. For the early Stoics the godhead was the acting force, the skilfully creating fire, which was without doubt thought of as matter, albeit as very fine matter. As a fiery breath, *pneuma,* the godhead pervades all matter. Hence the godhead is all-immanent and all that exists is the original substance or godhead which manifests itself in various ways. In the godhead as *logos spermatikos* lie the germs of all existence. Such notions well-nigh inevitably lead to a pantheistic conception of God: God and the world are ultimately identical.

If we compare with this statements of Seneca's, great changes appear to have taken place concerning the conception of God. For him God no longer seems to be that *logos spermatikos* which is active in the

1 Rom. 3 : 21 ff., v. 25 in particular; 8 : 3, 32; 2 Cor. 5 : 18-21; Gal. 4 : 4; Phil. 1 : 6; 2 : 13; 2 Cor. 1 : 9; 1 Cor. 10 : 13; 1 Thess. 5 : 24; 1 Cor. 8 : 5 f.; Eph. 4 : 6; 1 Cor. 15 : 24.
2 *Eph.* 3 : 1-12.

world, but a godhead which may be distinguished from the world, which rules and governs it:

> All things are made up of matter and of God; God controls matter, which encompasses him and follows him as its guide and leader. 1
> Matter lies sluggish, a substance ready for any use, but sure to remain unemployed if no one sets it in motion. Cause, however, by which we mean reason, moulds matter and turns it in whatever direction it will, producing thereby various concrete results. 2

God is called 'the great creator and ruler of the universe', 3 'the God under whose guidance everything progresses', 4 'the arbiter of the universe', 5 'the Divine Creator', 6 'the Builder of the universe'. 7

This God is beyond space and time, and is also omnipresent. 'God is near you, he is with you, he is winthin you', 8 'he does service to mankind, everywhere and to all he is at hand to help.' 9 Such an omnipresent God knows the most secret human thoughts. Hence the fact that we may conceal our thoughts from our fellow-men is of no avail to us. For they are known to God. 'Nothing is shut off from the sight of God. He is witness of our souls, and he comes into the very midst of our thoughts.' 10

Neither does Seneca refrain from applying the title of father to God. Of the good man he says: 'he is God's pupil, his imitator, and true offspring, whom his all-glorious parent, being no mild taskmaster of virtues, rears, as strict fathers do, with much severity', 11 he is the God and Father of us all, 12 whom we should honour with gratitude as we should our human fathers. 13 Thus Seneca ostensibly presents us

---

1 *Ep.* 65. 23.
2 *Ep.* 65. 2.
3 *Prov.* 5. 8.
4 *Ep.* 107. 9.
5 *Ep.* 16. 5.
6 *Ep.* 113. 16: *divinus artifex.*
7 *Ep.* 119. 15: *mundi conditor*; cf. *Helv.* 8. 3: *formator universi . . . deus potens omnium; N.Q.* ii. 45. 1: *rector custosque universi . . . operis huius dominus et artifex; N.Q.* vii. 30. 3: *ipse qui ista tractat, qui condidit, qui totum hoc fundavit deditque circa se; Ep.* 65. 19: *rerum formator . . . istius artifex mundi; Ep.* 44. 1: *omnes, si ad originem primam revocantur, a dis sunt; Ep.* 90. 1: *deorum immortalium munus, quod vivimus, philosophiae quod bene vivimus; Ben.* vii. 31. 2: *. . . di omnium rerum optimi auctores; Ep.* 71. 14: *cuncta temperans deus.*
8 *Ep.* 41. 1.
9 *Ep.* 95. 47.
10 *Ep.* 83. 1.
11 *Prov.* 1. 5.
12 *Ep.* 110. 10; cf. *Ben.* ii. 29. 4.
13 *Ben.* iv. 19. 3.

with the picture of a father who takes care of everything and is kind
and well-disposed towards mankind. [1]

All this apparently implies the existence of a very personal God.
Seneca seems to be saying that there is an I — thou relationship between
God and man, that God bestows especial care upon each and every
one of us. But this is only illusionary. Perhaps the simplest way of
drawing attention to the basic contrast between Paul and Seneca on
this point is by saying that Seneca is in the last resort not serious when
he speaks of a personal God. Or in order to avoid appearing to
throw suspicion on the subjective seriousness of a man like Seneca
this should perhaps be formulated differently: he cannot really be
serious when he testifies to a belief in a personal God and in an I —
thou relationship between God and man. This can often be easily
demonstrated by reference to the context, the setting in which these
words which seem to speak of a personal God are placed. Mentioned
above were places where God is described as 'the great creator and
ruler of the universe'. One such passage is *Prov.* 5. 8. But if we look
at the context in which Seneca uses this expression, we see it in quite
a different light. It is preceded in *Prov.* 5. 7 by the following:

> Fate guides us, and it was settled at the first hour of birth what length
> of time remains for each. Cause is linked with cause, and all public
> and private issues are directed by a long sequence of events. Therefore
> everything should be endured with fortitude, since things do not, as
> we suppose, simply happen — they all come.

Hence in *Prov.* 5. 8 it can only be said to be:

> a great consolation that it is together with the universe we are swept
> along; whatever it is that has ordained us so to live, so to die, by the
> same necessity it binds also the gods. One unchangeable course bears
> along the affairs of men and gods alike. Although the great creator
> and ruler of the universe himself wrote the decrees of Fate, yet he
> follows them. He obeys for ever, he decreed but once.

It is plain that with such a 'creator and ruler of the universe' an I —
thou relationship is out of the question. The only line of conduct for
the good man is 'to offer himself to Fate', the fate to which the
'creator and ruler of the universe' is also subjected.

Likewise when Seneca calls God the Father, the context should
be closely examined. An instance of this is also to be found in the
De Providentia, where God is alluded to as the 'all-glorious parent',

---

[1] Cf. also *Ben.* iii. 28. 2: *parens*; *Ben.* iv. 8. 1: *omnium parens.*

parens ille magnificus. Equally noteworthy is the fact that in the same passage Seneca also speaks of the gods in the plural:

> I shall reconcile you with the gods, who are ever best to those who are best. For Nature never permits good to be injured by good; between good men and the gods there exists a friendship brought about by virtue. Friendship, do I say? Nay, rather there is a tie of relationship and a likeness, since, in truth, a good man differs from God in the element of time only; he is God's pupil, his imitator, and true offspring, whom his all glorious parent, being no mild taskmaster of virtues, rears, as strict fathers do, with much severity. [1]

The train of thought is obvious. God, the sublime father, brings up his children just as good human fathers do: strictly and without spoiling them. If the virtuous man subjects himself to the fate that inexorably controls his life, then there is nothing that can really harm him. Accordingly it is in the nature of things that the good governing of the world by the gods, which runs its inevitable course, can never really harm the good man. For the wise man is 'above Fortune', *supra fortunam.* [2] Thus between the gods and man there can exist a bond of friendship brought about by virtue. There is no question here of a bond of trust; the felicitous relationship is brought about by the virtue of the wise man who readily submits himself to fate with the result that no evil can befall him.

This is indeed radically different from what Paul means by 'the God and Father of our Lord Jesus Christ, the Father of mercies and God of all comfort' (2 Cor. 1 : 3), whose mercy and love alone bridge the deep chasm between the holy God and sinful man. Consequently Seneca does not actually conceive of a God who cares for each individual personally, because he makes no clear distinction between this 'care' and fate, destiny, fortune. 'Fate guides us — cause is linked with cause', this really amounts to the 'care' of the gods being equivalent to the inexorable enactment of the laws of nature. A human being can submit himself voluntarily, but submission to an unchanging fate bears no resemblance to a personal relationship, neither on the part of God nor on the part of man. And since Seneca virtually identifies God's care with the workings of the laws of nature, he can never take a decisive step in the direction of theism, but remains confined to pantheism.

Hence it is not to be wondered at that Seneca feels justified in

---

[1] *Prov.* 1. 5.
[2] *Brev. Vitae* 5. 3; cf. *Const.* 8. 3: *fortuna ... quotiens cum virtute congressa est, numquam par recessit.*

giving God all these names. He is the ruler and guardian of the universe, the soul and spirit of the world, the lord and creator of this work, to whom every name is appropriate. [1] Neither is it surprising that in answer to the question what is God, Seneca can say: the spirit of the universe, the *mens universi,* and a little further on: all you see and all you do not see. His true greatness which is greater than can be conceived, is only acknowledged, if he is said to be everything alone, if he rules his work from within and without. [2] It is evident from such statements that Seneca does not really rise above the pantheism of the early Stoics, and that he can therefore never be completely serious when speaking of a personal God whose dealings with men are on an I — thou basis. Seneca's God is, when all is said and done, fate, nature, and his 'deeds' are the decrees of fate, the enactment of the laws of nature. 'God' or the 'gods' are ultimately nothing but figuratively used, friendly terms for the irresistible fate, for which man is no match, and to which he voluntarily submits, if he has any wisdom.

So it is understandable that for Seneca acceptance of and acquiescence to God's will are the same as submission to the laws of nature. [3] Nature governs this visible kingdom by change; regular change which may be perceived by man. Seneca goes on to say:

> It is to this law that our souls must adjust themselves, this they should follow, this they should obey. Whatever happens, assume that it was bound to happen, and do not be willing to rail at Nature. That which you cannot reform, it is best to endure, and to attend uncomplainingly upon the God under whose guidance everything progresses; for it is a bad soldier who grumbles when following his commander. [4]

Time and again this identification of God with nature and fate is to be met with in Seneca. He repeatedly asserts that these are all the same for him. It is solely a matter of a change of name. When someone says: ' "It is nature who supplies me with these things," ' Seneca asks:

> But do you not understand that, when you say this, you merely give another name to God? For what else is Nature but God and the Divine

---

[1] N.Q. ii. 45. 1, 2, 3; cf. M. Spanneut, *Le Stoïcisme des Pères de l'Église,* 1957, p. 398 f.

[2] N.Q. i. praef. 13; cf. Th. Schreiner, *Seneca im Gegensatz zu Paulus,* 1936, p. 196; Spanneut, *op. cit.,* p. 294, 404.

[3] The will of God = the law of the universe *Ep.* 71. 16; cf. *Ep.* 54. 7; 74. 20; 76. 23; 96. 2; 107. 9-12; *V.B.* 15. 4; *Prov.* 5. 6.

[4] *Ep.* 107. 8, 9.

Reason that pervades the whole universe and all its parts? You may, as often as you like, address this being who is the author of this world of ours by different names; it will be right for you to call him Jupiter Best and Greatest .... If likewise you should call him Fate, it would be no falsehood; for since Fate is nothing but a connected chain of causes, he is the first of all the causes on which the others depend. Any name that you choose will be properly applied to him if it connotes some force that operates in the domain of heaven — his titles may be as countless as are his benefits. 1

It is just as correct to say that one owes certain gifts to God as to nature, for:

In whatever direction you turn, you will see God coming to meet you; nothing is void of him, he himself fills all his work. For this reason, O most ungrateful of mortals, it is futile for you to say that you are indebted, not to God, but to Nature, for there is no Nature without God, nor God without Nature, but both are the same thing, they differ only in their function. 2

When from his place of exile Seneca comforts his mother by reminding her that another human being can only exercise the slightest and most worthless control over us, since universal Nature and our own virtue accompany us everywhere, he says:

Believe me, this was the intention of the great creator of the universe, whoever he may be, whether an all-powerful God, or incorporeal Reason contriving vast works, or divine Spirit pervading all things from the smallest to the greatest with uniform energy, or Fate and an unalterable sequence of causes clinging one to the other — this, I say, was his intention, that only the most worthless of our possessions should fall under the control of another. 3

Hence it is not surprising that continual reference is made by Seneca to the rule of nature. 4

It is frequently apparent that what sounds personal is really meant impersonally. 'Obedience to God' acquires quite a specific meaning, when the context makes it plain that it means the acceptance of all the hardships 'the very constitution of the universe' may bestow upon us: 5

---

1 *Ben.* iv. 7. 1, 2; cf. E. Vernon Arnold, *op. cit.,* p. 218 ff.
2 *Ben.* iv. 8. 1, 2.
3 *Helv.* 8. 3.
4 *N.Q.* iii. 10. 3; 15. 1, 3; 27. 2, 3; vi. 1. 12 etc.
5 Compare in this respect two statements which bear a superficial resemblance to each other: *Ep.* 78. 7: 'No man can suffer both severely and for a long time; Nature, who loves us most tenderly, has so constituted us as to make pain either endurable or short'; 1 Cor. 10 : 13: 'God is faithful, and he will not let you be tempted beyond your strength, but with the temptation will also provide the way of escape, that you

This is the sacred obligation by which we are bound — to submit to the human lot, and not to be disquieted by those things which we have no power to avoid. We have been born under a monarchy; to obey God is freedom. 1

Imitation of the gods can be mentioned in the same breath as living according to nature: 'It is our aim to live according to Nature, and to follow the example of the gods.' 2 The will of the gods is identified with an unalterable law:

... the gods are constrained by no external force, but their own will is a law to them for all time. What they have determined upon, they do not change, and, consequently, it is impossible that they should appear likely to do something although it is against their will, since they have willed to persist in doing whatever it is impossible for them to cease from doing, and the gods never repent of their original decision. 1

Accordingly the principal features of Seneca's conception of God clearly emerge as rationalistic monism and harsh determinism. God may be considered to be on the same level as the unalterable laws of nature and the unwavering course of fate. It is because of reason that he is present everywhere, in man too. In that sense God is omnipresent, omnipotent, eternal.

Some of Seneca's utterances and sayings do not seem to fit into this pattern. Seneca himself occasionally appears to be conscious of this and of the dilemma in which it places him with respect to his fundamental principles. In one of his letters to Lucilius he writes of the great importance of philosophy in the life of man. It moulds our minds, guides our actions and shows us what we should and should not do. He then lets an imaginary opponent say:

"How can philosophy help me, if Fate exists? Of what avail is philosophy, if God rules the universe? Of what avail is it, if Chance governs everything?"

Seneca counters this objection as follows:

Whether the truth, Lucilius, lies in one or in all of these views, we must be philosophers; whether Fate binds us down by an inexorable law, or whether God as arbiter of the universe has arranged everything, or whether Chance drives and tosses human affairs without method, philosophy ought to be our defence. She will encourage us to obey God

---

may be able to endure it'; or *Ben.* iv. 25. 1: 'It is our aim to live according to Nature, and to follow the example of the gods'; Eph. 5 : 1: 'therefore be imitators of God, as beloved children.'

1 *V.B.* 15. 6, 7.
2 *Ben.* iv. 25. 1.
3 *Ben.* vi. 23. 1.

cheerfully, but Fortune defiantly; she will teach us to follow God and endure Chance. But it is not my purpose now to be led into a discussion as to what is within our own control, — if fore-knowledge is supreme, or if a chain of fated events drags us along in its clutches, or if the sudden and the unexpected play the tyrant over us .... [1]

Accordingly Seneca here puts three alternatives into the mouth of his adversary: the world is governed by Fate, God, or Chance. And in his answer he acknowledges these diverse possibilities. Unfortunately, however, he does not go into the matter more closely, and leaves unexplained the relationship between the *inexorabilis lex* of fate and the *arbiter deus universi*. At all events — and this is what is remarkable — he evidently momentarily assumes that they are not identical. The *Deus-fatum* and the *Deus-providentia* exist side by side.

This is not the only time that Seneca shows recognition of this distinction. In other places too the foundation of his Stoic conception of God appears to be shaken. When he writes, 'Although the great creator and ruler of the universe himself wrote the decrees of Fate, yet he follows them. He obeys for ever, he decreed but once,' [2] the emphasis is of course on the fact that God too is subservient to Fate; but it may also be gathered from this that God once dictated the decrees of Fate, that he was once in command. Was God at one time above Fate, although he is now bound up with it?

And when eternal will, *aeterna voluntas*, is ascribed to the gods, this inevitably suggests that they are living persons. [3]

The relationship between God and man is sometimes dealt with in Seneca's writings in a manner that is much more fervent, and more personal than would seem possible in view of the basic structure of Seneca's thought, as for instance when he argues that if life runs contrary to our expectations, this must be accepted, for the gods willed it so. And what the gods have decreed is naturally better. [4] Seneca frequently makes statements advocating the surrender of the individual to a personal God: 'Let man be pleased with whatever has pleased God'. [5]

When Seneca assumes that man can be grateful to God, [6] when he can even say that towards men God has the mind of a father, and

---

[1] *Ep.* 16. 4-6.
[2] *Prov.* 5. 8, see above p. 37.
[3] *Ben.* vi. 23. 1.
[4] *Ep.* 98. 4, 5.
[5] *Ep.* 74. 20; cf. *Ep.* 16. 5; 71. 16; 76. 23; 96. 1, 2; *Prov.* 5. 6.
[6] E.g. *Ep.* 15. 10.

loves them deeply, [1] that God is at the service of the human race, ready to help everywhere and everyone, [2] that we human beings are loved more by the immortal gods than any other creatures, [3] all such statements suggest the warmth and ardour of a personal relationship. But, as has already been seen, closer inquiry makes it plain that Seneca's conception is far more rational, impersonal and lacking in warmth than these statements would suggest. When he remarks that the gods are an active influence in men's lives, [4] or that they give man effectual assistance, [5] he is really referring to the godhead's immanent activity in man's better self.

From all this it is evident that the distinction between a personal god and an impersonal godhead is one made by us, and that in his writings Seneca himself was scarcely aware of it. With the exception of a single instance (*Ep.* 16. 4-6) Seneca never perceived the existence of any dividing line. He did not see any definite antithesis between *deus* on the one hand and *lex, fatum, fortuna* on the other. If we give careful thought to this matter which is so important in an estimation of Seneca's relationship to Paul, we are obliged to conclude that for Seneca the godhead was on the whole impersonal, and that any remarks he makes which seem to point in another direction do not modify in any essential way the basic pattern of his thoughts. Only once does Seneca deviate on this point from the traditional Stoic view, but then he does so quite unconsciously. This means that in his conception of God he differs fundamentally from Paul. Of course to some extent we also approach Paul's letters with a pre-conceived idea of an antithesis between a personal and impersonal God, which is never stated by the Apostle himself, but in his letters it is made abundantly clear that the God and Father of our Lord Jesus Christ is a personal and all-powerful God who, unfettered to fate or the laws of nature, pursues His way of salvation from the creation of the world until the close of the age.

The antithesis between Seneca and Paul with respect to the conception of God naturally impinges on various other provinces. It obviously dictates their attitude towards *prayer*, for example. Here Seneca displays the same ambivalent attitude that has been observed

---

[1] *Prov.* 2. 6.
[2] *Ep.* 95. 47.
[3] *Ben.* ii. 29. 6; cf. *Prov.* 2. 6, 7.
[4] E.g. *Ep.* 95. 50; *Ben.* iv. 32. 1; *Prov.* 4. 7; cf. *Ep.* 93. 8.
[5] *Ep.* 41. 2, 5.

in his conception of God. For by identifying God with destiny and nature, he robs prayer of all meaning. At most it is for him an edifying expression of acquiescence to ineluctable fate.

Sometimes Seneca writes in the form of a prayer, thus seeming to suggest acquiescence to the will of a personal God, as for instance when he quotes Cleanthes's prayer at the end of *Ep.* 107:

> Lead me, O Master of the lofty heavens,
> My Father, whithersoever thou shalt wish.
> I shall not falter, but obey with speed.
> And though I would not, I shall go, and suffer,
> In sin and sorrow what I might have done
> In noble virtue. Aye, the willing soul
> Fate leads, but the unwilling drags along.

The opening lines of this hymn seem to give utterance to a supplicatory, acquiescent acceptance of the will of a sovereign God, but further on it becomes plain that acquiescence to the inevitable is the true theme. Man should do this uncomplainingly. For then he accepts fate as a guiding force; inner rebellion against it is of no avail, as he will then be dragged along against his will. Epictetus also quotes this prayer and it is he who attributes it to Cleanthes. [1] Augustine quotes it as if it were by Seneca himself. [2] The last line of the prayer, as quoted by Seneca, is missing in Epictetus. Some scholars deem it to have been derived from Cleanthes, while others are of the opinion that it has been appended by Seneca. [3] At all events, both the prayer as a whole and the last line in particular are entirely compatible with Seneca's pattern of thought; the same sentiments are also expressed in the concluding lines of the letter, which follow immediately upon this prayer:

> Let us live thus, and speak thus; let Fate find us ready and alert. Here is your great soul — the man who has given himself over to Fate; on the other hand, that man is a weakling and a degenerate who struggles and maligns the order of the universe and would rather reform the gods than reform himself. [4]

Hence this passage which at first glance appears to be the formulation of a prayer to the sovereign God, proves to be basically nothing but a testimony to a joyful submission, wherever possible, to the unalterable enactment of fate. Precisely the same things that are said in this

---

[1] *Ench.* 53.

[2] *Civ. Dei* 5. 8: *Annaei Senecae sunt, nisi fallor, hi versus.*

[3] Cf. Achilles Beltrami, *L. Annaei Senecae ad Lucilium Epistulae morales*, II, 1949, p. 172, note to line 5.

[4] *Ep.* 107. 12.

prayer are also said elsewhere by Seneca, but then not in the form of a prayer:

> All that the very constitution of the universe obliges us to suffer, must be borne with high courage. This is the sacred obligation by which we are bound — to submit to the human lot, and not to be disquieted by those things which we have no power to avoid. 1

Here too the synonymity of God and fate is assumed. If a really personal prayer of acquiescence is not conceivable on such a basis, still less is of course a prayer in which God is asked something. For supplication is quite useless if all coming events are pre-ordained. Seneca himself makes this plain:

> Let me uphold the rigid sect that takes exception to such rites and regards vows as but comfort to a heart ill at ease. The fates perform their function in a far different way from that supposed; they are not moved by any prayer nor changed by pity nor by favour. Their course is irrevocable; once they have entered upon it they flow on by unalterable decree. 2

To Marcia who has lost her son, and who torments herself with the thought that he might have lived longer, Seneca has this to say:

> His life has not been cut short, nor does Chance ever thrust itself into the years. What has been promised to each man, is paid; the Fates go their way, and neither add anything to what has once been promised, nor subtract from it. Prayers and struggles are all in vain; each one will get just the amount that was placed to his credit on the first day of his existence. 3

It is foolish to shed tears because one was not born a thousand years earlier, or later:

> You have been cast upon this point of time; if you would make it longer, how much longer shall you make it? Why weep? Why pray? You are taking pains to no purpose. 4

Seneca advises Lucilius that it is time he gave up the old-fashioned method of praying, such as was practised by his parents:

> What need is there of vows? Make yourself happy through your own efforts; you can do this, if once you comprehend that whatever is blended with virtue is good, and that whatever is joined to vice is bad. 5

---

1 *V.B.* 15. 6, 7.
2 *N.Q.* ii. 35. 1, 2.
3 *Marc.* 21. 6.
4 *Ep.* 77. 11, 12.
5 *Ep.* 31. 5.

It is folly to ask God to grant one things one can attain by one's own efforts:

> You are doing an excellent thing, one which will be whole-some for you, if, as you write me, you are persisting in your effort to attain sound understanding; it is foolish to pray for this when you can acquire it from yourself. We do not need to uplift our hands towards heaven, or to beg the keeper of a temple to let us approach his idol's ear, as if in this way our prayers were more likely to be heard. God is near you, he is with you, he is within you. [1]

Let us make an end to those prayers which we have learnt from our nurses, our tutors or our mothers in youth:

> How long shall we go on making demands upon the gods, as if we were still unable to support ourselves. [2]

It may to some extent be said of these passages, that they do not condemn prayer itself, but an all too hasty use of it by persons who are not willing to exert themselves, [3] or who ask for the fulfilment of ordinary material desires. [4] But in all these utterances on prayer there is most certainly an echo of what is stated most clearly in the first two quotations: [5] if fate has already pre-ordained everything, a prayer, in which a request is made, is completely useless. It can achieve nothing.

It might be expected that Seneca would accept the consequences of this and counsel people to abandon prayer entirely. However, he does not do so. On the contrary, he not only assumes that people pray, but he even urges them to do so. It is by no means dishonourable to make supplications to the gods. [6] Writing about lightning he says among other things that if the lightning is favourable, one must beg the gods to realize their promises; if it is unfavourable, one must ask them to stave off their threats. [7] Seneca vehemently denies the assertion that the gods are unconcerned about the world:

> He who says this does not hearken to the voices of those who pray and of those who all around him, lifting their hands to heaven, offer vows for blessings public and private. Assuredly this would not be the case, assuredly all mortals would not have agreed upon this madness of ad-

---

[1] Ep. 41. 1; cf. N.Q. iii. praef. 14; Ep. 95. 50.
[2] Ep. 60. 1, 2; cf. Ep. 32. 4; 10. 5; Brev. 11. 1; Pol. 4. 2; Ben. vi. 38. 1.
[3] Ep. 31. 5; 41. 1.
[4] Ep. 60. 1, 2.
[5] N.Q. ii. 35. 1, 2; Marc. 21. 6.
[6] Ben. ii. 1. 4.
[7] N.Q. ii. 33.

dressing divinities that were deaf and gods that were ineffectual, unless
we were conscious of their benefits that sometimes are presented unasked,
sometimes are granted in answer to prayer — great and timely gifts,
which by their coming remove grave menaces. 1

Accordingly he urges Lucilius to thank the gods for having heard
his former prayers and also to continue to call upon them in prayer:

> pray for a sound mind and for good health, first of soul and then of
> body. And of course you should offer those prayers frequently. Call
> boldly upon God; you will not be asking him for that which belongs
> to another. 2

The question inevitably comes to mind how Seneca, who with
the views he held on fate must have been quite unable to see any
useful purpose served by supplicatory prayers, nevertheless repeatedly
advocated prayer. Now and then he seems to have sensed this inconsistency himself. In the *De Beneficiis* he writes:

> We petition even the gods, whose knowledge nothing escapes, and,
> although our prayers do not prevail upon them, they remind them
> of us. 3

If this is the aim of prayer, one wonders whether there is anything
to be gained by it: the gods, after all, know everything, and are therefore hardly in need of man's prayers to remind them of him. This
is not why men send up their prayers, they do so in order to ask a
boon, they hope to obtain something by praying, something other
than just the attention of the gods.

In his work *Naturales Quaestiones* Seneca himself raises this point:
if there is a *fatum,* then everything must proceed according to an
inexorable plan, hence there can be no place for prayer. If, on the
other hand, we take prayer and the possibility of its being heard as
our starting-point, it is conceivable that the course of events might
be altered by prayer. But then fate does not reign inexorably. It may
be observed that it is precisely in this book that Seneca clings most
tenaciously to the idea of the indissolubility of the bonds of Fate. 4
Nevertheless, he argues, prayers are not unavailing, since there are
openings in the chain of events which may be filled in various ways.
If this is so — is the obvious rejoinder — then the iron rule of
destiny is disturbed. Then there is apparently something on which

---

1 *Ben.* iv. 4. 2.
2 *Ep.* 10. 4; cf. *Ep.* 31. 2.
3 *Ben.* v. 25. 4.
4 *N.Q.* ii. 35. 1, 2, see above p. 45.

fate has no hold. Then there are matters which have not been pre-
ordained by destiny, then there is a weak link in the chain. And this
would consequently mean that the fixed course of events would at
certain moments be controlled by prayer. In connection with exorcizing
the danger of lightning Seneca discusses the question whether it is
possible to stave off the threat of fate. Whether expiatory sacrifices
and similar rites can ward off danger, sometimes mitigating it, sometimes deferring it. Then he says:

> Meantime we have so much in common with the persons last mentioned
> in holding that vows are of service, but without prejudice to the power
> and sway of fate. Some things are in fact left by the immortal gods in
> such a state of suspense as to turn to the advantage of worshippers if
> they employ prayer to heaven and take vows upon them. This, then,
> is so far from being opposed to fate that it is actually a part of fate. [1]

If Seneca is here arguing that the course of fate is not disturbed
by prayer, then the moment and contents of the prayer must of
necessity be predetermined. Only then does it form a link in an un-
interrupted chain. But then nothing remains of man's freedom to
pray, or of the possibility of a genuine answer to his prayers. Hence
it is quite understandable that Seneca expects a counter-attack to prove
that all our actions are dictated by omnipotent fate. Seneca then claims:

> When I come to treat of that subject, I will explain how, without in-
> fringing the power of fate, something may still be left to human choice.
> For the nonce, I have explained the point at issue, viz. how, consistently
> with an order fixed by fate, perils from prodigies may be averted through
> expiation and sacrifice, inasmuch as they do not conflict with fate,
> but, on the contrary, are assumed by the very law of fate. [2]

But, continues his imaginary opponent, is there any point in consulting
the *haruspex* if it is already pre-ordained that one will make an expiatory sacrifice? For then it will be made even if they do not advise it.
Seneca replies:

> He does so far good in that he is the instrument of fate. In a like manner,
> when recovery from illness seems the work of fate, it is due at the same
> time to the doctor, because the boon of fate passes through his hands in
> order to reach us. [3]

It is regrettable that Seneca did not carry out his apparent plan of
writing at greater length on this subject, since, even after this answer,

[1] N.Q. ii. 37. 2.
[2] N.Q. ii. 38. 3.
[3] N.Q. ii. 38. 4.

it is not clear how he can really believe in man's freedom to pray
or commit an act of propitiation and in the god's freedom to hear
his prayers. Fate obliges man to pray or offer expiatory sacrifices or it
prevents him from doing so, but either way man's apparent free choice
is, according to Seneca, part of the predetermined course of events,
from which no true deviation is made.

Hence Seneca desires to leave some scope for prayer, but is really
unable to do so because he first and foremost wants to hold fast to
the idea of the inexorable fulfilment of destiny. On no account does
he wish to abandon his central thesis which he has just restated prior to
this passage in answer to the question 'What do you understand by
fate?' His reply is:

> I suppose it is the binding necessity of all events and actions, a necessity
> that no force can break. If you believe that such a power can be prevailed
> upon to change through sacrifice or the head of a snowwhite lamb,
> you know little about the Divine dispensation. 1

Accordingly prayer can be no more than a cog in the tremendous mechanism of ineluctable destiny. 2

This is all very far removed from the way in which Paul speaks
of prayer. He always assumes as a matter of course that prayer is
meaningful and has a part to play in the whole life of the Church. In
all his letters he makes repeated references to prayer, in particular to
mutual intercession, and without doubt these references are not merely
an edifying way of saying that we think of each other or that we
ought to do so. In well-nigh all his letters he assures his churches
that he prays for them:

> without ceasing I mention you always in my prayers. 3 I thank my God
> in all my remembrance of you, always in every prayer of mine for you
> all making my prayer with joy. 4 We always thank God, the Father of
> our Lord Jesus Christ, when we pray for you. 5

He is no less insistent in asking for the intercession of a church on
his behalf:

---

1 N.Q. ii. 36; white animals were sacrificed to propitiate the lightning, probably
because it came from heavenly regions.

2 Cf. de Bovis, p. 205: 'un des mécanismes de la Nécessité Universelle'; Robert
M. Grant, *Miracle and Natural Law*, 1952, p. 10 f.: '...since the order of nature
was immutable, prayer to the gods was useless'; D. Loenen, *Eusebeia en de cardinale
deugden*, 1960, p. 46 f.

3 Rom. 1 : 9.

4 Phil. 1 : 3, 4.

5 Col. 1 : 3; cf. 1 Cor. 1 : 4; Eph. 1 : 16; Phil. 1 : 9; Col. 1 : 9; 1 Thess. 1 : 2;
2 Thess. 1 : 3, 11; Philem. 4.

You also must help us by prayer, so that many will give thanks on our behalf for the blessing granted us in answer to many prayers. 1 I appeal to you, brethren, by our Lord Jesus Christ and by the love of the Spirit, to strive together with me in your prayers to God on my behalf, that I may be delivered from the unbelievers in Judea, and that my service for Jerusalem may be acceptable to the saints, so that by God's will I may come to you with joy and be refreshed in your company. 2 Pray at all times in the Spirit, with all prayer and supplication. To that end keep alert with all perseverance, making supplication for all the saints, and also for me, that utterance may be given me in opening my mouth boldly to proclaim the mystery of the gospel, for which I am an ambassador in chains; that I may declare it boldly, as I ought to speak. 3

And just as he asks the church in Rome 'to strive together with me in your prayers to God on my behalf' (Rom. 15 : 30), so also does he know that Epaphras is 'always remembering you earnestly in his prayers' (Col. 4 : 12).

In this intercession many requests are made for the joy and strength of the Gospel, for the courage required to preach the Gospel, and also for more concrete things. The principal and most frequent is that God may grant that both the Apostle and the Church fit into the order of salvation as willingly and well-preparedly as possible, that this order of salvation be abundantly realized in them, in their lives, communal life, and in the world. When Paul gives thanks to God, he does so first 'because of the grace of God which was given you in Christ Jesus' (1 Cor. 1 : 4), and 'for your partnership in the gospel from the first day until now' (Phil. 1 : 5). And when he asks for the churches to pray for him, he does so first 'that God may open to us a door for the word, to declare the mystery of Christ' (Col. 4 : 3).

Accordingly he is able to exhort the churches to pray constantly, while such prayers are apparently bound together closely with the joy of living according to the Gospel (1 Thess. 5 : 17). The churches should not be anxious, for they can make known to God their wishes by prayer (Phil. 4 : 6). In the middle of his discussion on the value of glossolaly, Paul mentions prayer in the churches; he reminds the Corinthians that they should not only pray with the spirit but also with the mind (1 Cor. 14 : 13-15). It is of great benefit to marital relations now and then to set aside time for prayer (1 Cor. 7 : 5).

Such prayer is never lacking in meaning, because it is addressed

---

1 2 Cor. 1 : 11.
2 Rom. 15 : 30-32.
3 Eph. 6 : 18-20; cf. Col. 4 : 3; 1 Thess. 5 : 25; 2 Thess. 3 : 1; Philem. 22.

to the God and Father of our Lord Jesus Christ, because He may be
invoked as abba, Father. For in Christ we have been adopted as His
sons. The churches have not received the spirit of slavery to fear
afresh, but they have received the spirit of sonship, on account of
which we may say: abba, Father. This Spirit bears witness with our
spirit that we are children of God (Rom. 8 : 15, 16; cf. Gal. 4 : 6).
It is, moreover, this Spirit who comes to our aid in our human weakness, when we do not know how we ought to pray (Rom. 8 : 26).
If we bear in mind how much a part the Holy Spirit is of God's
work of salvation — He is the 'guarantee' (Eph. 1 : 14; 2 Cor. 1 : 22;
5 : 5), the first fruit (Rom. 8 : 23), a typical gift of the end of time,
who holds out promise of the fulfilment —, then we realize how
prayer too, abundant, fully convinced prayer, is involved in the whole
order of salvation, which has been revealed in Christ and which will
be continued until the day of Jesus Christ.

Prayer is part of the whole message of rejoicing in the Lord (Phil.
4 : 4). If God did not even spare His own Son but gave Him up for
us, then it is plain that He will give us all things with Him (Rom.
8 : 32). If Christ is on God's right hand and pleads for us, what is
there left to separate us from the love of God in Christ (Rom. 8 :
34 ff). Then it goes without saying that the faithful may approach
God with confidence.

Indeed, it goes without saying. For what has been said of prayer
in the New Testament in general may equally well be applied to Paul:
'Das Charakteristikum des urchristlichen Betens ist die einzigartige Er-
hörungsgewissheit.' [1] It is remarkable that nowhere in the Pauline
epistles is there any explicit mention made of the possibility or the
certainty of prayers being heard, despite the fact that this is taken
for granted by Paul. This does not mean that prayer here too, though
in a different way, is a part in the mechanism of the machinery of
salvation, that it automatically becomes operative like a new law, that
it acquires a magic influence over God's actions, and hence is of
effect within the framework of a new law of cause and result. There is

---

[1] *Th. W.* II, p. 802; cf. K. Barth, *Die kirchliche Dogmatik* iii. 3, p. 323; 'Das
ist die Gnade Gottes gegenüber dem sündigen Menschen, dass er ihn nicht nur zur
Demut des Knechtes und zur Dankbarkeit des Kindes, sondern zur Vertraulichkeit
und Kühnheit seines Freundes beruft, an die Seite seines Thrones, an seine eigene
Seite, dass er ihm nicht nur erlaubt, sondern gebietet, ihn anzurufen in der bestimm-
ten Erwartung, dass er ihn nicht nur hören, sondern eben erhören werde, dass sein
Bitten also nicht nur subjektive, sondern auch objektive Bedeutung, nämlich Bedeutung für sein eignes Tun haben werde.'

one place in the Pauline epistles where the Apostle refers to a very personal matter which he has brought before the Lord in prayer. He has prayed three times to the Lord concerning an ailment which has been most troublesome to him, 'that it should leave me'. He receives the following answer: 'My grace is sufficient for you, for my power is made perfect in weakness' (2 Cor. 12 : 7-10). This is not an answer to his prayer in the usual sense of the word. But still it does not lead Paul to speak about the problem of the effect of prayer. He evidently continues to believe that God can do something in answer to prayer that He would not have done without prayer, or that He can leave undone something that He would otherwise not have left undone.

This is a characteristic difference between Paul and Seneca: Paul's way of thinking and living revolves around his unshakable belief in the God and Father of Jesus Christ, which inevitably causes him to see prayer too against the background of the living God's proclamation of salvation; Seneca is obliged to argue about prayer in terms of his conception of God, and to incorporate it as best he can in a logical train of thought, which is in harmony with a particular theory of the universe. For him the notion 'god' is in itself a subject to be reflected upon, and the upshot of a closely reasoned, intellectual argument. This notion is one logically constructed by human thought, which of course also demands a justification of prayer. Such a difference is only to be expected in view of the divergent notion of God. Seneca, who time and again identifies God with nature and fate, can never achieve that unreasoned confidence in the possibility of communion between God and man in prayer, in which man calls upon God, because God has first called him. [1]

It is plain that the difference in the point of departure may also lead to a great divergence in practical conduct. An example of this is to be found in Seneca's attitude towards *suicide*.

In antiquity suicide was frequently practised, and was accepted by many as the obvious means of escape from all sorts of distress, misery and oppression. To us it is sometimes astounding how insignificant

---

[1] Cf. *Th. W.* iii, p. 111 f.: 'Die zahllosen Zeugnisse lebendigen Betens im NT sind ebenso viele Zeugnisse für den persönlichen Gott, an den das Urchristentum glaubte, sind zugleich Zeugnisse dafür, in welchem Sinne hier der Begriff der Persönlichkeit Gottes verstanden werden muss: Der Gott des NT ist ein Gott, zu dem der Mensch Du sagen darf, wie man nur zu einem personhaften Wesen Du sagen kann. Dieses Du Sagen des Menschen zu Gott aber ist die Antwort auf das Du. mit dem Gott den Menschen angerednet hat'; cf. also Th. Schreiner, op. cit., p. 53-62.

were the reasons why many of the ancients committed suicide, sometimes quite resignedly, and often with the complete approval of their
nearest connections, and within sight of their families and friends. Of
the latter Seneca's own suicide is a striking, but not exceptional
example. [1] Appalled though we may be by the suicides in antiquity
which are recorded with almost monotonous regularity, [2] we may
nevertheless be sure that the Romans themselves, and certainly those
who quite placidly and voluntarily made an end to their lives, did not
react thus. On the whole their attitude was quite the reverse; they
did not consider suicide as a sin against the gods, but often looked
upon an exaggerated attachment to life as ignominious and cowardly.

Suicide was, however, occasionally condemned in antiquity, and
some of these condemnations must certainly be ascribed to religious
beliefs. An instance of this is to be found in *Phaedo* 62C in which it is
said that the gods look after us and we human beings are among
their possessions. Socrates asks Cebes:

> "Then wouldn't you yourself be angry if one of the creatures you pos-
> sessed were to put an end to itself without your signifying that it was
> your wish for it to die? And if there were any punishment you could
> inflict, would you not inflict it?"
> "Certainly."
> "Well, perhaps that shows that it isn't unreasonable that a man ought
> not to put an end to himself until God brings constraint upon him, as
> he does now upon me." [3]

Generally speaking, however, suicide was not condemned. On the
contrary, it was usually considered to be closely linked with the will
of God. Socrates, too, does not wholly condemn it in the *Phaedo*,
adding as he does a clause open to various interpretations: 'until God
brings constraint upon him'. He is, as is evident from the words 'as
he does now upon me', alluding to his own case, and it is possible
that he would not have deemed suffering or misery to be such a
ἀνάγκη; Seneca on the other hand is quite convinced that God sometimes shows it to be his wish that a man should choose to leave this

[1] Tacitus, *Ann.* 15. 61 ff.
[2] Cf. C. F. Georg Heinrici, *Hellenismus und Christentum*, 1909, p. 23: 'Geradezu
erschütternd sind die praktischen Folgerungen, welche die römischen Aristokraten
der Kaiserzeit aus diesen Anschauungen zogen; die Belege für den famosae mortis
amor (Horat., *Ars poet.* 469) sind eines der düstersten Blätter der Annalen des
Tacitus.'
[3] Plato's *Phaedo*, trans. with Introduction and Commentary by R. Hackforth, Cam-
bridge, 1955.

life. It is a privilege which man has received from God, that he is
free to leave this life at any moment, if it should oppress him to greatly.

Seneca does, however, sharply condemn those who are rash and
cowardly in their acceptance of such a means of escape. He too is
sometimes shocked to observe:

> what trifling reasons impel men to scorn life. One hangs himself
> before the door of his mistress; another hurls himself from the house-
> top that he may no longer be compelled to bear the taunts of a bad-
> tempered master; a third, to be saved from arrest after running away,
> drives a sword into his vitals. Do you not suppose that virtue will be
> as efficacious as excessive fear? 1

Seneca apparently censures those who take refuge in suicide because
they are bored with life. 2 The dangers to be avoided are twofold:

> For we need to be warned and strengthened in both directions, — not
> to love or to hate life overmuch; even when reason advises us to make
> an end of it, the impulse is not to be adopted without reflection or at
> headlong speed. The brave and wise man should not beat a hasty
> retreat from life; he should make a becoming exit. And above all, he
> should avoid the weakness which has taken possession of so many, —
> the lust for death. For just as there is an unreflecting tendency of the
> mind towards other things, so, my dear Lucilius, there is an unreflecting
> tendency towards death; this often seizes upon the noblest and most
> spirited men, as well as upon the craven and the abject. The former
> despise life; the latter find it irksome. 3

We must know exactly where to draw the line. There are situations
which urge us to depart this life, but others by no means justify such
a decision. Seneca, himself, gives some examples of where he thinks
the line should be drawn:

> I shall not abandon old age, if old age preserves me intact for myself,
> and intact as regards the better part of myself; but if old age begins
> to shatter my mind, and to pull its various faculties to pieces, if it
> leaves me, not life, but only the breath of life, I shall rush out of a
> house that is crumbling and tottering. I shall not avoid illness by seeking
> death, as long as the illness is curable and does not impede my soul.
> I shall not lay violent hands upon myself just because I am in pain;
> for death under such circumstances is defeat. But if I find out that the
> pain must always be endured, I shall depart, not because of the pain,
> but because it will be a hindrance to me as regards all my reasons for

---

1 *Ep.* 4. 4.
2 *Tranqu. an.* 2. 15.
3 *Ep.* 24. 24, 25; cf. 30. 15.

living. He who dies just because he is in pain is a weakling, a coward;
but he who lives merely to brave out this pain, is a fool. [1]

Sometimes the proper feelings of others ought to be taken into
account when suicide is being contemplated:

> For one must indulge genuine emotions; sometimes, even in spite of
> weighty reasons, the breath of life must be called back and kept at our
> very lips even at the price of great suffering, for the sake of those
> whom we hold dear; because the good man should not live as long as
> it pleases him, but as long as he ought. He who does not value his wife,
> or his friend, highly enough to linger longer in life — he who obstinately
> persists in dying — is a voluptuary .... It gives proof of a great heart
> to return to life for the sake of others; and noble men have often done
> this. [2]

Seneca's own behaviour set an example for this: when in youth he
was sometimes so sick and miserable that he nurtured plans of suicide,
the thought of his old father restrained him. [3]

It must, however, be borne in mind that Seneca interprets this
solicitude for others as a concession to the emotions. For when he
writes about suicide — and he does so extremely often —, it is
frequently noticeable that he looks upon it as a decision for which
the individual is himself responsible. The wise man possesses sovereign
power over his own life. He ought not to depart this life for frivolous
reasons, *ex frivolis causis*. And the wise man will be prevented from
doing so by his reason, but he has complete freedom to decide whether
he has more urgent reasons to do so than mere *frivolae causae*. Ultimately he is responsible to no one else but himself, his own reason.

Therefore Seneca always thinks of suicide primarily as an expression of the confident courage of the wise man who refuses to be
deprived of his freedom in any way, who, quite independent of all
other persons and emotions whatsoever, only allows his actions to be
dictated by his own reason. [4] He alone can determine the right moment
to escape the *male vivere* and seek the *bene mori*. [5] He must decide
when the time has come 'that the foulest death is preferable to the
fairest slavery', as it had in the life of that German whom Seneca
extols so exuberantly and who choked himself in the latrine with the
sponge,

---

[1] *Ep.* 58. 35, 36.
[2] *Ep.* 104. 3, 4.
[3] *Ep.* 78. 1, 2; cf. *N.Q.* iv Praef. 17.
[4] See e.g. *Ep.* 4. 5; 24. 25; 69. 6.
[5] *Ep.* 70. 6; elsewhere too Seneca refers to the *bene mori*, e.g. *Tranqu. an.* 11. 4.

which was devoted to the vilest uses .... Yes, indeed; it was not a
very elegant or becoming way to die; but what is more foolish than
to be over-nice about dying ?What a brave fellow! He surely deserved
to be allowed to choose his fate! [1]

Time and again the possibility of suicide, of a voluntary departure
from life is for Seneca a sign of man's freedom, proof of the fact that
he cannot be enslaved in any way against his will for:

> in any kind of servitude the way lies open to liberty. If the soul is
> sick and because of its own imperfection unhappy, a man may end its
> sorrows and at the same time himself .... In whatever direction you
> may turn your eyes, there lies the means to end your woes. See you that
> precipice? Down that is the way to liberty. See you that sea, that river,
> that well? There sits liberty at the bottom. See you that tree, stunted,
> blighted, and barren? Yet from its branches hangs liberty. See you
> that throat of yours, your gullet, your heart? They are ways of escape
> from servitude. Are the ways of egress I show you too toilsome, do they
> require too much courage and strength? Do you ask what is the highway
> to liberty? Any vein in your body! [2]

Seneca often refers to suicide as the path to liberty. [3] He repeatedly
mentions Cato as an example of how to die manfully. He proved that
he was free by making an end to his life. [4] Hence suicide is glorified
in a constantly recurring hymn to freedom.

The ever present opportunity to depart this life is a gift of the
gods. It sometimes seems as if man is obliged to live under an ines-
capable constraint. This would be an evil. Seneca quotes a passage from
Epicurus: "It is wrong to live under constraint; but no man is constrained to live under constraint" upon which he comments:

> Of course not. On all sides lie many short and simple paths to freedom;
> and let us thank God that no man can be kept in life. We may spurn
> the very constraints that hold us. [5]

It is God who has arranged matters so that we are never imprisoned
in this life for ever. When it is a case of *necessitas* (cf. Socrates'
ἀνάγκη), God himself opens up the way for us to escape from this
necessitas.

---

[1] *Ep.* 70. 20, 21; cf. *Ep.* 77. 15: *vita, si moriendi virtus abest, servitus est*; *Ep.*
91. 15: *Nihil horum indignandum est. In eum intravimus mundum, in quo his
legibus vivitur. Placet; pare. Non placet; quacumque vis, exi*; *Ep.* 117. 21; *N.Q.* vi.
32. 4.

[2] *Ira* iii. 15. 3, 4.

[3] *Ep.* 12. 10; 26. 10; 66. 13; 70. 5, 12, 16, 23, 24; 77. 15; *Marc.* 20. 3; cf. E.
Benz, *Das Todesproblem in der stoischen Philosophie,* 1929, p. 73 ff.

[4] *Ep.* 13. 14; *Ep.* 24. 6-8; *Prov.* 2. 10; *Const.* 2. 3.

[5] *Ep.* 12. 10.

God has seen to it that man can never be kept in this life against his will. Whatever the trouble God says to man:

> Above all, I have taken pains that nothing should keep you here against your will; the way out lies open. If you do not choose to fight, you may run away. Therefore of all things that I have deemed necessary for you, I have made nothing easier than dying. I have set life on a downward slope: if it is prolonged, only observe and you will see what a short and easy path leads to liberty. I have not imposed upon you at your exit the wearisome delay you had at entrance. Otherwise, if death came to a man as slowly as his birth, Fortune would have kept her great dominion over you. [1]

As may be expected Seneca emphatically opposes those philosophers who condemn suicide:

> You can find men who have gone so far as to profess wisdom and yet maintain that one should not offer violence to one's own life, and hold it accursed for a man to be the means of his own destruction; we should wait, say they, for the end decreed by nature. But one who says this does not see that he is shutting off the path to freedom. The best thing which eternal law ever ordained was that it allowed to us one entrance into life, but many exits .... This is the one reason why we cannot complain of life: it keeps no one against his will. [2]

Hence it is by no means contrary to the godhead's will if the wise man at some time or other chooses to make an end to his life. Indeed, it is precisely because of the divine order of things that he is at all times at liberty to make an end to himself. God himself has opened up the way for him to free himself from any sort of slavery. In the *necessitates ultimae,* if the utmost pinch of need arrives, [3] he is never imprisoned for ever, because God always holds open the door for him, *patet exitus.* [4] Is this a manifestation of the loving care of a God who is involved in human destiny, whose solicitude accompanies a human being on all his travels? Or does Seneca here, too, despite the personal sounding phrases which he frequently uses, really mean something far more impersonal? Is it not nature whose laws have ordained that a human being can enter life only along one road, but can leave it along many, that the road to life is fraught with difficulties, but that the road away from it is open at all times? At all events as elsewhere in Seneca, here, too, in these statements on suicide

---

1 *Prov.* 6. 7; cf. Ep. 17. 9.
2 *Ep.* 70. 14, 15.
3 *Ep.* 17. 9.
4 *Prov.* 6. 7.

the word God might well be replaced by other words, without it being detrimental to the sense as a whole. In fact Seneca does this himself when he says that life does not hold us prisoner, and that an eternal law, an *aeterna lex,* has ordained that we should have one entrance into life, but many exits. [1] It is striking that Seneca should also use this same expression *aeterna lex* at the beginning of his *De Providentia* to indicate the wonderful order of the universe: the flight of the stars, the swift revolution of the heavens is ruled by eternal law, *aeternae legis imperio.* [2] Who is it who gives us freedom, that gift for which we may be grateful? A God who in this way, and at a particular time, shows how much he cares for man? Or is this freedom incorporated in the natural order of things, so that man can, whenever he desires, make use of the possibilities embodied in nature? I believe that Seneca intended the latter. But it is characteristic that here, too, there is for him no essential difference between the various modes of expression. God, nature, life, the eternal law are all different ways of saying the same thing. [3]

It is plain that fundamental differences emerge between Seneca's estimation of suicide and Paul's preaching of the Gospel. No immediate comparisons can of course be made, since Paul nowhere speaks of suicide or the possibility of it. At the most those places can be compared where Paul writes of a desire to depart. 'We would rather be away from the body and at home with the Lord' (2 Cor. 5 : 8). 'My desire is to depart and be with Christ, for that is far better' (Phil. 1 : 23). But how vastly different are these texts from Seneca if we read them both in their setting! Even the quoted passages testify to the fact that death is only desired in so far as it holds forth a prospect of being at home with the Lord. Hence Paul does not really long for death; he longs to be with Christ. But if Christ can still use him here on earth, he will of course choose life. Although Paul is often prepared to loose his life, he never glorifies death jubilantly, not

---

[1] *Ep.* 70. 15, 14.

[2] *Prov.* 1. 2.

[3] Cf. A. Bonhöffer, *Epiktet und das Neue Testament,* 1911, p. 6 f., where he says in connection with Epictetus's ideas on suicide: 'Wenn der Philosoph, der sittlich Gebildete je in die Lage kommt, seinem Leben selbst ein Ende zu machen, so tut er es ja *in völligstem Einklang mit dem Willen der Gottheit,* ohne eine Spur von Bitterkeit gegen sie, ohne auch nur im geringsten deshalb an ihrer fortdauernden Liebe und Weisheit zu zweifeln. Man kann diese Anschauung sonderbar und verkehrt finden, aber von einem Konflikt zwischen göttlicher Vorsehung und dem Recht des Menschen auf sein eigenes Leben kann auf dem Standpunkt der Stoa keine Rede sein.'

even when it means martyrdom for Christ's sake, as did Ignatius who feared that the intervention of the church in Rome might at the last moment prevent his dying for Christ (Ign. *Rom.* 4). Paul writes with great restraint about the question of life and death, also in those two places where he clearly expresses his personal desire to be with the Lord. It is not death upon which his mind centres but Christ, in life and in death:

> So whether we are at home or away, we make it our aim to please him.
> For we must all appear before the judgment seat of Christ, so that each
> one may receive good or evil, according to what he has done in the
> body (2 Cor. 5 : 9, 10).

In Phil. 1 he finally and emphatically chooses life instead of death, even though he by no means disguises the fact that he personally desires 'to depart and be with Christ', that for him 'to die is to gain' (Phil. 1 : 23, 21). Life and death are not important in themselves, but 'it is my eager expectation and hope that I shall not be at all ashamed, but that with full courage now as always Christ will be honored in my body, whether by life or by death' (Phil. 1 : 20). For him 'to live is Christ' and 'if it is to be life in the flesh, that means fruitful labor for me' (Phil. 1 : 21, 22). Even if it is 'far better' to depart and be with Christ, 'to remain in the flesh is more necessary on your account' (Phil. 1 : 24). Accordingly, however difficult the choice may be for him personally, Paul finally chooses life and not death, despite the fact that death means 'to depart and be with Christ'. Death in itself is not idealized, a heroic death is not glorified, instead Christ and the service of the Lord in the Church are the centre of attention. [1]

But even if immediate points of comparison are lacking with respect to the subject of suicide, Paul must certainly have encountered situations in his life which Seneca would have deemed to be *ultimae necessitates,* from which man may and can escape by turning towards the path to freedom. Paul never, however, mentions the distress and misery in his life in order to illustrate by his attitude in such circumstances the courage and determination that can be displayed by man; it may even be said that it is only by chance that we know of what he had been through; that is to say because Paul felt compelled by his opponents' attitude to allude to this subject. Therefore he only speaks of it against his will, really considering the mention of his experiences to be a foolishness on his part. But because his opponents are en-

---

[1] Cf. K. Barth, *Die kirchliche Dogmatik,* iii. 2, p. 779 f.

deavouring to depreciate the work he has done as a servant of Christ, he is obliged to write about his sufferings. [1]

What is remarkable with respect to his writing about the heavy external pressure that was brought to bear on his life is that he is nearly always referring to the suffering which he voluntarily takes upon himself as a servant of Christ. To put it bluntly: by far the greater part of his sufferings would never have befallen him, had he not been an ambassador of Christ, and striven to deliver his Lord's message as faithfully as possible. These trials and tribulations are his lot because he preaches the Gospel. Hence right from the start the troubles and distress which Paul experiences as a result of his working as a servant of Christ assume a quite different character from that of Seneca's *ultimae necessitates,* the distress and misery into which man is thrown by fate or the godhead. If suffering is entailed in the work that he does as a servant of Christ in this world, he will even gladly submit himself to it, because it is an integral part of God's work of salvation in Christ. Such suffering is ultimately suffering in fellowship with Christ and is therefore something in which one may rejoice. Paul knows himself to be a member of a very special generation, the generation 'upon whom the end of the ages has come' (1 Cor. 10 : 11). It is a characteristic of the end of time that it will bring many trials and afflictions to those who are in Christ, in whose life, death and resurrection the close of the age is made manifest, in whom the mystery which has been hidden for ages and generations is now revealed to his saints (Col. 1 : 26). Now that the Messiah has appeared in Jesus Christ, and the decisive close of the age has been ushered in accordingly, the suffering which belongs to that time has also been entered upon. With this, suffering is instantly placed in a much broader perspective. This eschatological suffering, which had its inception in the sufferings and death of Jesus Christ, is upheld in the sufferings of those who belong to Him. The suffering of the Apostles and of the churches is suffering in fellowship with Christ. [2] Therefore Paul feels so much comfort, even when in the greatest distress, that he can pass on the comfort that he himself knows to others. [3] Particularly in the pericope in which Paul testifies to the fact that 'as we share abundantly in Christ's sufferings, so through Christ we share abun-

---

[1] 2 Cor. 11 : 21-33; cf. 1 Cor. 4 : 11-13; 2 Cor. 4 : 8, 9; 6 : 4-10.
[2] Cf. 2 Cor. 4 : 17, 18; 1 Thess. 3 : 3, 4; 2 Cor. 1 : 5; Rom. 14 : 7, 8; Rom. 8 : 17; 2 Cor. 4 : 10 f.; Phil. 3 : 5-11; Gal. 6 : 17; Col. 1 : 24.
[3] 2 Cor. 1 : 3-7.

dantly in comfort too' (2 Cor. 1 : 5) there are expressions evocative
of a situation which Seneca would most surely have regarded as one
in which a human being has a right to choose the path to freedom
which God, nature, life, fate has left open to him: 'we were so utterly
unbearably crushed that we despaired of life itself. Why, we felt that
we had received the sentence of death' (2 Cor. 1 : 8, 9; cf. 1 Cor.
15 : 32), but even, or rather precisely, in a situation such as this
Paul immediately points to the victorious God of salvation, saying:

> but that was to make us rely not on ourselves but on God who raises the
> dead; he delivered us from such a deadly peril, and he will deliver
> us; on him we have set our hope that he will deliver us again (2 Cor.
> 1 : 9, 10).

Paul never loses courage, and is able to bear with and accept life,
even rejoicing in it, because he knows of the existence of the God and
Father of our Lord Jesus Christ, the Father of mercies and God of all
comfort (2 Cor. 1 : 3), who calls and is faithful (1 Thess. 5 : 24),
who will never let him be tempted beyond his strength (1 Cor.
10 : 13).

Consequently it is ultimately Paul's particular message concerning
God and Jesus Christ which prevents even the thought of the possibility
of suicide from arising. The living God, who by means of His re-
deeming work has granted man salvation, and can grant deliverance
at any given moment, is the giver of a liberty of a very different
nature from the freedom that Seneca's god always holds open in the
iter ad libertatem. For Paul the only *bene mori* [1] is living and dying
for Christ's sake; to be liberated from all other forms of slavery is to
be the slave of Christ. Suffering with Christ is in all circumstances
one of those experiences which may be rejoiced in as rewarding for
Christ's sake.

And so it may be seen that the difference between Paul's and
Seneca's attitude towards suicide is not merely an incidental side-issue,
but that it touches on the very heart of the matter: their divergent
conception of God. The permissability and frequently even the un-
reserved acceptance of suicide are by no means incongruous with Seneca's conception of God's rule, and of providence. Hence there is little
to be gained by examining this question separately, only to bring to
light extenuating circumstances. [2] What concerns us here is the exist-

---

[1] See above p. 55.
[2] Thus e.g. Kreyher, pp. 109-12; G. A. van den Bergh van Eysinga, *De Wereld
van het Nieuwe Testament*, 1929, p. 228 f.

tence of a choice of starting-points. Once this choice has been made, it gives rise to a variety of consequences. One of the scholars who attempt to defend the Stoic school on this point is quite justified in saying that the Stoic attitude towards suicide is entirely consistent with the Stoic belief in providence. But when he goes on to say that 'suicide after mature consideration is a natural and reasonable action in keeping with the words of the poet: "das Leben ist der Güter höchstes nicht", in which the heroism of Christian martyrdom will ultimately also have its roots', [1] then he is placing on one and the same level two notions which, if examined carefully, are virtually incomparable, belonging as they do to two entirely different worlds. Heroism, for instance, is a term which the first Christians, if they were thoroughly familiar with Paul's letters, would never have been able to use, and which therefore right from the start gives rise to such enormous misunderstandings with respect to the death of Christians, that its application must inevitably lead to a distortion of Christian motives and most certainly of Paul's motives. Martyrdom means bearing witness not to one's own courage and confidence in one's freedom but to Jesus Christ, to the salvation, which God has granted us in Him, which is given to man and is not innate in him. To testify to this the Christian is prepared to suffer and die, but it is plain that this death has nothing in common with the road to freedom which the Stoics believed was held open by God, in order that man might not be obliged to lose his own moral dignity. It is not surprising that those with no insight into the motives of the Christian martyr's death should depreciate it, measuring it by the standards of the perfectly controlled, calm way of dying of the Stoics; that Epictetus spoke slightingly of the way the Galileans died as ὑπο ἔθους, [2] while Marcus Aurelius referred to it as κατὰ ψιλὴν παράταξιν, not λελογισμένως καὶ σεμνῶς καὶ ὥστε καὶ ἄλλον πεῖσαι ἀτραγῴδως. [3]

---

[1] G. A. van den Bergh van Eysinga, *op. cit.*, p. 229; Kreyher too compares this attitude with that of the Christian martyrs.

[2] Epict. *Diss.* iv. 7. 6.

[3] Marc. Aurelius, *In semet ipsum* xi. 3. 2; cf. A. J. Festugière O.P., *L'idéal religieux des Grecs et l'Évangile*, 1932, p. 269: 'Le seul mot ἀτραγῴδως précisément employé dans un blâme au sujet des chrétiens, nous est un témoignage sûr. C'est toute la fierté grecque, et sa pudeur hautaine, qui vient effleurer ici.'

CHAPTER THREE

MAN

If we make a comparison between Paul and Seneca's anthropological ideas, then here, too, we are confronted by the different nature of their writings. Paul's letters were not written to inform us of his theology, and even less to give us an account of his anthropology. In order to be able to say something about his beliefs concerning mankind — and it will become apparent that this is not completely impossible — we have to bring together texts and passages from letters which Paul himself usually intended to be read in quite a different connection. Paul does not give us a coherent doctrine concerning man, his mental and physical capacities, his spiritual life, his possibilities, his emotions, his virtues and abilities. In Paul we seek in vain for a theory concerning the relationship between the body and soul. If we wish to give a systematic description of his anthropology we shall have to be prepared for the fact that there are frequent hiates. The subject is only touched upon by Paul in passing, and even then this is never done for the sake of anthropology as such. Nevertheless his fundamental ideas on man do not remain a mystery to us. It may even be said that it is easier to give an account of what Paul thought of mankind than of what is said on this subject in the gospels. At least there are in Paul relatively long passages which may serve as the raw material for the construction of an anthropology. [1] But even then we must not forget that Paul never writes about this subject from a theoretical anthropological interest, that is to say from an interest in man as such. Even when he does write about man he is really concerned with one thing only: God's salvation in Christ. Romans 7, for example, which contains numerous statements that are of great significance in the construction of Paul's anthropology, only acquires the meaning Paul intends it to have, if we view it within the framework of the complete description of the salvation-occurrence in Rom. 1-8. Whatever Paul says about the body, soul, spirit, conscience, heart or

---

[1] Cf. W. G. Kümmel, *Das Bild des Menschen im Neuen Testament,* 1948, p. 20: 'Ist doch Paulus der einzige Zeuge des N.T., der in grösserem Umfang direkte Aussagen über das Wesen des Menschen macht und die anthropologischen Begriffe seiner Zeit in reichlichem Masse verwendet.'

flesh is never said because of his interest in man as such, and even
when he writes more extensively on such matters, he is only mentioning
them in passing, his thoughts being completely occupied by what God
does in Christ through the Holy Spirit.

This may be readily illustrated by one particular point and one
text. The question has sometimes been raised whether Paul thought
of man as dichotomous or trichotomous. Everything tells in favour
of the former, but there is one text in particular by reason of which
it has been argued that Paul was strongly inclined towards trichotomy,
namely 1 Thess. 5 : 23, where man is said to comprise of 'spirit and
soul and body'. But it is immediately obvious from the context that
it is by no means Paul's intention to enrich his readers' knowledge of
man; the accent does not lie on the anthropological aspect, but on the
theological, Christological, soteriological aspect of this text: 'May the
God of peace himself sanctify you wholly; and may your spirit and
soul and body be kept sound and blameless at the coming of our Lord
Jesus Christ.' If we do give this text our attention from an anthropological view point, we cannot but notice that such attention is really
out of proportion to the meaning which this fortuitous trichotomous
remark has for Paul himself. If we are interested in Paul's anthropological ideas we must of course examine a text such as this with
care, and the problem has frequently been contemplated as to whether
pneuma should be taken to refer to the human or the holy, divine
Spirit.

Calvin already remarked upon the singularity of this trichotomy
in his commentary on this passage. [1] He rejects the interpretation
which makes *anima* refer to the *motus vitalis,* and *spiritus* to the *pars
hominis renovata.* For then, he goes on to say, Paul's prayer would
be absurd. Indeed, Paul would not have to pray for the Holy Spirit,
who after all already belongs to God's world, who here on earth
already points towards the complete salvation of the coming aeon,
in the words of 1 Thess. 5 : 23. Whether Calvin's own interpretation
in which he makes *spiritus* refer to the *ratio vel intelligentia* and *anima*
to the *voluntas et omnes affectus* is correct seems to me doubtful. Barth [2]

---

[1] A. Tholuck, *Joannis Calvini in Novum Testamentum Commentarii,* Vol. VI,
1834, p. 301: 'Notanda est autem haec hominis partitio: nam aliquando homo sim-
pliciter corpore et anima constare dicitur, ac tunc anima spiritum immortalem signi-
ficat, qui in corpore habitat tamquam in domicilio.'
[2] K. Barth, *Die kirchliche Dogmatik,* iii. 2, 1948, p. 427.

who quotes Calvin dismisses the latter's interpretation. He himself rejects the trichotomy, [1] but admits:

> Die einzige Bibelstelle, die man in dieser Hinsicht als undeutlich ansprechen könnte, ist 1 Thess. 5 : 23. Es ist zuzugeben, dass diese Stelle hart klingt: wegen der nur leise differenzierten Aneinanderreihung der drei Begriffe und noch mehr wegen des Umstandes, dass Paulus hier auch den Geist als der Bewahrung bedürftig, als nicht *per se* vollständig bewahrt zu bezeichnen scheint.

And he goes on to say:

> Die, wenn auch leise Differenzierung, in der der "Geist" der Seele und dem Leib gegenübergestellt werden, muss entscheidend beachtet werden, weil die Stelle, wenn sie vom „Geist" wirklich als von einem Dritten neben Seele und Leib reden würde, nicht nur bei Paulus, sondern auch im übrigen A. und N. T. ganz allein stehen würde [2]

In spite of Luke 1 : 46 f. and Heb. 4 : 12 Barth insists that 1 Thess. 5 : 23 is the only scriptural passage which might be said to be lacking in clarity in this respect. He paraphrases the passage as follows:

> Er selbst, der Gott des Friedens, heilige euch in der Ganzheit eures Seins, und es werde euer Geist (der diese Ganzheit eures Seins begründet und garantiert) und mit ihm die Seele und der Leib ohne jede Einbusse bewahrt in der Wiederkunft unseres Herrn Jesus Christus.

And further:

> Sie [die Parusie] bringe ihnen die Erhaltung ihres ganzen menschlichen Seins durch denselben Geist, durch den es jetzt schon begründet und konstituiert ist .... Was wir auch vom Geist des Menschen sonst zu hören bekommen, es geht jedenfalls immer um ein Zentrum seines Wesens und seiner Existenz, das neben Seele und Leib kein Drittes, sondern *in* Leib und Seele zugleich *über* und *jenseits* von beiden zu suchen, das als der Repräsentant der göttlichen Schöpfungsgnade gegenüber dem Ganzen des Wesens und der Existenz des Menschen zu verstehen ist. [3]

It is obvious that the text itself contains no distinction such as is made here by Barth. There is no mention of the spirit constituting the foundation of the whole of man's being. Barth's attempt to ascribe such a particular function to the spirit in this text, so that it is in any case not on one line with body and soul, arises from a desire to remove from this text too — according to him the only scriptural passage where this is necessary — as much as is possible of the trichotomy, so that man may subsequently be spoken of as body and soul. But from this text

---

[1] As the Fourth Constantinopolitan Council did already in 869-70; see Henricus Denzinger, *Enchiridion Symbolorum*, 1946, 338 can. 11.

[2] K. Barth, op. cit., pp. 426, 427.

[3] K. Barth, op. cit., p. 436 f.

it is by no means possible to infer that the spirit is to be found in the body and soul, and at the same time above and beyond both.

Naturally many commentators have observed the singularity of 1 Thess. 5 : 23 and have pondered the trichotomy of this text. [1] It is rightly pointed out by an increasing number of scholars that no anthropological emphasis should be laid on the trichotomy in it, and that an entirely incorrect accent is given, if an attempt is made to unravel the relationship between 'spirit and soul and body' anthropologically. Equally correct is the observation that in this passage *pneuma* is not a reference to the Holy Spirit. This identification is still disqualified by Calvin's argument that it would make Paul's prayer absurd. Paul would never place soul and body on one line with the Holy Spirit. Consequently the word *pneuma* refers to man's own spirit (cf. Rom. 8 : 16; 1 Cor. 2 : 11). When Paul mentions 'spirit and soul and body' side by side with one another, he wishes this to mean no more nor less than the complete man, and he does not consider these terms anthropologically at all. One of the most recent commentators on 1 Thess., W. Neil, draws a good parallel here:

He [Paul] is speaking rhetorically, not theologically .... A modern preacher would urge his congregation to put their 'hearts and souls' into an evangelistic mission, with an equal disregard for psychological exactitude.

Neil also quite properly observes that Paul was just as 'unconcerned about psychology' here as Jesus was in Mark 12 : 30. [2] Comparison with texts such as Deut. 6 : 5 and Mark 12 : 30 is indeed a step in the right direction. There, too, we are guilty of incorrect emphasis if we endeavour to determine what each individual word in the enumeration means exactly. There, too, the true accent should fall on the complete man. [3]

---

[1] P. Feine, *Theologie des Neuen Testaments*, [7]1936, p. 273: 'Singulär in anthropologischer Hinsicht ist bei ihm 1 Thess. 5, 23'; W. G. Kümmel, op. cit., p. 24, also thinks that, if 1 Thess. 5 : 23 is intended trichotomously, it is unique in this respect.

[2] W. Neil, *The Epistle of Paul to the Thessalonians*, 1950, p. 133 f.

[3] Cf. *Th. W.* VI, p. 433, note 685: 'Der Segenswunsch ist wohl traditionell, vielleicht liturgisch, besagt also wenig über das paul. Verständnis des Menschen. Die Kombination kann zufällig sein wie Dt 6, 5'; John A. T. Robinson, *The Body, A Study in Pauline Theology*, 1957, p. 27, quotes a commentary by Wheeler Robinson on this passage: 'The enumeration is not systematic, but hortatory, to emphasize the completeness of the preservation; it should be compared with the somewhat similar enumeration of Deut. 6 : 5'; cf. also R. Bultmann, *Die Theologie des Neuen Testaments*, 1948, p. 202; W. D. Stacey, *The Pauline View of Man*, 1956, p. 123 f.

Such a text must of course be discussed extensively by dogmatists and commentators. What Paul says or does not say, just how much or how little, must be weighed in the balance. Particularly when there is a lack of anthropological material, a strong inclination arises to determine exactly how much anthropological information can be distilled from the relatively few passages that seem to possess anthropological significance. But with a passage like this it becomes immediately obvious that such an interest is really out of all proportion to Paul's own interest in this subject, and that the anthropoligical aspect which is certainly not of prime importance in this text is being placed in the foreground. The anthopological statement is incidental and entirely within the framework of God's work of salvation in Christ. Such a statement about man has first to be forcibly detached from its context before it can be properly examined from an anthropological point of view.

This example also demonstrates that Paul does not refer to man without referring to God and Christ. What he says about man can never be isolated from his message of God's historical work of salvation. Anthropology is indissolubly bound up with the whole of Paul's kerygma.

The great contrast between Paul's approach to this subject and Seneca's is immediately apparent. To begin with the titles of Seneca's writings are of significance in this respect: *De Vita Beata, De Tranquillitate Animi, De Constantia Sapientis, De Otio, De Brevitate Vitae, De Ira.* Even without knowing anything about the contents, it is immediately clear from the titles of these works that man is their subject, that he, his happiness, his peace of mind, his constancy, his emotions are the centre of interest. Here we learn how a man should act, if one takes into account his nature, his talents, his difficulties, his inner conflicts and his pleasures, how he can control himself, how he can develop himself, how he can mould his character. To be sure, Seneca also wrote *De Providentia,* but when reading this work one soon observes that there, too, the central theme is the notion that the imperturbableness and inviolability of the philosopher should be an example to man in dealing with the uncertainty of this *providentia divina* in all situations. The contrast might almost be formulated as follows: Seneca always speaks first of man and from man's point of view and only in connection with this — and then usually in passing — does he speak of the divinity; for Paul what God has done, does and will do in Christ is always of prime importance and man is only mentioned insofar as is necessary in this connection.

If we begin to examine Seneca's anthropological ideas it becomes
apparent that they are characterized by a strongly marked dualism of
body and spirit. Seneca always speaks rather contemptuously of the
body, sometimes a little jestingly, sometimes complaining bitterly of
man's state on earth, of the fact that during his life he is at the mercy
of his body. The body, often referred to as the *corpusculum,* [1] the
puny, miserable body, is only a shell, a garment worn for a time,
a strait jacket, a prison. It thus goes without saying that Seneca can
comfort a mother on the loss of her son by asserting that it is only
the body of her son that has been lost:

> Only the image of your son — and a very imperfect likeness it was —
> has perished; he himself is eternal and has reached now a far better
> state, stripped of all outward encumbrances and left simply himself.
> This vesture of the body which we see, bones and sinews and the skin
> that covers us, this face and the hands that serve us and the rest of
> our human wrapping — these are but chains and darkness to our souls.
> By these things the soul is crushed and strangled and stained and, im-
> prisoned in error, is kept far from its true and natural sphere. It con-
> stantly struggles against this weight of the flesh in the effort to avoid
> being dragged back and sunk; it ever strives to rise to that place from
> which it once descended. There eternal peace awaits it when it has passed
> from earth's dull motley to the vision of all that is pure and bright. [2]

Hence there is no reason for Marcia to visit her son's grave repeatedly:

> what lies there is his basest part and a part that in life was the source
> of much trouble — bones and ashes are no more parts of him than
> were his clothes and the other protections of the body. He is complete
> — leaving nothing of himself behind, he has fled away and wholly
> departed from earth; for a little while he tarried above us while he was
> being purified and was ridding himself of all the blemishes and stain
> that still clung to him from his mortal existence, then soared aloft and
> sped away to join the souls of the blessed. [3]

In exile on Corsica Seneca is able to comfort his mother by saying
that:

> the mind can never suffer exile, since it is free, kindred to the gods,
> and at home in every world and every age; for its thought ranges over all
> heaven and projects itself into all past and future time. This poor body,
> the prison and fetter of the soul [*corpusculum hoc, custodia et vinculum
> animi*], is tossed hither and thither; upon it punishments, upon it

---

[1] Cf. Fritz Husner, *op. cit.,* pp. 109-15.
[2] *Marc.* 24. 5.
[3] *Marc.* 25. 1.

robberies, upon it diseases work their will. But the soul itself is sacred and eternal, and upon it no hand can be laid. 1

It might be thought that this rather ostentatious contempt for the body is connected with the nature of the writings that have hitherto been quoted: the *Consolationes*. When wishing to comfort someone who has suffered a loss, one sometimes grasps any means of consolation available. Among the consoling thoughts with which someone in mourning could be cheered, is also as great as possible a depreciation of the life in the body. However, this disregard does not appear to be restricted to Seneca's consolatory writings alone. It occurs repeatedly in his other writings. For instance, in one of his letters he writes that philosophical studies:

> elevate and lighten the soul, which is weighted down by a heavy burden and desires to be freed and to return to the elements of which it was once a part. For this body of ours is a weight upon the soul and its penance [*animi pondus ac poena*]; as the load presses down the soul is crushed and is in bondage, unless philosophy has come to its assistance and has bid it take fresh courage by contemplating the universe, and has turned it from things earthly to things divine. 2

Seneca expresses contempt for the body in a variety of similes: the spirit lives in the body as beneath a heavy burden, *gravis sarcina*; the body is a weight and a penance for the spirit, *pondus ac poena*; the spirit is in the body as in fetters, *in vinculis,* as in prison, *carcer*. He is also able to write about the body as *caro ista,* that flesh which will never make him fear. 3 The body and the spirit are two companions, the latter of whom can always break with the former if he thinks fit. They are not partners on equal terms. The spirit will always assume the right of control. 'To despise our bodies is sure freedom', *contemptus corporis sui certa libertas est.* 4

It sometimes seems as if Seneca can hardly find words strong enough to express his contempt:

> Man's primary art is virtue itself; there is joined to this the useless and fleeting flesh, fitted only for the reception of food, as Posidonius remarks. This divine virtue ends in foulness, and to the higher parts, which are worshipful and heavenly, there is fastened a sluggish and flabby animal. 5

---

1 *Helv.* 11. 7; cf. *Pol.* 9. 3, 8.

2 *Ep.* 65. 16.

3 Cf. *Ep.* 24. 17: *grave corporis mei pondus*; *Ep.* 92. 33: *onus necessarium*; *Helv.* 11. 6: *gravis sarcina*; *Ep.* 76. 25; 79. 12.

4 *Ep.* 65. 22.

5 *Ep.* 92. 10; cf. *Ep.* 120. 17: *corpus tam putre.*

Why do we love this body of ours so foolishly, this most fleeting thing, [1] that is not a home, 'but a sort of inn (with a brief sojourn at that) which is to be left behind when one perceives that one is a burden to the host.' [2] 'Survey everything that lies about you, as if it were luggage in a guesthouse', Seneca exhorts the dying, for they are passing through 'the last hour of the body but not of the soul'. [3]

Our spirit which wishes to rise is always impeded by our bodies. Therefore we must constantly strive to overcome the defects of our bodies by reason. [4] Only a dull mind which has surrendered to the body does not aspire to higher things. [5] Luxury may for instance enslave the mind to the body. [6] But this is not inevitable. Man's whole being is not enslaved. It is true that the mind is imprisoned in the body as in a jail, that bodies are at the disposition of masters, that fate has surrendered the body to a master; a master can buy and sell a body but man's better part cannot be delivered into bondage. The mind is autonomous, *sui iuris*. [7]

It is self-evident that the outcome of such an attitude is disregard to a lesser or greater degree for the body's comfort. The body is nothing but a necessary evil. It cannot be dispensed with. Therefore it should not be entirely neglected, but the more apparent it is that it is of secondary importance, the better:

> I confess that we all have an inborn affection for our body; I confess that we are entrusted with its guardianship. I do not maintain that the body is not to be indulged at all; but I maintain that we must not be slaves to it. He will have many masters who makes his body his master, who is over-fearful in its behalf, who judges everything according to the body. We should conduct ourselves, not as if we ought to live for the body, but as if we could not live without it. Our too great love for it makes us restless with fears, burdens us with cares, and exposes us to insults. Virtue is held too cheap by the man who counts his body too dear. We should cherish the body with the greatest care; but we should also be prepared, when reason, self-respect, and duty demand the sacrifice, to deliver it even to the flames. [8]

---

1 *Ep.* 58. 23 cf. *Marc.* 11. 3: *imbecillum corpus et fragile.*
2 *Ep.* 120. 14.
3 *Ep.* 102. 24.
4 *Ep.* 58. 27.
5 *Ep.* 71. 14.
6 *Ep.* 90. 19.
7 *Ben.* iii. 20. 1, 2.
8 *Ep.* 14. 1, 2; cf. Georges Pire, op. cit., 1958, pp. 105 f., 116, 195.

'The body is to be regarded as necessary rather than as important', [1] hence it is sound and wholesome to make no more concessions to the body than are necessary for good health. It should be treated rather harshly so that it may not be disobedient to the mind. [2] It should never be forgotten that the body should only be looked after for the sake of the mind. [3] If the body is nothing but a necessary evil, an *onus necessarium*, man should not be its lover, *amator*, but only its overseer, *procurator*. It must be borne in mind that no man is free who is a slave to his body. [4]

Hence at all times man should first care for his mind, and then for his body which will not be difficult to look after, if all that is desired is good health. Indeed a cultured man regards all exaggerated physical training with contempt:

> It is indeed foolish and very unsuitable for a cultivated man, to work hard overdeveloping the muscles and broadening the shoulders and strengthening the lungs. For although your heavy feeding produce good results and your sinews grow solid, you can never be a match, either in strength or in weight, for a first-class bull. Besides by overloading the body with food you strangle the soul and render it less active. Accordingly, limit the flesh as much as possible, and allow free play to the spirit. [5]

Rigorous physical training entails many inconveniences. Any excessive concern for the body is pernicious, therefore:

> whatever you do, come back soon from body to mind. The mind must be exercised both day and night, for it is nourished by moderate labour .... Cultivate that good which improves with the years [6]

From these repeated expressions of contempt for the body and from the stress Seneca lays upon caring for the body only as much as is necessary, it becomes clear that ultimately the mind alone is of importance; the body is only important insofar as it is indispensable for mental activity. [7] It is a man's mind which determines his true worth:

---

1 *Ep.* 23. 6.

2 *Ep.* 8. 5; cf. *Ep.* 21. 11.

3 *Ep.* 92. 1.

4 *Ep.* 92. 33; cf. *V.B.* 4. 4; 5. 4; this is one of the many images which Seneca derives from legal practice in order to describe the relationship between the body and the soul, cf. F. Husner, op. cit., pp. 45-51.

5 *Ep.* 15. 2.

6 *Ep.* 15. 5.

7 From passages like *Ep.* 14. 1, 2; 15. 1, 2; 5. 4; 73. 16 Husner draws the conclusion that side by side with the dualistic estimation we also find a 'nicht-feindliche Leibbewertung'. This in my opinion is incorrect. Although contempt for the body may

When you wish to inquire into a man's true worth, and to know what manner of man he is, look at him when he is naked; make him lay aside his inherited estate, his titles, and the other deceptions of fortune; let him even strip off his body. Consider his soul, its quality and its stature, and thus learn whether its greatness is borrowed, or its own. [1]

The mind is so independent and free that it refuses to be confined in the prison of the body and will not be prevented from following its own impulses, from pursuing mighty ideas and travelling into the infinite, a companion to the heavenly bodies, *comes caelestibus*. [2]

Man's spirit is of divine origin. In the midst of all those things which cannot withstand the encroachment of old age, one must search for something which can:

And what is this? It is the soul, — but the soul that is upright, good, and great. What else could you call such a soul than a god dwelling as a guest in a human body [*deus in corpore humano hospitans*]? A soul like this may descend into a Roman knight just as well as into a freedman's son or a slave. For what is a Roman knight, or a freedman's son, or a slave? They are mere titles, born of ambition or of wrong. One may leap to heaven from the very slums. Only rise "And mould thyself to kinship with thy God". [3]

And so we see that a great human soul bears a convincing testimony to its divine origin:

When a soul rises superior to other souls, when it is under control, when it passes through every experience as if it were of small account, when it smiles at our fears and at our prayers, it is stirred by a force from heaven. A thing like this cannot stand upright unless it be propped by the divine. Therefore, a greater part of it abides in that place from whence it came down to earth. Just as the rays of the sun do indeed touch the earth, but still abide at the source from which they are sent; even so the great and hallowed soul, which has come down in order that we may have a nearer knowledge of divinity, does indeed associate with us, but still cleaves to its origin; on that source it depends, thither it turns its gaze and strives to go, and it concerns itself with our doings only as a being superior to ourselves [4]

---

not be expressed with equal violence everywhere, the above-cited passages certainly testify—especially when read in their context—to an obvious contrast between soul and body. In all events Husner acknowedges: 'Trotzdem hinterbleibt aber dem Leser der Schriftenmasse Senecas als Gesamteindruck durchaus die dualistisch-pessimistische Färbung, die strengere, finsterere Beurteilung, für die sich verschiedene Gründe anführen lassen', Fritz Husner, op. cit., pp. 29 f., 139.

[1] *Ep.* 76. 32.
[2] *Ben.* iii. 20. 1; cf. *Clem.* iii. 1. 5.
[3] *Ep.* 31. 11, the quotation is from Virgil, *Aeneid*, viii. 364 f.
[4] *Ep.* 41. 5.

There is a quality in man that is 'the peculiar property of man', *pro-prium hominis*, that can neither be given nor snatched away from him. What is that? 'It is soul, and reason brought to perfection in the soul. For man is a reasoning animal [*rationale animal*].' [1]

Here the radical dualism in Seneca's anthropology is clearly revealed. The spirit, the soul, has its origins in another world and really still belongs to the world of God, in the same way that the sun's rays which shine on earth still really belong to the sun. Therefore it may be said of a mind which has freed itself as far as possible from the body, in order to dwell upon heavenly phenomena, that it is, as it were, nourished by these, grows and, freed from its chains, returns to its place of origin, *in originem redit*, while its divinity is proved by the fact that it delights in the divine, and is not occupied by what is strange to it but by what is its own. [2] And this spirit which thus repeatedly demonstrates its divine origin is peculiar to man, *proprium hominis*. All man's material possessions are really no part of him; they only go to make up his environment which is transient. If a man wishes to glory in anything, he should glory in what is really his, his soul which is his permanent possession. It is not hard to hold on to this possession. All that is necessary is to live in accordance with one's nature. The general madness of mankind has made this difficult, but it is in reality by no means so. [3] Anyone who wishes to can remain in permanent possession of his soul: 'the soul itself is sacred and eternal, and upon it no hand can be laid.' [4]

Of human reason, too, it may be said that it is 'nothing else than a portion of the divine spirit [*pars divini spiritus*] set in a human body.' [5] Just as divine reason is above all things and subject to none, so is ours, too, because it is derived from divine reason. [6]

This enables Seneca to say that God does not only come to man, but he enters into him also. 'No mind that has not God, is good. Divine seeds are scattered throughout our mortal bodies.' It is only a matter of cherishing these seeds. If the good husbandman attends to them and nurtures them, they shall blossom up disclosing their true origin, but a bad husbandman will kill them, as does infertile and marshy soil. [7]

---

[1] *Ep.* 41. 8.
[2] *N.Q.* i. Praef. 11 f.
[3] *Ep.* 41. 8.
[4] *Helv.* 11. 7.
[5] *Ep.* 66. 12.
[6] *Ep.* 92. 1.
[7] *Ep.* 73. 16.

From this it must follow that man is a mixture of the divine and human, *mixtum divini humanique*. [1] On the one hand part of God's mind has flowed into the heart of man, [2] and he belongs by virtue of his soul and reason in the divine world, on the other he is, despite this, bound to his body, his despicable body in which he is imprisoned during his earthly life.

The soul is the divine part of man. But what is this soul? Is it spiritual or material? Where does it reside? Seneca realizes that such questions are not easily answered and that many divergent answers are given. [3] Sometimes he indicates that he considers the soul to be material in some way or other: 'The goods of the body are bodily; so therefore must be the goods of the soul. For the soul, too, is corporeal'. [4] Elsewhere he can refer to the *animus* as a certain form of *spiritus*, but then the question naturally arises as to how material he considers the *spiritus* to be. [5] He is apparently thinking of the soul as something material when he says that the human body is held together by the pressure of the air, and that the breath keeps it functioning; and then he goes on to ask what sets our *animus* in motion, if it is not breath? [6]

So although Seneca knows quite well that all kinds of difficult questions arise as soon as one wishes to form a clear idea of the nature of the soul or the spirit, this knowledge does not for an instant deter him from dwelling repeatedly upon this fundamental anthropological dualism: the body is the inferior, contemptible part of man, the prison, the chains fettering the mind. The soul, the spirit, is the divine part of man. Between these two there is a radical difference. The spirit, the soul, may not be able to do without the body entirely, nevertheless

---

[1] *Ep.* 102. 22.

[2] *Ep.* 120. 14.

[3] *N. Q.* vii. 25. 2, where he cites various opinions adhered to in antiquity with respect to this problem; see Paul Oltramare, *Sénèque, Questions naturelles*, Vol. II, 1929, p. 326, note 1.

[4] *Ep.* 106. 4; here as elsewhere Barker's translation differs considerably from this one: 'The various forms of bodily good are material, so therefore are those of the spirit, for the spirit itself is material.' E. Phillips Barker, *Seneca's Letters to Lucilius*, ii, 1932, p. 214. The Latin reads: *Quae corporis bona sunt, corpora sunt; ergo et quae animi sunt. Nam et hoc corpus est.*

[5] *Quid enim est aliud animus quam quodam modo se habens spiritus?*, *Ep.* 50. 6. Here too the translations vary quite considerably: Gummere (in Loeb) translates: 'For what else is the soul than air in a certain state?' Barker: 'For what else is spirit than a special mode of gaseous matter?' Pohlenz, *Stoa* II, p. 160, quotes this passage as evidence that 'die Seele' is understood to be 'Pneuma'.

[6] *N.Q.* ii. 6. 6; cf. *N.Q.* vi. 18. 6.

it must pay as little attention to it as possible. The life of the spirit is what really counts.

Paul's anthropological ideas are very different. As soon as we examine the meaning of those anthropological terms which are used by both writers the profound difference comes to light. In the first place both speak about the body. *Corpus* is as has been said, for Seneca the inferior, contemptible part of man. This is by no means what σῶμα means for Paul. We have various clear indications of this:

(1) The future life in the resurrection is not envisaged by Paul as a life outside the body, but in the body, albeit not in the same body we have here on earth, but in a 'spiritual body' (1 Cor. 15 : 44), in a 'glorious body' (Phil. 3 : 21; cf. 1 Cor. 15 : 50). If we compare with this what Seneca says to Marcia concerning the death of her son, that he would be liberated from the burden of the body in the life after death, we observe the fundamental difference between Seneca's and Paul's attitude towards the body. It is inconceivable that Paul, who shared the attitude which seems to have vexed Celsus and Porphyry so greatly, [1] should have envisaged an immortality of the soul freed from the burden of the body as man's final and absolute salvation.

(2) Paul would never have been able to write as he does on fornication in 1 Cor. 6 : 12-20 if he had made a sharp distinction between body and soul. His adversaries in the church at Corinth may well have been persons who believed in the Platonic dualism of body and soul, to which Seneca also adhered, and who therefore drew specific conclusions from this with respect to their moral behaviour: the soul, the spirit, is confined in the body as in a prison, but nevertheless it cannot be sullied by what that contemptible body does. It does not matter what the body does, the soul remains fundamentally unaffected by it. It is obvious that such a belief could easily be used to defend sexual libertinism, as was done later in certain Gnostic circles: fornication can be considered as an adiaphoron which does not essentially threaten the purity of the divine soul. In contrast with this Paul emphasizes the fact that what a human being does with his body does not only affect the physical side of life but his whole being. Hence Paul exhorts the members of the Church to remember that:

> your body is a temple of the Holy Spirit within you, which you have from God. You are not your own; you were bought with a price. So glorify God in your body (1 Cor. 6 : 19, 20).

---

[1] Origen, *Contra Celsum* v. 14; Porphyry, Frag. 94.

It is inconceivable that such a statement should come from Seneca. For him the soul, the spirit, could glorify the gods, but this is impossible for the contemptible body which always threatens the purity of the spirit.

These two examples make it clear that Paul writes about the body in quite a different way from Seneca. Contempt for the body as such is out of the question. The word is used repeatedly without any adverse pathos. When Paul, for example, speaks of being 'absent in body' (1 Cor. 5 : 3) or of a 'bodily presence' (2 Cor. 10 : 10), he simply means his personal absence or presence. And so it is that σῶμα could frequently be taken to mean 'person', 'I', 'myself'. 1

In those passages in which Paul does not intentionally make the body the subject of his discourse but speaks of it in passing, in a context quite unrelated to anthropology, it is abundantly obvious that for him the body is an intrinsic part of man's whole being. Sometimes Paul interchanges 'your members' with 'yourselves' (Rom. 6 : 13) or 'to yield yourselves' with 'to yield your members' (Rom. 6 : 16, 19), cf. how in 1 Cor. 6 : 15 he says 'your bodies are members of Christ' and in 1 Cor. 12 : 27 'you are the body of Christ and individually members of it'. Paul's use of alternatives is proof of the fact that he by no means regards the body as a negligible, and contemptible part of man, but as an essential part of his person.

Consequently there is no question of everything the body does being contemptible in itself; what is important is the use to which man puts his body. This body can be subjected to various forces. It is not evil in itself, but if sin reigns over it, then it is being put to sinful purposes:

> Let not sin therefore reign in your mortal bodies, to make you obey their passions. Do not yield your members to sin as instruments of wickedness, but yield yourselves to God as men who have been brought from death to life, and your members to God as instruments of righteousness. For sin will have no dominion over you, since you are not under law but under grace. What then? Are we to sin because we are not under law but under grace? By no means! Do you not know that if you yield yourselves to any one as obedient slaves, you are slaves of the one whom you obey, either of sin, which leads to death, or of obedience, which leads to righteousness? But thanks be to God, that you who were once slaves of sin have become obedient from the heart to the standard of teaching to which you were committed, and, having been set free from sin, have

---

1 Gal. 6 : 17; 2 Cor. 4 : 10; 1 Cor. 13 : 3; 9 : 27; Rom. 4 : 19; 1 Cor. 7 : 4, 34; Rom. 1 : 24; 12 : 1; 8 : 13; 2 Cor. 5 : 10.

become slaves of righteousness. I am speaking in human terms, because of your natural limitations. For just as you once yielded your members to impurity and to greater and greater iniquity, so now yield your members to righteousness for sanctification (Rom. 6 : 12-19).

Paul neither speaks contemptuously about the body nor with elation about the soul, the ψυχή It is in the first place remarkable that the word ψυχή is never used by Paul in those parts of his letters dealing with his expectations concerning the future life. Here and there the continued existence of the soul immediately after death, in an intermediate state between death and resurrection, is perhaps assumed, but even then the soul is nowhere mentioned by name (2 Cor. 5 : 1 ff.; Phil. 1 : 23).

But even apart from these pericopes the soul is never discussed with the elated pathos so characteristic of Seneca. Paul's use of the word 'soul' is particularly reminiscent of the Hebraic Old Testament use of nefeš. [1] Accordingly, in Paul as in other books of the New Testament the word *psyche* can frequently be best translated by 'life'. [2] A comparison of various translations shows that where earlier translators have often used the word 'soul', more recent ones have written 'life'. [3] Similarly musical instruments such as the flute or the harp are called 'life-less', ἄψυχα (1 Cor. 14 : 7). Paul uses πᾶσα ψυχή in the neutral sense of the Old Testament (Rom. 2 : 9; cf. 13 : 1). Like *soma, psyche* can now and then also be rendered with 'person', hence also with a personal pronoun. When Paul professes 'I will most gladly spend and be spent for your souls', 'for your souls' does not mean much more than 'for you' (2 Cor. 12 : 5); in another verse the R.S.V. has replaced the translation 'my soul' by 'me': 'I call God to witness against me' (2 Cor. 1 : 23). This is also the case in 1 Thess. 2 : 8 where the translation 'our own selves' no longer bears any traces of the original *psychai*:

> So, being affectionately desirous of you, we were ready to share with you not only the gospel of God but also our own selves, because you had become very dear to us.

---

[1] Cf. e.g. Johs. Pedersen, *Israel, Its Life and Culture,* i-ii, 1946. pp. 99-181, where what is characteristic is at once stated clearly: 'Such as he is, man, in his total essence, is a soul. In the O.T. we are constantly confronted with the fact, that man, as such, is a soul' (p. 99). 'That which the Israelite understands by soul is, first and foremost, a totality with a peculiar stamp' (p. 100).

[2] Rom. 11 : 3 (a reference to 1 Kings 19 : 10); 16 : 4; 2 Cor. 1 : 23; Phil. 2 : 30; 1 Thess. 2 : 8.

[3] Cf. J. N. Sevenster, *Het begrip psyche in het Nieuwe Testament,* 1946, p. 4 ff.

Again and again the word *psyche* is used either alone or in compounds without the least pathos. [1] From this it is clear that ψυχή and its compounds are not only used to mean the external, material, physical life but also to denote the inner life, or a certain conviction and desire; there is, however, nowhere any question of glorifying the soul as the true essence of man, or as the divine part of him, the only part really to matter.

Neither does the word spirit, *pneuma,* applied in the anthropological sense to man generally, that is to say, not in the sense of the Holy Spirit, signify the exalted, divine part in man. The analysis of 1 Thess. 5 : 23 disclosed that it is used together with soul and body to signify the complete man, but that Paul has not the slightest intention of conveying that this *pneuma* is a very special part of man. In 1 Cor. 7 : 34, too, the expression 'in body and spirit' is evidently used to signify the complete man. Like *soma* and *psyche, pneuma* may now and then be replaced by a personal pronoun without it being detrimental to the sense. [2]

Hence *pneuma,* too, is not used by Paul to signify a particular part, a separate divine organ in man. When one observes that 'body', 'soul' and 'spirit' could all three sometimes be rendered simply by the personal pronoun, it is obvious, first, how little distinction is made between these anthropological terms, and, secondly, that they are certainly not used in antithesis. From this it may be gathered that man, natural man, is visualized by Paul as a unity, and that the dualism underlying Seneca's anthropological ideas is absolutely foreign to him.

Perhaps the difference between Paul's and Seneca's approach to anthropological questions is most apparent from the fact that they use similar words in entirely different meanings.

At first sight the inner struggle between the higher and the lower instincts in man, as this is repeatedly depicted in Seneca's writings, does not seem to lack parallels in the Pauline epistles. In Seneca, the individual life led by the *animus* and *anima* and their inner strength guarantee to a certain extent that man's struggle against his baser physical self is never hopeless, although it may of course be hard enough and call for great exertion. It would sometimes seem as if

---

[1] μιᾷ ψυχῇ Phil. 1 27; σύμψυχοι Phil. 2 : 2; εὐψυχῶ Phil. 2 : 19; ἰσόψυχοδ Phil. 2 : 20. In a more or less derogatory sense ψυχικός is even used in 1 Cor. 2 : 14; 15 : 33, 46.

[2] 1 Cor. 16 : 18; 2 Cor. 2 : 13; 7 : 13; Rom. 1 : 9; Gal. 6 : 18; Phil. 4 : 23; Philem. 25. As neutral as psyche: Phil. 1 : 27; 2 Cor. 12 : 18.

Paul also refers to such an inner struggle. Kreyher, for instance, places side by side with Rom. 8 : 9, 13:

> you are not in *the flesh*, you are in the *Spirit*, if the Spirit of God really dwells in you . . . . if you live according to *the flesh*, you will die, but if by *the Spirit* you put to death the deeds of the body you will live.

a quotation from a letter of Seneca's:

> you should consider whether one has a right to call anything good in which God is outdone by man. Let us limit the Supreme Good to the soul [Kreyher translates: "Das höchste Gut muss im *Geiste* wohnen"] . . . . The sum total of our happiness must not be placed in *the flesh*. 1

If we underline flesh and spirit, as Kreyher has done, striking parallels between Paul and Seneca do indeed seem to exist, when they speak of a struggle between these two. Kreyher is able to find more than one such parallel. Paul says:

> I know that nothing good dwells within me, that is, in my flesh . . . . I delight in the law of God, in my inmost self, but I see in my members another law at war with the law of my mind (Rom. 7 : 18, 22). *The desires of the flesh are against the Spirit* and the desires of the Spirit are against the flesh; for these are opposed to each other (Gal. 5 : 17).

Does this resemble what Seneca writes:

> This vesture of the body which we see, bones and sinews and the skin that covers us, this face and the hands that serve us and the rest of our human wrapping — these are but chains and darkness to our souls [Kreyher: Verdunkelungen der Geister]. By these things the soul is crushed and strangled and stained . . . *It constantly struggles against this weight of the flesh* [Kreyher: Das ist sein ganzer schwerer *Kampf mit dem Fleische*] in the effort to avoid being dragged back and sunk. 2

Paul writes: 'we walk not according to *the flesh* but according to *the Spirit* (Rom. 8 : 4). Is this not very similar to Seneca's:

> Never shall this *flesh* drive me to feed fear, or to assume any pretence that is unworthy of a good man . . . *the soul* shall bring all quarrels before its own tribunal [Kreyher: *Der Geist* beansprucht in allen Stücken den Vorrang]? 3

---

1 *Ep.* 74. 16; Kreyher, p. 85; cf. R. Liechtenhan, 'Die Überwindung des Leides bei Paulus und in der zeitgenössischen Stoa', *Zeitschr. für Theologie und Kirche*, N.F. Vol. 3, 1922, p. 397 f.: 'Seine [Paulus'] Auffassung des Gegensatzes von Fleisch und Geist ist aus dem alttestamentlichen Denken allein nicht zu verstehen. Die Rolle des Fleisches als des hemmenden und sündlichen Elementes erinnert stark an die stoische Auffassung vom Leib als Kerker und Fessel der Seele.'

2 *Marc.* 24. 5, Kreyher, p. 84.

3 *Ep.* 65. 22; Kreyher, p. 84 f.; Barker translates: 'the spirit will assume all right of control'; Lat.: *animus ad se omne ius ducet.*

Is it not so, that we frequently find in Paul traces of that struggle between the flesh and the spirit which is often described by Seneca so vividly? Does not Paul also, when endeavouring to counter the dissipation and fornication in the Corinthian church, make an urgent appeal to his readers' knowledge of the fact that their bodies are a temple of the Spirit (1 Cor. 6 : 19)? Such statements would seem to bear a strong resemblance to Seneca's descriptions of the inner struggle between the *animus,* the *anima* and baser physical sensuality.

Nevertheless this resemblance is illusory. In reality these words which Kreyher quotes as having parallels in Seneca, have for Paul quite a different meaning, since here he does not use spirit, *pneuma,* to signify part of the natural man but to denote the Holy Spirit which is given by God in Christ. It is 'the Holy Spirit within you, which you have from God' (1 Cor. 6 : 19; cf. Rom. 8 : 15; Gal. 4 : 5, 6). This Spirit is accordingly never the property of man as such, of the natural man, prior to Christ, but of the Church, of those to whom God has granted it. Therefore in 1 Cor. 6 : 19 Paul does not address mankind in general, but the Church. For this Church may be considered to be in possession of the Spirit. This Spirit belongs within the framework of the history of salvation which is God's plan for mankind and the world. Since the coming of Christ He has been present in the Church and He points to the beginning of the fulfilment.

Consequently it is not surprising that this Spirit is clearly distinguished from man's spirit as such. From this it is manifest that this Spirit has no place in the common conception of anthropology but that it belongs to the salvation-history, the new creation (2 Cor. 5 : 17), to 'the new nature, created after the likeness of God in true righteousness and holiness' (Eph. 4 : 24). 'Created after the likeness of God' — how passively this is expressed! The subject here is the 'new' man who has not cultivated, formed and developed his own spirit but is created by God; who has received from God the Holy Spirit. This Spirit is not the same as man's own spirit and hence Paul makes a clear distinction between them (Rom. 8 : 16; 1 Cor. 2 : 10 f.). And so it must be concluded that in these texts, which Kreyher considered to be striking parallels, Paul and Seneca mean two different things with the word 'spirit', and this accordingly gives their utterances distinctly different meanings.

Neither do Paul and Seneca mean the same thing when they speak of the flesh in the texts quoted above. When Seneca mentions the flesh, *caro ista* (*Ep.* 65.22), *inutilis caro et fluida* (*Ep.* 92.10), *cum hac gravi carne certamen* (*Marc* 24. 5), it may be seen from the context that he means the body, upon which, with the aid of this expression, he heaps all his contempt. But for Paul 'flesh', σάρξ, is by no means the same as the body. For him it is a rather complex notion containing a number of gradations of moral judgment. [1] It can signify man's physical presence without any depreciating connotation. 'All flesh' is often used in the Hebraic Old Testament sense simply to mean 'all people', 'each'. [2] Accordingly, this word, too, could sometimes be replaced by a personal pronoun (e.g. in 2 Cor. 7 : 5). The expression 'flesh and blood' signifies man in all his human weakness and transitoriness as opposed to God or 'the principalities and powers' (Gal. 1 : 16; 1 Cor. 15 : 50; Eph. 6 : 12). It is man in his entirety — so certainly not only in his body — as opposed to the Holy Spirit, the *pneuma,* which comes from God and is therefore everlasting. Similarly 'the life in the flesh' can sometimes simply mean man's life on earth without any derogatory connotations. [3]

Side by side with this, however, we find 'flesh' is also used depreciatingly, so that the expression 'according to the flesh', for example, is not only employed unemotively, [4] but also, when used in conjunction with a verb, frequently to indicate sinful behaviour. [5] When 'flesh' signifies the power which brings about man's sinful behaviour, Paul is by no means thinking solely of the carnal appetite, the emotions and passions of the body, but also of a certain ethical or religious self-exaltation and pride, for example, the fulfilment of the Jewish law (Gal. 3 : 3), the pride of the pious Israelite in all the privileges and honorary titles which give a man confidence in his own strength (Phil. 3 : 3-7), pride in one's own wisdom or particular spiritual talents (1 Cor. 1 : 26; 2 Cor. 11 : 18).

From this it is quite clear that for Paul 'the flesh' does not necessarily mean a particular part of man but, like sin, it sometimes signifies a superhuman power which can control man, and then not only his body but also his soul, his spirit, his reason, his inner self. Man may be wholly subjected to this power, and be its slave. This should also be borne in mind with respect to the antithesis between the flesh and the Spirit. In Rom. 8 : 4 ff. and Gal. 5 : 16 ff. it is not, as in Seneca,

---

[1] Cf. *Th. W.* VII, p. 124 ff.
[2] Rom. 3 : 20; 1 Cor. 1 : 29; Gal. 2 : 16.
[3] See e.g. Gal. 2 : 20; Phil. 1 : 22; 2 Cor. 10 : 3.
[4] Rom. 4 : 1; 9 : 3; 1 Cor. 10 : 18; Gal. 4 : 29; Rom. 1 : 3; 9 : 5.
[5] 2 Cor. 1 : 17; 5 : 16; 10 : 2, 3; Rom. 8 : 4.

a question of an inner struggle between the various parts of man, but
of a struggle involving the whole of man, both his body, his soul,
and his human spirit, against God, against the *pneuma* which comes
from without, from God. Paul is dealing with man's rejection of, and
even hostility towards, the new life which God is bringing him in the
Holy Spirit. Hence for Paul the human spirit is not by nature a firm
bulwark against the evil appetites and passions of the body as it is for
Seneca. The latter promises the man 'for whom true pleasure will be
the scorn of pleasures', *cui vera voluptas erit voluptatum contemptio,*
the bliss of a 'mind that is free, lofty, fearless and steadfast — a mind
that is placed beyond the reach of fear, beyond the reach of desire,
that counts virtue the only good, baseness the only evil', [1] of a spirit
'that rejoices only in virtue', the power of which is unconquerable. [2]
Paul does not recognize such a spirit in natural man. He would have
considered it as part of the flesh, to which belong also human arrogance, confidence and pride in one's own strength which are anta-
gonistic to the *pneuma,* the Holy Spirit given by God. For Paul the
only really significant dividing-line runs not between the various parts
which go to make up a human being — it has been seen how indis-
tinctly he separates these — but between the complete man, body,
soul and spirit (or whatever other names these attributes are given)
on the one hand and that which comes from God, that which God
grants in Christ on the other. All of Paul's anthropological ideas are
dominated by the central salvation-occurrence.

Once this fundamental difference has been clearly perceived, the
careful reader will not allow himself to be misled by superficial verbal
parallels and will be doubly on his guard against misunderstanding
when these do occur. For instance, the expression 'the sinful body'
in Rom. 6 : 6 could for the reader unacquainted with Paul's anthropological ideas appear to be used in Seneca's sense of the body as such
being sinful, evil, despicable. But on close examination it becomes
clear that it means something else entirely, namely: the body insofar
as it is the instrument of sin. This gives the text quite a different
significance. For then the body is not sinful in itself, but can be
subjected to the power of sin, can become its instrument. It all depends
what power governs the body; to which purpose it is put.

Rom. 7 : 24, 'Who will deliver me from this body of death' could,

---

[1] *V.B.* 4. 3.
[2] *V.B.* 4. 2: *animus virtute laetus; invicta vis animi.*

if isolated from its context, be reminiscent of Seneca who repeatedly compares the body with a prison, or with chains in which the soul is fettered. For Seneca refers to the parts of the body as 'chains and darkness to our souls' (*Marc.* 24. 5); as 'this poor body, the prison and fetter of the soul' (*Helv.* 11. 7), as 'this prison of the body, in which the mind is confined' (*Ben.* iii. 20. 1). Of the soul he says that it is 'in bondage' (*Ep.* 65. 16). After such statements by Seneca concerning the relationship between body and soul, there seems to be a strong case for interpreting Rom. 7 : 24 as a cry for deliverance from the body. But in reality Paul wishes to say something entirely different, namely, who will deliver me from this body which is subject to that death I have spoken of above; from this body over which sin reigns and therefore death. This is a cry for deliverance from that body which is irrevocably doomed to die if it is a slave to sin. Hence for Paul it is not the body as such that is the prison, the chains, but the fact that the body can be at the mercy of death which is allied to sin, that it can be in the power of the flesh. Sin, death, the flesh are powers which can reign over the body, but which are in no way inherent in the body. [1]

Similarly it would be a mistake to interpret Rom. 8 : 13, 'if by the Spirit you put to death the deeds of the body you will live,' as if it had been written by Seneca, as if contempt were being shown for 'the deeds of the body' and admiration for the human spirit which restrains the body. From the context it is plain that Paul is referring to the Holy Spirit and the body when it is subjected to the flesh. This is abundantly clear from the immediately preceding passage: 'So then, brethren, we are debtors, not to the flesh, to live according to the flesh — for if you live according to the flesh you will die, but ... (Rom. 8 : 12, 13a).

Likewise care should be taken not to misunderstand the expression 'the redemption of our bodies' in Rom. 8 : 23. As is so often the case the translation is a matter of exegesis, since the genitive in ἀπολύτρωσις τοῦ σώματος ἡμῶν can be interpreted in various ways. It has some-

---

[1] Cf. R. Bultmann, *Theologie des Neuen Testaments*, I, 1948, p. 197 in connection with Rom. 7 : 24: 'so ist das σῶμα das von der σάρξ beherrschte, der Sünde verfallene Ich, und der Ruf geht nicht auf die Befreiung vom σῶμα überhaupt, sondern von diesem von der σάρξ durchwalteten σῶμα und das heisst im Grunde von der σάρξ.' I do not agree that Paul elsewhere approaches Hellenistic-Gnostic dualism, as Bultmann claims with respect to 2 Cor. 5 : 1 ff.; 2 Cor. 12 : 2-4; 1 Cor. 7 : 1-7, p. 198 f.

times been suggested that this is a *genitivus separativus* and that what is meant here is the redemption from the physical body. [1] This is, however, improbable. It is not a question here of redemption from the body, but of the body. The body, too, is redeemed, and has its part in the coming glory. The parallel in verse 21 points in this direction: just as 'the creation will be set free from its bondage to decay and obtain the glorious liberty of the children of God', so too may we expect 'the adoption as sons' with its special glory, since our bodies which are dead because of sin (8 : 10) are freed from that mortal fate and put on immortality (1 Cor. 15 : 52, 54). [2] This text has quite justifiably been linked with a text like 2 Cor. 5 : 4, where Paul appears to shrink from being unclothed, and then not clothed in the body of the resurrection, [3] while it has also been quoted as proof of the fact that:

> from the very beginning Docetism was rejected as the most destructive of temptations, a sort of dark anti-gospel, proceeding from Anti-Christ. [4]

A notion which occurs quite frequently in the writings of both Paul and Seneca is that of *the conscience*. It is therefore perhaps worthwhile comparing how they use it. In Seneca we come across the word a great deal, [5] and the important place it occupies in his works justifies Pohlenz's statement that:

> Es ist für uns das erste Mal in der griechisch-römischen Philosophie, dass das Gewissen in dieser Weise als lebendige Macht gewürdigt wird. [6]

It is indeed a living force. For the conscience is not a word or notion about which Seneca argues or philosophizes in a purely theoretical

---

[1] As e.g. R. Bultmann, op. cit., p. 198.

[2] Cf. *Th. W.* IV, p. 355: 'Die ἀπολύτρωσις τοῦ σώματος ist R8, 23 nicht die Erlösung vom Leibe, sondern die Erlösung des Leibes.'

[3] Otto Schmitz, *Das Lebensgefühl des Paulus,* 1922, p. 109.

[4] G. Florovsky, The Gospel of Resurrection, in *Paulus-Hellas-Oikumene, An Ecumenical Symposium,* 1951, p. 75. He mentions in this connection 1 John 4 : 2, 3; Rom. 8 : 23; 2 Cor. 5 : 4; cf. also Ch. de Beus, *Paulus, Apostel der vrijheid,* n.d., p. 126: 'The full gift of becoming children of God will not be granted until the future. It consists, according to Rom. 8 : 18b-23, in the redemption of our bodies, which does not mean from the body, but the glorification of the whole of man's being, of which the body is a part.'

[5] J. Dupont, 'Syneidèsis aux origines de la notion chrétienne de conscience morale', in *Studia Hellenistica,* Ed. L. Cerfaux and W. Peremans, 5, 1948, p. 124: 'la notion de conscience joue un rôle capital dans la morale de Sénèque'; C. A. Pierce, *Conscience in the New Testament,* 1955, p. 118: 'the word is very common in the Latin Stoic writers .... perhaps above all [in] Seneca.'

[6] Pohlenz, *Stoa* I, p. 317.

manner, but one whose meaning and workings in man's everyday life he demonstrates.

Let us deal first with the meaning of the word: the basic meaning of conscientia is of course 'a joint knowledge with some other person', a sense in which Seneca occasionally uses it. There are, he says in one of his letters, people who will tell everything, even their most intimate affairs to anyone they meet, but there are others who fear to share their knowledge with their closest friends. [1] Elsewhere he speaks of faithful friends 'whose knowledge of you you fear less than your knowledge of yourself.' [2]

However, Seneca — and he is certainly not alone in this — more often uses the word to denote man's knowledge of his own actions, words and thought. Accordingly, the conscientia is that part of man which, as it were, shares his knowledge of these matters:

> The mind of the wise man is like the ultra-lunar firmament; eternal calm pervades that region. You have, then, a reason for wishing to be wise, if the wise man is never deprived of joy. This joy springs only from the knowledge that you possess the virtues [ex virtutum conscientia]. [3]

Wickedness makes us miserable, virtue makes us happy. If it is a virtue to be grateful, then it goes without saying that the consciousness of gratitude, conscientia grati, belongs to a divine and blessed spirit. [4] 'All worry has been banished because of the consciousness of true love', ex conscientia veri amoris dimissa omnis anxietas. [5] This knowledge we have of what happens within us is of course clearly expressed in the sibi conscius esse, being conscious of one's own self, to which Seneca repeatedly refers. [6]

If this consciousness influences man morally, arousing certain feelings in him, then the notion conscientia is very similar to what we normally understand by conscience:

> The ingrate dwells in fear of the gods, who are the witnesses of all ingratitude, he is tortured and distressed by the consciousness of having thwarted a benefit. [7]

This implies the existence of a bad or good conscience. The days of the innocence of the human race, generis humani innocentia, that long

---

[1] Ep. 3. 4: etiam carissimorum conscientiam reformidant.
[2] Tranqu. an. 7. 3: quorum conscientiam minus quam tuam timeas.
[3] Ep. 59. 16.
[4] Ep. 81. 21.
[5] Ben. vi. 42. 1.
[6] Ira i. 20. 3; Ep. 71. 36.
[7] Ben. iii. 17. 3.

past golden age, *antiquum illud saeculum,* are over. [1] It is only in the
life of the philosopher that this innocence makes its return. But even
there it has become something else, because the wise man has held
on to it through all kinds of experiences and in the face of many
affects. Never again is it the original innocence of the golden age. [2]

Now that the golden age of innocence is past the problem of the
good or bad conscience arises. What a world of difference there is
between the mental state and outward appearance of a man with a
troubled conscience and one who can rejoice in a clear conscience.
The troubled conscience may reveal itself in a man's behaviour, for
example, in his silence, as was so with Cinna, when Augustus spoke
to him about his plan to murder the emperor. When this plot was
disclosed in all its details, Cinna remained silent 'not because of his
compact, but because of his conscience'. [3] Cinna's conscience began
to make itself heard, evidently as one troubled, although *conscientia*
is used here as elsewhere in the absolute sense. [4] A troubled conscience
may also be brought to light by blushing. Seneca frequently refers to
this phenomenon. In *De Beneficiis* he records how the emperor Tiberius would pay the debts of numerous Romans, on condition that
they publically explained to the senate why they were in debt. This
was help, an imperial subsidy, but it was no benefit, since it was not
something one could think of 'without a blush'. [5] To a certain extent
it is in a wrongdoer's favour if he can still blush. For there are those
who are such consummate villains that they can commit evil without
a blush. How many men there are who do not blush at theft, who
glory in adultery! [6]

And yet the consequences of a crime, of evil, usually have to be
taken in the long run. The price to be paid is the constant uneasiness
of a tormented conscience. How terrible is the true state of the man,
who is in fear of his fellow men and the gods as the witnesses and
avengers of his crimes, who has gone so far that he can no longer
change his conduct:

> For added to all the rest, this is still cruelty's greatest curse — that one
> must persist in it, and no return to better things is open; for crime must

---

[1] *Clem.* ii. 1. 3.
[2] Cf. *Marc.* 9. 5; *Ben.* iii. 13. 1; v. 17. 2; *Ep.* 79. 14: 94. 69.
[3] *Clem.* i. 9. 10.
[4] *Ep.* 97. 15; 105. 7; 43. 4.
[5] *Ben.* ii. 8. 2; cf. *Ira* ii. 2. 1; *Marc.* 24. 3; *Ep.* 11. 1; 50. 5.
[6] *Ep.* 87. 23.

be safeguarded by crime. But what creature is more unhappy than the man who now cannot help being wicked.

In what a miserable position is the man:

who resorts to the sword because he fears the sword, who trusts neither the loyalty of friends nor the affection of his children; who, when he has surveyed what he has done and what he intends to do, and has laid bare his conscience burdened with crimes and torturings, often fears to die, but more often prays for death, more hateful as he is to himself than to his servitors. 1

A bad conscience, 'even in solitude, is disturbed and troubled'. 2 Evil even fears the dark; the crime may remain safely hidden, but the criminal never feels safe. Crimes may not be discovered, but they never leave the mind at rest; the first and greatest punishment for sinners is to have sinned. The punishment for a crime is the crime itself: 3

Good luck frees many men from punishment, but no man from fear . . . . even men who hide their sins can never count upon remaining hidden; for their conscience convicts them and reveals them to themselves. But it is the property of guilt to be in fear. 1

A *mala conscientia* always makes a man feel unsafe. Even in his dreams he is tormented by anxiety. If the conversation turns to another's guilt, he immediately thinks of his own. Of him it may be said: 'A wrongdoer sometimes has the luck to escape notice but never the assurance thereof.' 5 All the pleasures and joys of life are spoilt for him. 6

How different is the life of a man with a good conscience! A bad conscience may even make a man nervous and uneasy when he is alone, a good conscience can call up witnesses and be quite unafraid of their judgment. If one's actions are honourable, everyone may know of them. 7 Wickedness fears the dark, 'a good conscience, how-ever, wishes to come forth and be seen of men'. 8 Then the uneasy, evil dreams, of which a man with a bad conscience is never free, vanish. 'Real tranquillity is the state reached by an unperverted mind

---

1 *Clem.* i. 13. 2, 3.
2 *Ep.* 43. 5.
3 *Ep.* 97. 12, 13, 14.
4 *Ep.* 97. 15, 16.
5 *Ep.* 105. 8.
6 *Brev.* 17. 1.
7 *Ep.* 43. 5.
8 *Ep.* 97. 12.

when it is relaxed.' [1] In contrast with the body whose good health is always temporary — the doctor can restore it, but cannot guarantee it and often has to visit the patient again and again — the mind,

> once healed, is healed for good and all. I shall tell you what I mean by health: if the mind is content with its own self; if it has confidence in itself .... [2]

The wise man wins the victory in every field. [3] But then he must take every care to keep his conscience unimpaired, [4] every precaution to see that it remains clear; [5] he must be resolute in saying: 'Nothing shall I ever do for the sake of opinion, everything for the sake of my conscience.' [6] If the conscience casts its vote plainly, other votes do not count and it will win by its vote alone and be able to undergo the greatest trials with fortitude, because its 'very heart is brimming with conscious virtue' *ipsum cor plenum bona conscientia.* [7] When asked whence springs the desire for the real good, Seneca answers:

> I will tell you: it comes from a good conscience, from honourable purposes, from right actions, from contempt of the gifts of chance, from an even and calm way of living which treads but one path. [8]

Accordingly, we see that there is a tremendous difference between the shame, the fear, the constant anxiety of the man with a bad conscience, and the inner freedom, the peace and firmly rooted tranquillity of the man with a good conscience. Seneca assumes that the conscience speaks quite clearly unless it has been dulled or even reduced to silence by consummate wickedness. The metaphors he uses to describe the conscience are varied, but they all indicate that the conscience makes itself plainly heard. It is the 'advocate with upright mind'. It is necessary that we:

> amid all the uproar and jangle of falsehood, hear one voice only. But what voice shall this be? Surely a voice which, amid all the tumult of self-seeking, shall whisper wholesome words into the deafened ear. [9]

We need 'a guardian, as it were, to pluck us continually by the ear'. [10]

---

[1] *Ep.* 56. 6.
[2] *Ep.* 72. 6, 7.
[3] *Const.* 19. 4.
[4] *Ep.* 117. 1.
[5] *Tranqu. an.* 3. 4; *V.B.* 19. 1.
[6] *V.B.* 20. 4.
[7] *Ben.* iv. 21. 5, 6.
[8] *Ep.* 23. 7.
[9] *Ep.* 94. 59.
[10] *Ep.* 94. 55.

'How wretched you are if you despise such a witness!' [1] He who listens to his conscience and has a good conscience, bears testimony to himself, but also by his conduct bears witness to the world and can at death,

> whenever Nature demands back his breath, or his reason releases it, depart, bearing witness that he has loved a good conscience and all good endeavour. [2]

Where, we may ask, does this voice, this witness, this guardian come from? After what has been said thus far, the answer is obvious: from God. For the most part we have to deduce this from statements in which Seneca does not mention the word *conscientia*, but nevertheless makes it clear enough that this is what he means, by, for instance, using the word *custos*, guardian, which he uses elsewhere as a metaphor for the conscience. A case in point is a passage which is most significant with respect to his beliefs concerning God:

> God is near you, he is with you, he is within you. This is what I mean, Lucilius: a holy spirit indwells within us, one who marks our good and bad deeds, and is our guardian. As we treat this spirit, so are we treated by it. Indeed, no man can be good without the help of God. [3]

It need hardly be said that in many passages where Seneca refers to the divine elements in man we may count the conscience among them; for example, where he maintains that a man's soul bears the seeds of goodness which may be roused by exhortation:

> The soul carries within itself the seed of everything that is honourable, and this seed is stirred to growth by advice, as a spark that is fanned by a gentle breeze develops its natural fire. Virtue is aroused by a touch, a shock. [4] Nature has laid the foundations and planted the seeds of virtue in us all. [5]

Elsewhere Seneca replies to the question as to "How we first acquire the knowledge of that which is good and that which is honourable" by saying:

> Nature could not teach us this directly; she has given us the seeds of knowledge, but not knowledge itself. [6]

In an appraisal of Seneca's conception of the conscience it is of

---

[1] *Ep.* 43. 5.
[2] *V.B.* 19. 1; 20. 5.
[3] *Ep.* 41. 1, 2.
[4] *Ep.* 94. 29.
[5] *Ep.* 108. 8; cf. *Ep.* 73. 16.
[6] *Ep.* 120. 3, 4; cf. Bertil Gärtner, *The Areopagus Speech and Natural Revelation,* 1955, p. 113 f.

course of great significance that the presence of the spirit means that there is an element of the divine in man. Accordingly, we do well to recall those passages in which Seneca speaks of the spirit as the divine part of man, that part of the divine spirit that has flowed down into the human heart, [1] the soul which is 'a god dwelling as a guest in a human body'. [2]

For Seneca the conscience is the voice of God, because it is the voice of the divine spirit in man, which testifies to the fact that God has entered into man. Or should we distinguish between God and the conscience? This is what Pohlenz does when he writes:

> Das Ziel des Menschen ist das Leben in Übereinstimmung mit der Natur, und er kann es dank seiner Anlage aus eigener Kraft erreichen. In seinem Gewissen hat er den untrüglichen Wegweiser für sein Handeln. Aber über diesem Gewissen steht als letzte Autorität noch die Gottheit, die es uns als Wächter beigegeben hat, die Gottheit, der wir unser Leben verdanken, der wir verantwortlich sind, der nichts von allem, was geschieht, entgeht. [3]

Seneca has indeed made statements which would seem to justify the making of such a distinction. Nevertheless, the question arises whether Seneca does not really maintain that everything takes place within man, because 'God' makes himself heard by means of the divine voice in man. Among the passages Pohlenz quotes from is *Ep.* 41. 2. It would seem that Pohlenz is giving the contents of this passage concerning the relationship between God and the conscience too great a 'personal' connotation by saying: 'Gott hat uns in unserem Inneren einen ständigen unentrinnbaren Wächter beigegeben.' What Seneca says is:

> 'God is near you, he is with you, he is within you... a holy spirit indwells within us, one who marks our good and bad deeds, and is our guardian.'

This is not the same as Pohlenz's formulation of the matter. In this holy spirit, in this *custos* — by this Seneca most assuredly means the

---

[1] *Ep.* 120. 14.
[2] *Ep.* 31. 11.
[3] Pohlenz, *Stoa* I, p. 320; cf. p. 317: 'Unsere geheimen Gedanken kennt ausser Gott nur einer; das sind wir selbst. Denn Gott hat uns in unserem Inneren einen ständigen, unentrinnbaren Wächter beigegeben, dem nichts verborgen bleibt, was wir tun, und dieser Wächter ist zugleich der unbestechliche Richter, dem wir für jeden unserer Gedanken und für jedes Wort, das über unsere Lippen kommt, Rechenschaft schulden. Es ist das Gewissen, die conscientia, das damit zur letzten Instanz über unser Verhalten erhoben wird, die uns lohnt und straft.'

conscience — God is in us. Saying that God has given us a guardian is putting far too personal a stress on God.

It cannot be denied that there are passages where Seneca does refer to the gods in a personal manner, for example, when he professes:

> I shall know that the whole world is my country, that its rulers are the gods, and that they abide above me and around me, the censors of my words and deeds. 1

Or when in another passage on the conscience he speaks of the gods 'who are the witnesses of all ingratitude', 2 or of the 'gods, whose knowledge nothing escapes'. 3 But it becomes clear what he means by this when we read how he begins another passage by saying, 'God comes to men', as if God comes to man in person from without, but then he immediately goes on to say:

> nay, he comes nearer, — he comes into men. No mind that has not God, is good. Divine seeds are scattered throughout our mortal bodies. 4

Elsewhere he states that, 'Nothing is shut off from the sight of God', but this too is qualified by:

> He is witness of our souls, and he comes into the very midst of our thoughts — comes into them, I say, as one who may at any time depart. 5

This is only another instance of something we have already observed repeatedly in Seneca's writings, namely, when it seems at first sight as if God is referred to personally, this appears on closer examination not to be the case. By saying that God has entered into man Seneca evidently wishes to express the belief that the divine part of man makes itself heard in the conscience. Hence it is incorrect to say that above the conscience there is the supreme authority of the godhead.

The fact that Seneca ultimately considers judgment and forgiveness to be man's own concern, and a matter for his own conscience, is made clear in a passage in *De Ira,* where, to be sure, the word conscience is not used, but it is quite evidently understood. Here Seneca says that he has formed the habit of examining his behaviour at the end of each day. When referring to this he employs words derived from legal terminology. He calls the habit '[appearing] before a judge every day', *cotidie ad iudicem venire,* and '[pleading] my cause before the bar of

---

1 *V.B.* 20. 5.
2 *Ben.* iii. 17. 3.
3 *Ben.* v. 25. 4.
4 *Ep.* 73. 16.
5 *Ep.* 83. 1.

self', *cotidie apud me causam dico*. A man who does this need not be afraid of his own errors, for he can say to himself: beware that you do not do it again. This time I shall forgive you. After such a self-examination which comprises accusation, plea for the defence and forgiveness, one can, if one hides nothing and omits nothing, sleep in peace:

> How delightful the sleep that follows this self-examination — how tranquil it is, how deep and untroubled, when the soul has either praised or admonished itself, and when this secret examiner and critic of self has given report of its own character! [1]

In this way man is his own prosecutor, judge, and intercessor, as Seneca explicitly says in one of his letters:

> As far as possible, prove yourself guilty, hunt up charges against yourself; play the part, first of accuser, then of judge, last of intercessor [*accusatoris primum partibus fungere, deinde iudicis, novissime deprecatoris*]. [2]

From this it is clear that it is scarcely possible to extract from Seneca's writings the notion of a godhead which has supreme authority above the conscience. For Seneca the last judgment is when man communes with the voice within him, which, because part of man is of divine origin, is the voice of God, but *in* man himself, because God has entered into man.

The question now arises whether Paul's conception of the office of the conscience closely resembles Seneca's. Can one say that he speaks of the conscience in almost the same way as Seneca? Pohlenz, for instance, is of the opinion that even before Seneca the conscience was a recognized philosophical concept, 'denn ganz ähnlich wie er würdigen es etwa gleichzeitig Philon und Paulus, obwohl sie aus jüdischer Überlieferung nicht einmal den Namen entnehmen konnten.' [3] That a close resemblance is sometimes seen is evident from the frequency with which statements of Seneca's are quoted, obviously as parallels, side by side with those texts in which Paul refers to the conscience. Windisch, for example, quotes beside 2 Cor. 1 : 12 Seneca's *Ep.* 43. 5; *V.B.* 19. 1; 20. 5, and then comments:

> Paulus stimmt mit den Griechen und Römern jedenfalls darin überein, dass das Zeugnis des Gewissens zur Bildung des Charakters, zur Prüfung

---

[1] *Ira* iii. 36. 2-4.
[2] *Ep.* 28. 10.
[3] Pohlenz, *Stoa* I, p. 317; id. *ZNW*, 1949, p. 78 f.

des eigenen Lebenswandels und zur Rechtfertigung gegenüber fremden Anwürfen gepflegt und gehört werden muss. [1]

Althaus writes in connection with another Pauline text concerning the conscience, Rom. 2 : 14 f., *inter alia*:

Paulus übernimmt mit dem hellenistischen Judentum, vor allem Philo, das Stichwort und den Grundgedanken der stoischen Ethik. — Wie in der Sache, mit der Behauptung des Naturgesetzes, das ins Herz geschrieben ist, knüpft Paulus auch mit dem Ausdruck „Gewissen" an ursprünglich stoische, dann popular-philosophische Gedanken seiner Zeit an, die vom hellenistischen Judentum aufgenommen waren. [2]

It is in the first place remarkable that the word συνείδησις occurs comparatively frequently in Paul, who is not likely to have taken it over from the Old Testament or Judaism, since it does not appear in the Old Testament, except in Eccles. 10 : 20, where it is used in an entirely different sence. In the Apocrypha the variant *syneidesis* for *eidesis* is doubtful. However, it does occur in Wisd. of Sol. 17 : 11 in the meaning 'conscience'. Accordingly the word only occurs in a work influenced by Hellenism and from a later period. It also occurs repeatedly in Philo. [3]

Judaism has no special word for 'conscience'. Now and then the word *lēb* approaches it in meaning. [4] But neither in Hebrew nor in Aramaic is there a word that covers the meaning of 'conscience' exactly. This implies that the word made its way into Judaism from outside, and that Paul too must have acquired it from these same sources. In view of this it is indeed striking that he uses it so frequently. The question remains, exactly how did Paul acquire the word? Was it from the Stoics or was it already in common parlance? [5]

The problem is whether he uses the word συνείδησις in the same sense as Seneca uses *conscientia*. Not without significance is the fact that Paul considers the conscience to be a universal human attribute.

---

[1] H. Windisch, *Der zweite Korintherbrief*, 1924, p. 54.

[2] Paul Althaus, *Der Brief an die Römer*, 1949, p. 21.

[3] Cf. H. Böhlig, Das Gewissen bei Seneca und Paulus, *Studien und Kritiken*, 1914, p. 18 ff.; J. Stelzenberger, op. cit., p. 194 f.; J. Bonsirven, S.J., *Le Judaïsme Palestinien*, ²1935, II, p. 11; W. D. Stacey, op. cit., p. 107.

[4] F. H. von Meyenfeldt, *Het hart (leb, lebab) in het Oude Testament*, 1950 (diss. Free University of Amsterdam), mentions various places in the O. T. where the word *leb* or *lebab* virtually has the same meaning as 'conscience': Gen. 20: 5, 6; 1 Sam. 24 : 6; 25 : 31; 2 Sam. 24 : 10; 1 Kings 2 : 44; 8 : 38; Job 27 : 6; Eccles. 7 : 22.

[5] The first possibility, although adhered to by many, is utterly rejected by C. A. Pierce, op. cit., p. 13 ff.; cf. also C. Spicq, *Saint Paul, Les Épitres Pastorales*, 1947, p. 29, in an excursus on 'La bonne conscience et la foi'; J. Dupont, op. cit., p. 123²; J. Stelzenberger, op. cit., p. 212 ff.

This is plainly implied in 2 Cor. 4 : 2, where Paul speaks of the way he has discharged his apostlehood in the world:

> We have renounced disgraceful, underhand ways; we refuse to practice cunning or to tamper with God's word, but by the open statement of the truth we would commend ourselves to every man's conscience.

With these words Paul does not allude only to the impression that his apostolic mission in word and deed will make on the churches, the Christians, but also to the impression it will have upon the Gentiles. He has in mind the conscience of every man who is reached by his preaching. This entails the assumption that the conscience makes itself heard in every man.

Such an assumption most probably also underlies the familiar pericope on authority, Rom. 13 : 5. Naturally this verse is firmly linked to the preceding verses, 3 and 4. 'To avoid God's wrath' refers back to the authorities' methods of punishment. If one resists authority and does wrong, one will experience its wrath. But that ought not to be the only reason for subjecting oneself to it. The conscience also acknowledges that authority acts rightly, both when it rewards what is good with its praise and when it punishes wrongdoing. Thus the conscience induces us to subject ourselves to authority. It is of course plain that Paul is first and foremost addressing Christians here. When he writes: 'there is no authority except from God' (v. 1) or 'he is the servant of God' (v. 4), it is clear that he is appealing to the attitude which Christians have towards authority by virtue of their faith. But when after verse 5 he immediately goes on to say: 'For the same reason you also pay taxes', he is alluding to something which is not only done by Christians, but by all citizens, Christian and Gentile alike. Although it is the members of the Church who are being addressed here in the first place, there is, I believe, no objection to our interpreting Paul's words to mean that every human conscience will approve of the action taken by authority with respect to those who do good or evil.

The question whether it is the Christians alone or together with the Gentiles to whom Paul is referring when he speaks of the conscience, is of particular importance in the exegesis of the well known text Rom. 2 : 14-16. This is usually regarded as the most significant passage on the conscience in the Pauline epistles, and not unjustifiably, since it is of great importance for our evaluation of Paul's conception of the revelation and of man as a whole. But it would be very one-sided to devote almost all our attention to this passage alone, thus neglecting the other passages where Paul treats the conscience more fully.

To whom does Paul refer with the word 'Gentiles', ἔθνη? Does he mean the Gentiles in general, or the Gentile Christians, that is to say those who were converted to Christianity from Gentiledom? It is plain that the answer to this question is of the utmost importance for the exegesis. Philologically speaking it is quite possible to take 'Gentiles' to mean Gentile Christians. The word is used by Paul several times in this sense, but then in contexts where misunderstanding is impossible. [1] Here, however, I consider this interpretation to be out of the question, despite the emphatic claims that are sometimes made for it. Karl Barth, for example, definitely excludes Rom. 2 : 14 f. from those passages (Rom. 1 : 18 f.; Acts 14 : 15 f.; 17 : 22 f. are mentioned) which are frequently quoted in defence of an extension of the revelation:

> Die Heiden, an denen die Weissagung von Jer. 31 : 33 in Erfüllung gegangen ist, sind nach dem ganzen Zusammenhang des Kapitels unzweideutig als Heiden*christen* zu verstehen. [2]

What Paul is saying in this chapter does not, however, point in this direction, far from it. Here he wishes to demonstrate that only those who are not only the hearers of the law but also doers of the law, may be justified by that law. The Jews have the law, but they do not act accordingly, and therefore can never be justified by that law. It might be said that the Gentiles cannot be judged according to the law, since they do not have it. But, says Paul, some Gentiles show by their conduct that they have the requirements of the law written on their hearts, 'while their conscience also bears witness'. This surely means the conscience of the Gentiles in general, as is also probably apparent from the ὅταν (not ἐάν) and the absence of the article before ἔθνη, so that 'when Gentiles, some Gentiles . . .' is meant. Hence this passage is not in contradiction with the very gloomy picture Paul paints of the moral conduct of the Gentiles in general in Rom. 1 : 24-32. The ὅταν indicates that what follows is one of the many facets of Gentiledom, Rom. 1 : 24-32 being another.

---

[1] Rom. 16 : 4; Gal. 2 : 12; Eph. 3 : 1.

[2] K. Barth, *Die kirchliche Dogmatik,* I, 2, 1945, p. 332; Barth has apparently changed his mind about the exegesis of this passage. The aforementioned exegesis is not yet to be found in *Der Römerbrief,* where ἔθνη is said to apply, not to Gentile Christians, but to Gentiles in general. There Barth refers, for example, to 'die Stimme des Gewissens, wie sie auch in den Gesetzlosen und Gottlosen redet', *Der Römerbrief,* ⁶1953, p. 43; cf. Max Lackmann, *Vom Geheimnis der Schöpfung,* 1952, p. 213 f. It is also applied to Gentile Christians in an article by F. Flückiger, 'Die Werke des Gesetzes bei den Heiden (Röm. 2, 14 ff.)', *Theologische Zeitschrift,* 1952, pp. 17-42, and in one by Bo Reicke, 'Syneidesis in Röm. 2, 15', *Theologische Zeitschrift,* 1956, p. 157 ff.

Further proof of the fact that Paul is referring to the Gentiles in general is the expression 'even though they do not have the law' (Rom. 2 : 14). Paul would not have said this of the Gentile Christians, who are repeatedly assumed to know the law of the Old Testament, and hence also 'have' it. Consequently the statement in Rom. 7 : 1: 'for I am speaking to those who know the law', is by no means proof of the fact that Paul was here addressing Jewish Christians alone. It is evident that Paul assumes that mixed Jewish Christian and Gentile Christian churches are familiar with the Old Testament, and hence also with the law. It is only of the Gentiles that Paul can say that, in contrast with the Jews, they have no written law.

Moreover, from Rom. 2 : 9 f., 12 onwards the subject is the contrast between the Jews and the Gentiles, a contrast which Paul repeatedly touches upon in this letter. [1] There are, however, no other passages where Paul alludes to a contrast between Jews and Gentile Christians. [2]

In view of all these factors it is virtually out of the question that Paul should be referring to Gentile Christians in Rom. 2 : 14-16, while it is evident from this text that Paul deems every man to have a conscience, or at least deems it possible for the conscience to speak in every man.

What, we may ask, does this conscience do? As an inner voice in a man it passes judgment on that man's actions, either endorsing them or censuring them. This is true of Paul's own conscience: for it tells him that he may boast, when he looks back on how he has lived in the world. Paul's conscience is his judge who passes judgment on what he has done (2 Cor. 1 : 12). In Rom. 9 : 1 also Paul appeals to his own conscience. At the beginning of the chapters on Israel he mentions how much he knows himself to be involved in what he is about to say about Israel: 'I have great sorrow and unceasing anguish in my heart.' His conscience bears witness that he is speaking the truth when he says how greatly this matter torments him. 'My conscience bears me witness', it is as if the conscience bears witness as a separate authority

---

[1] Rom. 1 : 5, 13; 9 : 24, 30; 11 : 11, 13, 25, etc.

[2] He contrasts Gentiles with Christians: Rom. 10 : 20; 1 Cor. 12 : 2, Gentile Christians with Jewish Christians: Rom. 16 : 4; Gal. 2 : 12, 14, but never Jews with Gentile Christians. G. Bornkamm points this out in his essay 'Gesetz und Natur, Röm. 2. 14-16' in the collection *Studien zu Antike und Christentum*, 1959, pp. 93-118; this remark p. 109, note 39; cf. also Herman Ridderbos, *Aan de Romeinen*, 1959, p. 60 f.

alongside the ordinary self. An independent witness, as it were, testifies side by side with Paul himself. Here, too, the conscience passes judgment.

It is significant that Paul adds 'in the Holy Spirit', which does not of course belong to 'my conscience' but to 'bearing witness'; Paul does not wish to speak of a conscience reposing in the Holy Spirit, but just as he speaks the truth in Christ, so too does the conscience testify in the Holy Spirit. Hence it would seem that we are not taking too much for granted if we deem it clearly stated by Paul that the testimony of the conscience, if it is a good testimony, belongs in the domain of the Holy Spirit. The conscience can only be called upon as a witness for the truth, if it is sanctified by the Spirit.

Paul is also referring to the judicial nature of man's conscience in 1 Cor. 4 : 4, despite the fact that there he does not use the word συνείδησις, but σύνοιδα. This verse is most important within the framework of the whole pericope 1 Cor. 4 : 1-5. In this pericope allusion is made to judgment from three different quarters on Paul's activities as an Apostle. The Corinthians have been rather critical of Paul. This is not what concerns him most. He wishes to point out that self-judgment is not the final judgment. The last judgment is in the hands of God and Christ. This does not necessarily mean that this judgment will always differ from a man's own judgment of himself. On the contrary, what Paul goes on to say: 'Then every man will receive his commendation from God' (v. 5b) conveys that he expects the Lord to confirm his own judgment of himself, namely: 'I am not aware of anything against myself'. But the possibility of these two judgments differing is not excluded. In all events, even if they should customarily agree, nobody is ever entitled to think that his own judgment of himself justifies him. Paul knows this to apply to himself: 'I am not thereby acquitted.' It is never the last judgment. [1]

In others too, Paul assumes the existence of such a voice as passes judgment within him. Second Corinthians 4 : 2 has already been mentioned. In 2 Cor. 5 : 11 likewise Paul appeals to the conscience of the members of the Church. He endeavours to convince his audience by preaching the Gospel. By means of this preaching he wishes to win people for this Gospel (cf. 1 Cor. 9 : 19-23). That this is his intention is already known to God, as it will be known to all at the day of

---

[1] Cf. R. Steinmetz, *Das Gewissen bei Paulus. Biblische Zeit- und Streitfragen*, 1911, p. 8 ff.

judgment, but the Apostle hopes that he will now also be revealed to the members of the Church as one whose only wish is to win people for the Gospel, and that their conscience will be outspoken in its judgment of him.

Further light is thrown on the Pauline conception of the conscience by the pericopes in First Corinthians which deal with the eating of food offered to idols, and in connection with this the acceptance of invitations to eat with Gentiles: 1 Cor. 8 : 7-13; 10 : 25-30. [1] Here mention is also made of the *conscientia antecedens,* that is to say the conscience which endorses or censures an action which has still to take place. It is clear from these passages that according to Paul no one should ignore the voice of his own conscience. All should listen to this voice. Paul decidedly considers himself to be among the 'strong' in Corinth: he has no objection to eating food offered to idols. He does not take the least exception to it personally. It does not make him uneasy in his mind. But there are those in the Church who are not yet free of idolatry. If such persons see someone who is stronger than they eating food offered to idols, they may be encouraged to do so themselves; but if they are not spiritually mature enough they will be morally destroyed by it. Paul is well aware that such an attitude is evidence of a 'weak conscience' (1 Cor. 8 : 10), but care should be taken not to injure such 'weak' brethren. Particularly those who are quite steadfast in their attitude towards these matters, 'all of us possess knowledge', would do well to remember that: ' "Knowledge" puffs up, but love builds up' (8 : 1). No one should be a party to the destruction of a 'brother for whom Christ died' (8 : 11). [2]

Paul also includes himself among the 'strong' in 1 Cor. 10 : 25-30. If one buys meat at the meat market one need not inquire anxiously where it comes from: 'Eat whatever is sold in the meat market without raising any question on the ground of conscience', and 'If one of the unbelievers invites you to dinner and you are disposed to go, eat whatever is set before you without raising any question on the ground of conscience' (1 Cor. 10 : 25, 27). But if a fellow guest, most

---

[1] See on this L. Batelaan, *De sterken en zwakken in de kerk van Korinthe,* 1942 (Diss. Free University of Amsterdam), in particular p. 37 ff.; J. Dupont, op. cit., (p. 84, note 5), p. 146 ff.

[2] Böhlig, op. cit., p. 18: 'Für den Träger ist es unbedingt verbindlich'; Steinmetz, op. cit., p. 17: 'Das Urteil des Gewissens ist für den Menschen subjektiv unbedingt verbindlich; das Gewissen ist auch dann eine Autorität, der sich der Mensch fügen muss.'

probably a weaker brother, suddenly says in an anxious tone of voice: ' "This has been offered in sacrifice," then out of consideration for the man who informed you, and for conscience sake — I mean his conscience, not yours — do not eat it' (1 Cor. 10 : 28 f.). For such a weak brother should be protected lovingly. If his conscience is uneasy, one must not injure him with one's own 'strong' behaviour.

This is an extremely important passage for Paul's conception of the conscience as a whole, since it shows that the promptings of the conscience do not possess unconditional validity. He himself is convinced that the conscience of the weak is at fault here, and has unnecessary scruples about buying meat at the market or accepting an invitation to eat with unbelievers. A weak conscience like this is still in the clutches of idolatry. It judges incorrectly.

Nevertheless, Paul does not urge the 'strong' to be unconditionally obedient to what *their* conscience bids them do, and to behave in accordance with their 'knowledge'. For if their conduct determined by that conscience should wound a 'weak' brother in the Church and confuse him so greatly that it would bring about his destruction, then their love for this brother for whom Christ died ought to influence their behaviour. Then they, 'the strong', should not allow their actions to be governed by the promptings of their conscience, correct though they may be, but by their loving consideration for the 'weak' conscience of their brother.

Hence however binding Paul deems the voice of the conscience to be for the individual, the conscience may not simply be regarded as God's final judgment in man. For, as has been seen, a conscience may be weak if it is still too greatly enthralled by idolatry. It is, in addition, striking that in Rom. 9 : 1 Paul adds 'in the Holy Spirit', and that in 1 Cor. 4 : 4 he virtually says that the judgment of one's own conscience may never in any event be regarded as the final judgment. The last judgment is the judgment of God or Christ on the day of judgment when all men will have to appear before the judgment seat of Christ (2 Cor. 5 : 10). It is plain from Rom. 2 : 16 that also in this pericope on the conscience the last judgment on the day of judgment is considered to be the truly decisive one, even though it is not so easy to fathom exactly how this verse is linked with the two preceding ones. [1]

---

[1] The transition has sometimes been considered so difficult that the verse has been taken for a later addition. As e.g. G. Bornkamm, op. cit., p. 116 f.

Accordingly it is a mistake to speak of 'natural revelation' in connection with Rom. 2 : 14 f. or Rom. 1 : 18-20. For Paul is not dealing with the question of a universal and a particular revelation here, at all events not explicitly. In both passages the subject under discussion is the place of the Gentiles in the history of salvation. In Rom. 1 : 18-20 Paul wishes to demonstrate that the Gentiles could have known God from the things He had created, and that they therefore cannot say that they do not know God; hence they are 'without excuse' in their moral wickedness. In Rom. 2 : 14 f. the question is whether, like the Jews, the Gentiles may also be judged according to whether they *do* the law. The Jews know the law but do not act accordingly. The Gentiles, too, may be judged by this standard, for they, too, have the law written on their hearts. It is in this connection that Paul mentions the conscience. In so doing, he by no means wishes to prove that man, by virtue of his inner life or his conscience, is close to God, but that the *complete* man is really *far* removed from God by nature. For men know what the law requires in their hearts, 'while their conscience also bears witness', but still they do not obey that law. Paul does not wish to open the eyes of his readers to God's revelation prior to Christ in creation or in the conscience, but to confront them as boldly as possible with God's revelation in Christ. He wishes to show that like the Jews who know the law as a written law, the Gentiles whose conscience tells them what the law requires also need the revelation of God's justice and mercy in Christ. [1]

If we compare the notion 'conscience' in Paul and Seneca, resemblance may be found not only in the names for the conscience: *conscientia*, συνείδησις, but also, for instance, in the fact that Seneca calls the conscience a witness, [2] while Paul speaks of the testimony, the bearing witness of the conscience. [3] The latter is all the more remarkable, since the word 'conscience' does not occur in the Old Testament and was introduced to Judaism from outside.

Furthermore for both Paul and Seneca the conscience judges, and its authority without doubt governs the person who hears its voice. No one, says Paul, has the right to force his opinion upon me (1 Cor.

---

[1] Cf. O. Cullmann, *Christus und die Zeit*, 1946, p. 160 ff.; R. Bultmann, *Theologie des Neuen Testament*, 1948, p. 212 ff.; W. G. Kümmel, *Das Bild des Menschen im Neuen Testament*, 1948, p. 26 f. D. Holwerda, *Commentatio de vocis quae est* ΦΥΣΙΣ *vi atque usu*, 1955, p. 85 f.

[2] *Ep.* 43. 5; *Ben.* ii. 10. 2.

[3] 2 Cor. 1 : 12; Rom. 9 : 1; 2 : 15.

10 : 29), a man is at liberty in his conscience. Accordingly, a 'weak conscience' should also be respected. Hence for both of them the conscience speaks with authority.

But this is where differences arise. For Seneca the conscience can pass the *final* judgment. In his self-examination and judgment man is his own 'accuser, judge, intercessor'. [1] He who subjects himself to an examination of his conduct at the end of the day may pass the final judgment upon himself and grant himself forgiveness, so that he may thereafter sleep soundly and peacefully. [2] Such a view is possible for Seneca because, according to him, God dwells in man, being present in his mind and reason. If parts of the divine spirit are present in man, it is axiomatic that man need not await any other judgment, once his conscience which is part of that divine spirit has passed judgment upon him.

Hence 1 Cor. 4 : 1-5 could almost be read as a reaction to what Seneca says in *De Ira* iii. 36. 2-4. According to Paul the judgment passed on a man by his conscience, even if it is not condemnatory, is not final. Only the Lord is in a position to pass the last judgment. The voice of the conscience is not always the voice of God: the conscience of the 'weak' in Corinth was at fault. It is only when it bears witness in the Holy Spirit that it may be called upon as a witness for the truth.

Naturally, too, the last judgment is one which pertains to the life and works of a man as a whole and which is passed on the day of judgment, the day when Christ comes again and judgment is passed after the resurrection of the dead. This can never be replaced by the judgment of the conscience, which is the reason why Paul also alludes to the last judgment in those pericopes dealing with the conscience (Rom. 2 : 16; 2 Cor. 5 : 10, 11).

Here too, the difference between Seneca's and Paul's conception of God, and hence also the difference in their ideas concerning the relationship between God and man, becomes obvious. For Paul the Stoic conception of an immanent God, of a God whose spirit pervades man and thus speaks directly through his conscience, is of course out of the question. In Paul the distance between God and man is preserved, even when he maintains that the Gentiles too have knowledge of God's written law by reason of their conscience. What use is this if sin

---

[1] *Ep.* 28. 10.
[2] *Ira* iii. 36. 2-4.

renders this knowledge of the law, written on their hearts, powerless. Man, every man, remains dependent, fully dependent, upon God's work of salvation. Hence it is of course quite impossible for Paul ever to consider the final judgment of a man's deeds as an action which takes place within a man. For him it is unalterably linked with the judgment seat of Christ (2 Cor. 5 : 10). Something of this action can, however, penetrate into this earthly life, if the conscience bears witness in the Holy Spirit (Rom. 9 : 1), because the Holy Spirit already belongs to the world of God. It is, however, not a part of man as such, but it is given to man by God. Here we have another example of the fact that it is sometimes precisely in those passages where there is complete verbal agreement, that the most essential differences emerge. Seneca too speaks of 'a holy spirit within us', [1] and from what follows it is apparent that he means the conscience: 'a holy spirit indwells within us, one who marks our good and bad deeds, and is our guardian.' He refers to a spirit which can dwell in every man, because 'God is near you, he is with you, he is within you.' [2]

Hence even when Paul makes use, frequent use, of a term which also often occurs in the writings of Seneca, he does so within a framework far removed from Seneca's range of ideas. In Paul these terms form part of the preaching of the Gospel by an Apostle of Jesus Christ, part of the description of God's work of salvation in Christ.

---

[1] *Ep.* 41. 2: *sacer intra nos spiritus.*
[2] *Ep.* 41. 1.

CHAPTER FOUR

THE LIFE OF THE INDIVIDUAL

The subject of this chapter brings us into the realm of ethics, where the difference in character between our sources asserts itself once more. Seneca writes very extensively on ethical problems, sometimes devoting entire essays to the subject. Certain ethical questions form the basis for a logically built up discourse, and while it is now and then difficult to follow Seneca's argument closely, the mainstream of his thoughts is usually clear enough for us to be able to form an accurate idea of his views concerning various ethical problems. Such problems were apparently of special interest to Seneca. The reason for this is obvious; Seneca felt himself to be a wise man who could give all kinds of persons good advice; he thought he understood mankind and the workings of man's mind and was therefore able to discover the failings both in others and in himself. If one comprehends the movements of the human soul, one can show one's fellow men the right road upon which to travel in life and also disclose to them how they can find the strength to follow that road. And so it is that many of Seneca's writings are treatises upon practical ethics in which he devotes all his attention to the struggles and sufferings of man, to man in his smallness and greatness, in order to show him how he thinks man should live. Reflections of an exclusively moral nature occupy a very important place in Seneca's writings. It is safe to say that Seneca was chiefly preoccupied with ethical problems, and hence also with the personal life of the individual and relationships between people.

It is characteristic of Paul's attitude towards ethics that they never form a chapter on their own but are always indissolubly linked with 'dogmatics' and 'theology', in short with the central kerygma. Paul's letters are not lacking in ethical exhortations and reprimands, but these do not spring from an isolated interest in ethical problems as such. Hence Paul never presents us with an ethical discourse as Seneca does. That a rounded-off set of moral principles, either personal or social, is not to be found in Paul, not even scattered throughout his writings, may quite justifiably be ascribed to the fact that his letters were written— as has already been mentioned— [1] in answer to certain questions or as

---

[1] pp. 23-25.

comment on particular events. The realization of this can sometimes be of the utmost importance to the interpretation of Paul's statements. It has, for instance, been concluded from 1 Cor. 7 : 2 that Paul's attitude towards marriage was for the greater part negative: to remain single is preferable, but marriage is necessary for those who cannot exercise self-control and would otherwise lapse into fornication. It is, however, important to bear 7 : 1 in mind: Paul is reacting here, as he is frequently in the letter, [1] to specific difficulties being experienced in the church at Corinth. He has apparently been asked a number of definite questions concerning this matter. Hence it is most certainly not Paul's intention to propound a complete set of marital ethics, and so, too, it is incorrect to assume that in 1 Cor. 7 : 2 Paul desires to indicate the one and only motive for marriage. Eph. 5 : 25-33 throws quite a different light upon this subject.

Hence the fact that the Pauline epistles deal with specific problems arising out of specific situations or in answer to questions brought up by one church or other, is one of the reasons why we look in vain for a complete set of ethical principles in Paul. Even more important than this, however, is that what Paul does say about ethics is never divorced from his theological standpoint. His ethics are not in a separate compartment from his theology, his life is not isolated from his beliefs. His opinions, his decisions, his actions constantly show themselves to be deeply rooted in his theology. The former cannot be understood without the latter. His ethical approach to even the most everyday matters is determined by theological considerations. [2]

We may, indeed, say that when we move away from the field of Pauline theology to that of ethics we scarcely feel as if we are embarking upon a new subject. When we read, for instance, about the Spirit in Paul's letters we are most certainly justified in considering ourselves confronted by theology. When Paul speaks of the working of the Sprit he embraces in this, man's whole life and being in Christ. The Church has received the Spirit by hearing with faith (Gal. 3 : 2, 5). There is a genuine tie between the salvation-occurrence in Christ and the fact that the Church is in possession of the Spirit. Originally mankind lived in slavery, under the law and in the flesh. But in the fullness of time God sent forth His Son to redeem mankind from the law so that men might receive adoption as God's sons; and finally God sent

---

[1] 1 Cor. 5 : 1; 6 : 1, 12 ff.; 8 : 1; 11 : 1; 12 : 1; 15 : 12.
[2] See e.g. 1 Cor. 8 : 4 ff., especially v. 11; 2 Cor. 8 : 9; Eph. 4 : 29, 30, 32; 5 : 1, 2; Phil. 2 : 5.

the Spirit of His Son into their hearts. [1] Belonging to Christ and possession of the Spirit are inseparably linked notions. [2] Possession of the
Spirit is only the beginning of the full glory that is to come. [3]

It is the glory of the Church and of the members of the Church
that the Spirit works in and among them. God gives the Spirit to man,
man does not bring Him forth out of himself. [4] The Spirit is the
author of certain *charismata*. [5] He enables man to fight against the
flesh. [6] Paul knows that he may appeal to the possession of the Spirit.
The Church may be exhorted to walk by the Spirit. [7] This may entail
effort and a struggle, [8] but it is never a hopeless struggle. The fruit
of the Spirit may be assumed to be present in the Church. [9] In it the
law is fulfilled by love. [10]

Where does theology end and ethics begin in this description by
Paul of the Spirit? It is indeed clear that no sharp dividing-line can
be drawn. When Paul speaks of the love felt by one human being
for another, he is really still thinking of the inscrutable love of God,
which is turned towards mankind. When he describes the forgiving-
ness, kindness and mercifulness of man towards man, he is describing mankind's response to God's forgiveness. When Paul mentions,
as he once does, the peace *in* man, 'the peace in believing', this also
is a direct reference to the peace God has granted man in Christ
(Rom. 15 : 13).

That Paul's ethics and theology are so indissolubly linked may be
attributed to the fact that both are entirely Christocentric. Being in
Christ, putting on Christ, being a new creature in Christ, being transformed by the renewal of the mind (Rom. 12 : 2), putting off the
'old' man who will be destroyed, and putting on the 'new' man who
is created according to God's will in true righteousness and holiness
(Eph. 4 : 22, 24), 'through Christ the world has been crucified to
me, and I to the world' (Gal. 6 : 14), — basically these are all
theological expressions, but at the same time they have a strong ethical

---

[1] Gal. 4 : 1-7; Rom. 7 : 4-6; 8 : 1-4.
[2] 1 Cor. 12 : 1-3; Rom. 8 : 9.
[3] Rom. 8 : 23; 2 Cor. 1 : 22; 5 : 5; Eph. 1 : 13, 14.
[4] Gal. 4 : 6; 1 Thess. 4 : 8; Rom. 8 : 14; Gal. 5 : 18; Rom. 8 : 26, 27.
[5] 1 Cor. 12 : 28; Rom. 12 : 6-8; Eph. 4 : 11.
[6] Rom. 8 : 4-9; cf. Gal. 5 : 16 ff.
[7] Gal. 5 : 16, 25.
[8] Cf. 1 Cor. 9 : 24-27; Phil. 3 : 12-14.
[9] Gal. 5 : 22; cf. Rom. 8 : 4.
[10] Gal. 5 : 13 f., 23; cf. Rom. 8 : 4; 13 : 8-10.

tendency. It is impossible to discuss Paul's ethics without discussing Christ. It is therefore somewhat arbitrary and could be misleading to deal with Paul's ethics as a subject apart, separating them from the context of his message for the sake of comparing them with Seneca's.

It has been necessary to examine closely the foundations upon which Paul's ethics lie, as it is of great importance for us to be aware, right from the start, of the widely differing approach to ethics of both writers. It will be clear from what has already been said that in Paul there is no place for an autonomous set of ethical principles, and that he does not take the individual human being as his point of departure but always sees him involved in some way or other in the entire salvation-occurrence.

Seneca's ethics are based on the notion that man has a free, autonomous personality, which in itself is of great value. After what has been said with respect to Seneca's anthropology it will be plain that man's most valuable attributes are his soul, his spirit and his reason. Such a notion must lead to a very different conception from Paul's of how man should live. In the Pauline epistles we find the view expressed that it is characteristic of the life of the Christian that he should realize what he already is, in Christ and within the framework of the salvation-occurrence, in which his faith enables him to share. That this salvation should be the basis for life is what really matters. For Seneca man's first duty is to mould himself into a free being, to cultivate himself, and to develop his personality. The origin of the notion 'person' most probably lies with Panaetius. The word is derived from the Latin *persona*, mask. [1] It is by no means accidental that Menander, who as a judge of human character first introduced individual personalities to the stage instead of types, already used the word 'character' in its modern sense. [2] The gradual development of the notion of the individual personality is indeed already perceptible in Hellenism. Panaetius may be said to have been the first to appreciate both scientifically and ethically the significance of the individual personality. The origin of our notion 'person' now becomes clear. As a Stoic Panaetius takes human nature in general as his point of departure. But in reality we only come into contact with human nature in the personal characteristics of each individual human being. Thus man

---

[1] Cf. W. Wiersma, 'De Stoa' in J. H. Waszink, W. C. van Unnik, Ch. de Beus, *Het oudste christendom en de antieke cultuur*, I, 1951, p. 318.

[2] Cf. Max Pohlenz, *Der hellenische Mensch*, 1947, p. 161. This book contains a section on 'Die Einzelpersönlichkeit', pp. 142-62.

has two faces; he wears, in the words of Panaetius who derives his image from the drama, two masks as it were and unites in himself two persons: among the Greeks the word πρόσωπον face, mask had long been applied to the person represented by it, and the Romans, who translated πρόσωπον with *persona*, followed this precedent. Accordingly Panaetius accepts for a fact that man can only live in harmony with nature, as is demanded by the Stoics, if he takes into consideration both his personal characteristics and his condition in life. It is clear that such an idea can easily lead to the doctrine promulgated by the Stoics, that each man should strive to develop a personality which makes full use of all its powers, which preserves its peace of mind in all circumstances, and which is capable of achieving by virtue of its inner strength a noble harmony within itself. The foundation and cultivation of the individual personality consequently becomes a moral duty. Of the Stoics it may indeed justly be said: 'so wird bei ihnen zuerst die Persönlichkeit zu einem massgebenden Prinzip'. [1] It is axiomatic that the cultivation of a harmonious personality can only thrive in a certain mental climate.

The glorification of the individual personality recurs repeatedly in Seneca. Time and again he takes as the starting point for his ethical exhortations the sublime picture of the noble personality. Wenn in his description of the happy life he starts to define the highest good, the *summum bonum,* he does so as follows:

> The highest good is a mind that scorns the happenings of chance, and rejoices only in virtue ... It is the power of the mind to be unconquerable, wise from experience, calm in action, showing the while much courtesy and consideration in intercourse with others. It may also be defined in the statement that the happy man is he who recognizes no good and evil other than a good and an evil mind — one who cherishes honour, is content with virtue, who is neither puffed up, nor crushed, by the happenings of chance, who knows of no greater good than that which he alone is able to bestow upon himself, for whom true pleasure will be the scorn of pleasures. [2]

He therefore goes on to exclaim:

> What prevents us from saying that the happy life is to have a mind that is placed beyond the reach of fear, beyond the reach of desire, that counts virtue the only good, baseness to only evil. [3]

---

[1] W. Windelband, *Lehrbuch der Geschichte der Philosophie,* ⁸1919, p. 139; cf. D. Loenen, *Eusebeia en de cardinale deugden,* 1960, p. 55.

[2] *V.B.* 4. 2.

[3] *V.B.* 4. 3.

Such a prodigious personality is deserving of the deepest respect. Seneca's glorification of such an awe-inspiring life is not free from pathos:

> If you see a man who is unterrified in the midst of dangers, untouched by desires, happy in adversity, peaceful amid the storm, who looks down upon men from a higher plane, and views the gods on a footing of equality, will not a feeling of reverence for him steal over you? Will you not say: "This quality is too great and too lofty to be regarded as resembling this petty body in which it dwells? A divine power has descended upon that man." [1]

Again and again Seneca bursts out into a lyrical glorification of the personality of the wise man:

> If we had the privilege of looking into a good man's soul, oh what a fair, holy, magnificent, gracious, and shining face should we behold — radiant on the one side with justice and temperance, on another with bravery and wisdom! And, besides these, thriftiness, moderation, endurance, refinement, affability, and — though hard to believe — love of one's fellow-men, that Good which is so rare in man, all these would be shedding their own glory over that soul. There, too, forethought combined with elegance and, resulting from these, a most excellent greatness of soul (the noblest of all these virtues) — indeed what charm, O ye heavens, what authority and dignity would they contribute! What a wonderful combination of sweetness and power! No one could call such a face lovable without also calling it worshipful. If one might behold such a face, more exalted and more radiant than the mortal eye is wont to behold would not one pause as if struck dumb by a visitation from above, and utter a silent prayer, saying: "May it be lawful to have looked upon it!"? And then, led on by the encouraging kindliness of his expression, should we not bow down and worship? [2]

Constant serenity is characteristic of the wise man's life, the only life which may be called truly healthy:

> I shall tell you what I mean by health: if the mind is content with its own self; if it has confidence in itself; if it understands that all those things for which men pray, all the benefits which are bestowed and sought for, are of no importance in relation to a life of happiness; under such conditions it is sound. [3]
> The effect of wisdom is a joy that is unbroken and continuous. The mind of the wise man is like the ultra-lunar firmament; eternal calm pervades that region, [4] it is consistent with itself throughout. [5]

---

1 *Ep.* 41. 4.
2 *Ep.* 115. 3, 4.
3 *Ep.* 72. 7.
4 *Ep.* 59. 16.
5 *Ep.* 31. 8; 35. 4.

Although Seneca repeatedly affirms that such a wise man is a rarity, that a good man, a *vir bonus* in the true sense of the word, and not one of the second grade, is like the phoenix which is born only once in five hundred years, [1] he elsewhere insists that the wise man is by no means only an ideal, never to be found in reality:

> There is no reason for you to say, Serenus, as your habit is, that this wise man of ours is nowhere to be found. He is not a fiction of us Stoics, a sort of phantom glory of human nature, nor is he a mere conception, the mighty semblance of a thing unreal, but we have shown him in the flesh just as we delineate him, and shall show him — though perchance not often, and after a long lapse of years only one. For greatness which transcends the limit of the ordinary and common type is produced but rarely.

Of Marcus Cato it may almost be said that he 'surpasses even our exemplar.' [2]

For Seneca the wise man with his imperturbable tranquillity is like a god, apart of course from the fact that he is mortal:

> It is impossible for any one either to injure or to benefit the wise man, since that which is divine does not need to be helped, and cannot be hurt; and the wise man is next-door neighbour to the gods and like a god in all save his mortality .... The man who, relying on reason marches through mortal vicissitudes with the spirit of a god, has no vulnerable spot where he can receive an injury. [3]

Seneca advises Lucilius to devote himself entirely to philosophy:

> Turn to her with all your soul, sit at her feet, cherish her; a great distance will then begin to separate you from other men. You will be far ahead of all mortals, and even the gods will not be far ahead of you. Do you ask what will be the difference between yourself and the gods? They will live longer. [4]

Such a man who cannot be thrown off his balance in any way, 'who has been saved from error, who is self-controlled and has deep and calm repose', [5] who evinces 'greatness of soul', [6] 'the unbroken calm of the happy soul', [7] a man strong and unyielding in disaster, not only averse to luxury but hostile to it, who neither seeks danger nor shrinks from it, who does not await destiny, but makes it, and

---

[1] *Ep.* 42. 1.
[2] *Const.* 7. 1.
[3] *Const.* 8. 2 f.; cf. *Prov.* 1. 5.
[4] *Ep.* 53. 11.
[5] *Const.* 9. 3.
[6] *Const.* 9. 4.
[7] *Ira* ii. 12. 6.

who goes forward to meet it, whether it be good or evil, fearlessly
and with composure, who is moved neither by the assaults of destiny
nor by its splendour, 1 — such a man 'is a spectacle worthy of the
regard of God as he contemplates his works.' 2 In fact, Seneca is sometimes even capable of placing the wise man above God. In the way
he bears life's troubles man can rise above God:

> In this you may outstrip God; he is exempt from enduring evil, while
> you are superior to it. 3 There is one point in which the sage has an
> advantage over the god; for a god is freed from terrors by the bounty
> of nature, the wise man by his own bounty. 4

Consequently de Bovis is not exaggerating when he writes on the
place of the wise man in Seneca:

> L'homme, le sage surtout, est le centre du monde. Il le crée pour ainsi
> dire . . . . il demeure le cardo autour duquel évolue son univers à lui.

And further on:

> Cet égocentrisme déterminé se manifestera sous des formes multiples. 5

Liechtenhan writes in the same vein:

> Dem Stoiker ist der Weise Mass und Ziel aller Dinge, der ganze Welt-
> lauf hat keinen anderen Zweck als dieses Prachtstück mit seiner Mannes-
> tugend und Seelengrösse hervorzubringen und ihm Glückseligkeit zu
> geben. 6

Indeed, everything revolves around the human personality which is
self-sufficient and pursues its royal way through this world, unmoved
and imperturbable, a sublime spectacle for mankind and the gods.

It goes without saying that Paul's thoughts move in quite a different
direction. Even a superficial perusal of the Pauline epistles will make
this clear. Some years ago in a controversy between the Roman Catholic
writer Gerard Brom and the Protestant O. Noordmans, the former
reproached the latter somewhat bitterly of having put various values,
such as personality and virtue, under a ban, and of regarding them

---

1 N.Q. iii. Praef. 13.
2 Prov. 2. 9.
3 Prov. 6. 6.
4 Ep. 53. 11.
5 De Bovis, op. cit., p. 107 f.; cf. Jean Laloup, op cit., p. 203: 'tout au long de
l'antiquité classique, l'idéal humain préconisé par l'arétè grecque ou la virtus romaine
se développe dans un climat individualiste: qu'il s'agisse d'une belle émulation, d'une
sagesse rationnelle ou d'une évasion vers la perfection, toujours l'homme est appelé
à se réaliser, à s'épanouir, à s'accomplir.'
6 R. Liechtenhan, op. cit. p. 395.

solely as 'names for heathen gods'. Brom goes on to exclaim indignantly:

> Are we to understand that just because these words, every one of which is to be found in the New Testament, are often made absolute in an impious fashion, they do not have any value left at all? This shift is a reaction typical of the Protestant attitude. 1

Hence according to Brom the notion 'personality' as a value is to be found in the New Testament. In a note we are given Eph. 4 : 24 as an example. But this text, the only one cited by Brom, is in direct opposition to what the Stoics in general and Seneca in particular understand by 'personality'. Seneca points, not without pride, to the man who is completely self-sufficient in his freedom and inner inviolability. Whereas Paul lays all the emphasis on what God does for man. The 'new' man is not something that man himself achieves or brings about in himself, but — and the use of the passive voice speaks volumes — the 'new' man is 'created after the likeness of God'. The Christian has to put on this 'new' man; he clothes himself in it, as in a garment, which he has not made himself but which has been given to him. Consequently it is impossible to use this text as illustration of the presence of the notion 'personality' in the Pauline epistles.

The same applies to various other passages in Paul's letters, which are sometimes quoted in order to show that the notion 'personality' occurs in his writings, even if he does not use the word. But those scholars who do this are forgetting that, even when the Apostle uses terms that are perhaps derived from Hellenistic and sometimes also Stoic thought, they acquire in his writings quite a different meaning and fulfil a different task, because they are employed within the framework of his account of the history of salvation. In his discussion of Pauline ethics Johannes Weiss, for instance, devotes a section to "Das Persönlichkeitsmotiv" 2 which he begins thus:

> Unter diesem Ausdruck fassen wir eine Reihe von Motiven zusammen, die das Gemeinsame haben, dass sie das Ideal einer vollkommenen (Röm 12, 2; Kol 1, 28; 4, 12) in sich ausgeglichenen, von jedem Übermass der Leidenschaft gereinigten Persönlichkeit aufstellen.

He then quotes from Paul's letters a number of passages, some of which I shall return to later in another connection, and others of which are mentioned here in order to show that Weiss sometimes does not

---

1 Gerard, Brom, *Gesprek over de eenheid van de kerk,* 1946, p. 103 f. He here carries on a polemical discussion with O. Noordmans, *Herschepping.*

2 Joh. Weiss, *Das Urchristentum,* 1917, p. 441 ff.

escape the danger of misconstruing certain texts in his endeavour to bring them under the heading of 'das Persönlichkeitsmotiv'. He says, for instance:

> Der schrankenlose Gebrauch der Freiheit, der nur allzuleicht in die Unfreiheit der Leidenschaft gegenüber umschlägt, der „Stärke" (Röm 15, 1) des freien Pneumatikers, die nur zu leicht den Adel und die Würde der Persönlichkeit in den Schmutz fallen lässt (1 Kor 6, 18), stellt er das Ideal gegenüber, Gott auch mit oder an dem Leibe zu verherrlichen (6, 20). [1]

Apart from the fact that the expression 'glorify God in your body' (1 Cor. 6 : 20) could not conceivably have been written by Seneca, what concerns us most here is the phrase 'den Adel und die Würde der Persönlichkeit in den Schmutz fallen [lassen]'. Is this really what is said in 1 Cor. 6 : 18 to which Weiss refers? Surely not. What does Paul maintain here? 'The immoral man sins against his own body.' Proof that this cannot be equated with besmirching the nobility and dignity of the personality is to be found in the following verse: 'Do you not know that your body is a temple of the Holy Spirit within you, which you have from God?' It is not the fact that the nobility and dignity of the human personality in general should not be degraded that Paul wishes to focus the attention on here but the Holy Spirit, which belongs within the framework of the history of salvation, which the members of the Church, not mankind in general, have received from God. Paul is not for a moment thinking of the glory of the human personality, but, if we may put it this way, of the glory of the Church of Christ, which has been received from God, the glory of the Church which knows that it does not rule over itself, because it has become the property of the Lord: 'You are not your own; you were bought with a price' (1 Cor. 6 : 19; cf. 1 Cor. 7 : 23).

Further on Joh. Weiss alludes to a 'Persönlichkeitsideal' which may be found in Gal. 5 : 22. It is true that the 'virtues' which are listed here would not be out of place in a description of a harmonious personality in the Greek style, but the opening words of the verse, 'the fruit of the Spirit', which are opposed to 'the works of the flesh' in Gal. 5 : 19 make it clear that Paul did not intend it as such. If we recall the antithesis between the flesh and the Spirit, discussed in the preceding chapter, it is impossible to imagine that Paul is outlining an ideal personality. If passages such as these are quoted as evidence

---

[1] ib., p. 441.

of this, then they are being construed in a way Paul never intended. [1]

Paul is constantly reminding Christians of their fellowship with Christ, of their being in Christ, and of their consequent ties with one another. Accordingly, instead of considering the members of the Church as personalities, or even as Christian personalities, he contemplates them in their relationship to each other, a relationship determined by their connection with Christ. The individual within the Church acquires his particular value by virtue of what Christ has done, not because he, the individual, is in himself a remarkable human personality. [2]

The difference between Paul's attitude and Seneca's towards this question may be illustrated by some passages where Paul's language appears to resemble Seneca's closely. In Phil. 4 : 11 Paul says: 'I have learned, in whatever state I am, to be content.' 'To be content, αὐτάρκης εἶναι has a Stoic ring. Αὐτάρκης, αὐτάρκεια are the words for self-sufficient, self-sufficiency. Paul is also familiar with the latter. [3] In his commentary upon 2 Cor. 9 : 8 Windisch remarks that αὐτάρκεια is: 'ein Zentralbegriff der kynisch-stoischen Lebenslehre', while Vincent says of αὐτάρκης in Phil. 4 : 11, that it is 'a favorite Stoic word':

> It expressed the doctrine of that sect that man should be sufficient unto himself for all things, and able, by the power of his own will, to resist the force of circumstances. [4]

That is to say that the word was used in connection with the man who is acquiescent and self-sufficient. As an illustration Vincent quotes Seneca's: 'the happy man is content with his present lot, no matter what it is, and is reconciled to his circumstances'. [5] Equally illustrative of this are some of Seneca's statements, which have already been quoted,

---

[1] Hence the notion 'personality' must be given quite a different content if it is to be used within the framework of Paul's ethics; cf. G. Delling, *Paulus' Stellung zu Frau und Ehe*, 1931, p. 153, who says of Paul: 'er kennt nicht den Willen zur Lebensganzheit, zur vollen Persönlichkeit. Er will nie ein an Leib und Seele vollkommener Mann im griechischen Sinn sein, sondern nur Sklave des Christus. Das ganz zu sein, bedeutet für ihn die Fülle der Persönlichkeit (Phil. 3, 12-15)'; see also R. Bultmann, *Glauben und Verstehen*, Vol. 2, 1952, p. 69.
[2] Cf. e.g. 1 Cor. 8 : 11; Rom. 14 : 15; Gal. 6 : 1-5; Phil. 4 : 2.
[3] 2 Cor. 9 : 8; 1 Tim. 6 : 6.
[4] H.Windisch, *Der Zweite Korintherbrief*, 1924, p. 278; M. R. Vincent, *Epistle to the Philippians*, 1922, p. 143; cf. Dom Jacques Dupont O.S.B., Συν Χριστωι *L'union avec le Christ suivant Saint Paul*, 1952, p. 119: 'L'adjectif αὐτάρκης est typique de l'idéal moral du stoïcisme'; Joh. Weiss, op. cit., p. 464, refers to Phil. 4 : 11-13 as 'jene an stoische Parallelen erinnernde Äusserung.'
[5] *V.B. 6. 2.*

in which he makes it plain that man should not only strive after self-sufficiency and contentment with respect to fate but also with respect to his own inner life. [1] The self-sufficiency of the Stoics consists in the spirit's contentment with itself, both as far as its fate and its own inner and moral life are concerned.

We cannot be sure whether Paul uses this well known *terminus technicus* of the Stoic school of philosophy consciously in Phil. 4 : 11. He need not necessarily have borrowed it from this source, since we know that αὐτάρκης was a word frequently used in daily life. [2] But even if he did adopt it from the Stoics he uses it in a different sense. The πάντα ἰσχύω of verse thirteen is reminiscent of Marcus Aurelius's τὸ αὔταρκες ἐν παντί. [3] But the addition, after 'I can do all things', of the words 'in him who strengthens me' naturally alters the meaning of this in itself Stoic sounding statement fundamentally. By virtue of the strength of Christ Paul is able to be content in whatever state he is. Lightfoot sums up the contrast most accurately:

> If the coincidence of imagery in these passages [he has quoted 1 Cor. 4 : 8, 10; 3 : 22, 23; 2 Cor. 6 : 10; 2 Cor. 9 : 8, 11; Phil. 4 : 11, 18] is remarkable, the contrast of sentiment is not less striking. This universal dominion, this boundless inheritance, is promised alike by the Stoic philosopher to the wise man and by the Christian Apostle to the believer. But the one must attain it by self-isolation, the other by incorporation. The requisite in the former case is a proud independence; in the latter an entire reliance on, and intimate union with an unseen power. It is ἐν τῷ ἐνδυναμοῦντι that the faithful becomes all-sufficient, all-powerful; it is ἐν χριστῷ that he is crowned a king and consecrated a priest. All things are his, but they are only his, in so far as he is Christ's and because Christ is God's. Here and here only the Apostle found the realization of the proud ideal which the chief philosophers of his native Tarsus had sketched in such bold outline and painted in these brilliant colours. [4]

---

[1] E.g. *V.B.* 4. 2 or *Ep.* 72. 7.

[2] Cf. *Th. W.* I, p. 466; J. H. Moulton and George Milligan, *The Vocabulary of the Greek Testament,* 1949, p. 93, where various examples are given of the meaning of αὐτάρκης = enough.

[3] *In semet ipsum* i. 16. 11.

[4] J. B. Lightfoot, *Saint Paul's Epistle to the Philippians,* ²1956, p. 305; cf. Vincent, op. cit., p. 143: 'Paul is not self-sufficient in the Stoic sense, but through the power of a new self — the power of Christ in him (Comp. 2 Cor. 3 : 5)'; K. Deissner, *Paulus und Seneca,* 1917, p. 30: 'während für den Stoiker die Unabhängigkeit von der Welt Sache der eignen Kraft ist, auf Zucht und Erprobung des Willens beruht, ist sie für Paulus ein göttliches Gnadengeschenk.' He says this in connection with Phil. 4 : 11 f., 13. R. Bultmann, *Das Urchristentum in Rahmen der antiken Religionen,* 1949, p. 207, also makes a clear distinction between the two in connection with this text.

A second example of an apparent resemblance in detail is to be found in a passage from Seneca which has already been mentioned, namely, where he describes what a wonderful spectacle a wise man must be, not only for mankind but even for the gods:

But lo! here is a spectacle worthy of the regard of God as he contemplates his works; lo! here a contest worthy of God, — a brave man matched against ill-fortune, and doubly so if his also was the challenge. I do not know, I say, what nobler sight the Lord of Heaven could find on earth, should he wish to turn his attention there, than the spectacle of Cato, after his cause had already been shattered more than once, neverteless standing erect amid the ruins of the commonwealth. 1

'Here is a spectacle. . . .' Seneca uses the word *spectaculum*. This same word is employed in the Vulgate for θέατρον in 1 Cor. 4 : 9:

I think that God has exhibited us apostles as last of all, like men sentenced to death; because we have become a spectacle to the world, to angels and to men.

But as soon as we read 1 Cor. 4 : 9 in its context (1 Cor. 4 : 6-13) the profound difference becomes plain. Paul, who is here warning his readers against self-importance and boasting, reminds them:

What have you that you did not receive? If then you received it, why do you boast as if it were not a gift? (v. 7).

Paul is ironical about the complacency of the Corinthians:

Already you are filled! Already you have become rich! Without us you have become kings! And would that you did reign, so that we might share the rule with you! (v. 8).

As it is, Paul says, we apostles are but miserable creatures. We apostles — Paul does not characterize himself and the others in their capacity of important individuals but in their work, their lives, in Christ's service as Apostles. And so it becomes clear that θέατρον *spectaculum*, is used quite differently from in Seneca. The latter wishes to glorify the figure of the wise man with this word. He uses it to express the highest praise for the self-confidence of the strong man, who is a delight even to the gods. Paul uses it to depict the Apostle in all his humility (cf. v. 10). He wants this word to be expressive of all the indignities, contempt and suffering which a life in the service of Christ entails. He probably had in mind the Roman gladiators whose task it was to fight to the death in front of an audience craving for sensation. For the Apostles are 'the refuse of the world, the offscouring

---

1 *Prov.* 2. 9.

of all things' (v. 13). [1] Moreover, here God is not the spectator of
the contest waged against life by the proud, free-willed man, but it is
God himself who 'has exhibited us apostles as last of all', in all their
weakness:

> die eben damit, als gottgewirkte, echte — nämlich Gottes — Kraft
> wird, so dass die Zuschauer etwas völlig anderes zu sehen meinen, als
> das wirkliche Geschehen, welches in jenem θέατρον sich abspielt. [2]

It is not surprising that it is in this connection that Paul warns
against boasting (1 Cor. 4 : 7). Noteworthy is the fact that the words
'boast' and 'boasting' scarcely occur in the New Testament except in
Paul who uses them frequently. According to him it is in direct conflict with belief in God's merciful gift, if a man boasts of anything, as,
for example, the Jew who boasts of the law (Rom. 2 : 17, 23) or of
his circumcision or his descent (Phil. 3 : 2-4), and the Greek of his
wisdom (1 Cor. 1 : 19 ff.) For man is in a position in which all
boasting is excluded (Rom. 3 : 27), and he is forgetting this if he
thinks he has anything that he has not been given (1 Cor. 4 : 7; cf.
1 Cor. 1 : 29). There is only one kind of boasting that is entirely
legitimate, and that is boasting of the Lord. [3] Consequently Paul knows
that if he boasts of things he has done or of his sufferings, even though
he may do so for Christ's sake, he is really acting foolishly (2 Cor.
11 : 16-21; 12 : 1). This knowledge causes him to make the paradoxical
statement that he will glory in his own weakness. [4] For Paul self-
confidence in man, 'confidence in the flesh' is a sinful, self-righteous,
arbitrarily triumphant attitude which can never exist in the presence
of God. 'Confidence in the flesh' is in antithesis to the 'glory in Christ
Jesus' (Phil. 3 : 3). There is no conflict between this and the fact
that Paul sometimes professes emphatically that his boast is that he
is an Apostle of Jesus Christ, for then he is not glorying in a human
self-confidence, but in what God has done to him and through him in
Christ (Rom. 15 : 17 f.; 1 Cor. 15 : 10).

Paul would have regarded everything Seneca says about the splendour of the independent human personality as self-glorification, as
'confidence in the flesh'. In his eyes Seneca's attitude would be

---

1 It is therefore unlikely that the use of this image here is derived from the
Stoics, as is thought by Carl Clemen, *Religionsgeschichtliche Erklärung des Neuen
Testaments*, 1924, p. 412; cf. ib., p. 318; Kreyher, p. 170 ff.

2 *Th. W.* III, p. 43.

3 1 Cor. 1 : 31; 2 Cor. 10 : 17; Gal. 6 : 17; cf. Rom. 5 : 11.

4 2 Cor. 11 : 30; 12 : 9; cf. Rom. 5 : 3.

running completely counter to the humility demanded by faith, to the realization that man has received everything from God, and can only exist by virtue of His mercy. [1]

Another way in which the difference between Paul and Seneca's attitude towards the individual may be illustrated is by examining their conception of *freedom*. For Seneca freedom is closely linked with the spiritual independence of the autonomous human being. Freedom is in the possession of the man who does not allow anything to disturb his mental balance, who is completely acquiescent in his acceptance of the fact that certain things are not within his reach, and who therefore realizes the foolishness of allowing himself to be deprived of his peace of mind either by the desire to possess such things or by their loss, or by the pleasures of the body. Freedom belongs to the man who has his passions completely under control, who refuses to be alarmed or intimidated by the treatment he receives from others, who is beyond all fear, and who knows that, if life should become too oppressive, there is always 'a door open', through which he can at any time depart this miserable life, in the same way that one can leave a room which is unpleasantly full of smoke.

A few quotations from Seneca will be sufficient to illustrate his conception of the free man. Seneca displays contempt for Cicero, who, when things go badly for him, writes in a letter to Atticus: ' "Do you ask what I am doing here? I am lingering in my Tusculan villa half a prisoner [*semiliber*]." ' To this *semiliber*, half free, Seneca takes exception:

> But, in very truth, never will the wise man resort to so lowly a term, never will he be half a prisoner — he who always possesses an undiminished and stable liberty, being free and his own master and towering over all others. For what can possibly be above him who is above Fortune? [2]

Seneca is convinced that lasting freedom of mind is possible:

> You understand, even if I do not say more, that, when once we have driven away all that excites or affrights us, there ensues unbroken tranquillity and enduring freedom; for when pleasures and fears have been banished, then, in place of all that is trivial and fragile and harm-

---

[1] Cf. Ulrich Wilckens, *Weisheit und Torheit*, 1959, p. 269: 'Der λόγος τοῦ σταυροῦ trifft das stoische Denken in seinem Ansatz, insofern der Glaube das Ende alles „Rühmens" bedeutet und d.h. im Blick auf die stoische Lehre: Das Ende eben jenes letzten und leidenschaftlichen Vertrauens auf den Logos, der das eigne Wesen des Menschen ist.'

[2] *Brev.* 5. 3.

ful just because of the evil it works, there comes upon us first a boundless joy that is firm and unalterable, then peace and harmony of the soul
and true greatness coupled with kindliness; for all ferocity is born from
weakness. 1

Therefore we must make our escape to freedom. But the only means
of procuring this is through indifference to Fortune. Then will be born
the one inestimable blessing, the peace and exaltation of a mind now
safely anchored, and, when all error is banished, the great and stable
joy that comes from the discovery of truth, along with kindliness and
cheerfulness of mind; and the source of a man's pleasure in all of
these will not be that they are good, but that they spring from a good
that is his own. 2

To obey God is freedom in the sense that he who voluntarily resigns
himself to his allotted fate enjoys complete spiritual independence:

All that the very constitution of the universe obliges us to suffer, must
be borne with high courage. This is the sacred obligation by which we
are bound — to submit to the human lot, and not to be disquieted by
those things which we have no power to avoid. We have been born
under a monarchy; to obey God is freedom. 3

Freedom is also to be found in the imperturbability which is un-
shaken whatever occurs:

not to put up with anything is not liberty; we deceive ourselves. Liberty
is having a mind that rises superior to injury, that makes itself the only
source from which its pleasures spring, that separates itself from all
external things in order that man may not have to live his life in dis-
quietude, fearing everybody's tongue. 4

He who wishes to be free, must not be a slave of his body:

No, I am above such an existence; I was born to a greater destiny
than to be a mere chattel of my body, and I regard this body as nothing
but a chain which manacles my freedom. Therefore, I offer it as a sort
of buffer to fortune, and shall allow no wound to penetrate through
to my soul. For my body is the only part of me which can suffer injury.
In this dwelling, which is exposed to peril, my soul lives free.

---

1 *V.B.* 3. 4; cf. the above quoted *V.B.* 4. 3.

2 *V.B.* 4. 5.

3 *V.B.* 15. 6, 7; this passage, especially the concluding words, *parere libertas est,*
is sometimes cited as a parallel to the expression in Jas. 1 : 25; 2 : 12: 'the law
of liberty', e.g. M. Dibelius, *Der Brief des Jakobus,* 81956, p. 111. Even though the
meaning of the expression is not readily understandable in James, and therefore much
disputed, we may at least be certain that James does not use it in the sense of
Seneca's *deo parere libertas est,* the meaning of which may be grasped from the
context. It is one of those 'parallels' which do not explain anything, and are therefore rather pointless in a commentary.

4 *Const.* 19. 2.

From this Seneca goes on to draw the conclusion that: 'To despise our bodies is sure freedom.' [1]

It has already been mentioned (p. 56) that Seneca regards suicide as an aspect of man's liberty. The soul is free to leave its dwelling, the body. It is a consolation for man that:

on all sides lie many short and simple paths to freedom. [2] Slavery is no hardship when, if a man wearies of the yoke, by a single step he may pass to freedom. O Life, by the favour of Death I hold thee dear! [3]

So little is necessary to equip man for the journey, 'a lancet will open the way to that great freedom, and tranquillity can be purchased at the cost of a pin-prick.' [4] As has already been indicated Seneca is in violent disagreement with those persons, who, calling themselves philosophers, believe that man has no right to take his own life. For then the road to freedom is closed. [5]

Consequently, for Seneca freedom is the supreme command which the self-sufficient, spiritually imperturbable, utterly placid man has over life, and even over death. [6] When Paul speaks of freedom, he means something entirely different, even in those passages in which his choice of words would seem to bear a superficial resemblance to the Stoic way of thinking. When, for example, he writes: 'all things are yours, whether .... the world or life or death or the present or the future, all are yours' (1 Cor. 3 : 21, 22), we are reminded of how in the *De Beneficiis* Seneca says that the mind of a wise man is master of all things, and that when we see such a mind 'we say that all things belong to him' *potentem omnium .... omnia illius esse dicimus.* [7] In the same book he says of the wise man that 'all things are his' [8]

---

[1] *Ep.* 65. 21, 22.

[2] *Ep.* 12. 10.

[3] *Marc.* 20. 3; cf. the above quoted (p. 56) *Ira* iii. 15. 3, 4; further *Ep.* 26. 10; 66. 13; 70. 5, 12, 23, 24; 77. 15.

[4] *Ep.* 70. 16.

[5] *Ep.* 70. 14.

[6] Cf. Ernst Benz, op. cit., p. 85 f.: 'Indem die stoische Lehre jedem Einzelnen das freie Verfügungsrecht über sich selbst innerhalb der Grenzen der sittlichen Gesetze zuerkannte, dehnte sich die persönliche Freiheit bis zur Negation der eigenen Existenz aus und erhob dadurch den Tod zum sittlichen Akt. *Der Tod als Phänomen verdient keine Beachtung; der Tod als Akt wird zentrales Problem der stoischen Ethik.* Die Selbstherrlichkeit der Lehre, die nicht genug die persönliche Freiheit des Einzelmenschen betonen konnte, machte vor dem letztem Ereignis, das „getan" werden musste, keinen Halt, sondern krönte den letzten physischen Vorgang zur letzten Heldentat der sittlichen Freiheit.'

[7] *Ben.* vii. 8. 1.

[8] *Ben.* vii. 2. 5.

and 'It is only the wise man who has all things, and has no difficulty in retaining them'. [1] That Paul wishes to express with these words quite a different idea from Seneca is made clear by the context. He writes them when endeavouring to impress upon the Corinthians how unseemly it is for a church of Jesus Christ's to split into factions formed around particular persons. As if the individual as such is ever of importance in the Church! Therefore Paul says:

> let no one boast of men. For all things are yours, whether Paul or Apollos or Cephas or the world, or life or death or the present or the future, all are yours; and you are Christ's; and Christ is God's.

This last addition suddenly gives quite a different twist to this seemingly Stoic notion. This is not the all-powerful philosopher who is boasting of his own strength and glory and summoning others to the same freedom, but the Apostle of Jesus Christ who is reminding a church that it is Christ's.

For Paul freedom is never the ultimate goal towards which human exertion should be directed. But freedom is possible, indeed, in the Church it is even a foregone conclusion, because Christ has made us free. 'For freedom Christ has set us free; stand fast therefore, and do not submit again to a yoke of slavery', Paul exhorts the Galatians (Gal. 5 : 1). To the Corinthians he says: 'Now the Lord is the Spirit, and where the Spirit of the Lord is, there is freedom' (2 Cor. 3 : 17). [2] Those who have been liberated by Christ, no longer live in slavery, but in freedom. Paul deems this freedom in Christ to be such a reality that he does not consider the bodily emancipation of a slave to be important. He should acquiesce in that state in which he was when he was called. For what is important has been done in Christ: the slave who is called in the Lord is a freedman of the Lord, while he who was free when called is a slave of Christ (1 Cor. 7 : 20-22). We do not obtain freedom by our own efforts, it is given to us in Christ. This does not mean that we enjoy the freedom of the spiritually completely independent man who has supreme command over his life. No, we have been redeemed by Christ and are now his property. It is precisely the fact that we are slaves of Christ's which makes us free.

Christ has set us free. He has already freed us and will one day free us completely from the dominion of 'the world rulers of this

---

[1] *Ben.* vii. 3. 2.

[2] Kreyher, p. 87, unjustly compares these words of Paul's with Ben. iii. 20. 1: 'the mind is its own master, and is so free.' Anyone who reads the context in Seneca will notice that he uses these words in a very different sense from Paul.

present darkness', against whom the Church still has to struggle in this aeon, and who will not be entirely subdued until Christ's final victory (Eph. 6 : 12). But in the world in which God's order of salvation has already gained the fundamental victory over the powers of chaos, the members of the Church no longer live in slavery, are no longer hopelessly subjected to evil forces, but enjoy the freedom that has been granted us in Christ.

There is another way in which we are free. In Christ we have also been set free from the law. This freedom is also one which we do not have in ourselves but which has been given us. The freedom, for which Christ has set us free, to which we have been called (Gal.. 5 : 1, 13), which we have in Christ Jesus, and of which we should not allow ourselves to be deprived by any spy (Gal. 2 : 4), is the knowledge that we never again need toil like slaves in living up to the law in order to come to God and His salvation. Those who belong to Christ no longer live under the yoke of rigid commandments, they no longer live under the whip-lash of morality.

Moreover, he who believes in redemption through Jesus Christ is also free from sin. In baptism we have died with Christ, 'We were buried therefore with him by baptism into death'. We are no longer the slaves of sin. He who is dead is free from sin. [1]

Hence freedom from evil forces, freedom from the law, freedom from sin belong to all who have by faith obtained part of God's gift of grace in Christ. By this freedom they may now live.

The magnificent perspective Paul sees in 'the glorious liberty of the children of God' (Rom. 8 : 21) is apparent from Rom. 8, where he maintains that the ultimate redemption of the whole of creation is directly linked with this freedom. 'For the creation waits with eager longing for the revealing of the sons of God' (Rom. 8 : 19). When the freedom, which the children of God already know here on earth, becomes one day a complete reality, when they are granted complete freedom from the law of sin and death (Rom. 8 : 2), then it will be the day of rejoicing for the whole of creation. Then creation which is still 'subjected to futility' (Rom. 8 : 20) will be released from its chains, then it need no longer groan in travail together, for then it will share in the glorious liberty of the children of God (Rom. 8 : 20, 22).

Once again it is plain from this that freedom and the whole of God's work of salvation in Christ are closely interwoven in Paul and

---

[1] Rom. 6 : 4-7; cf. Rom. 6 : 17, 18, 20-22; 8 : 2.

that, like the whole of the salvation-occurrence, freedom is also still awaiting completion.

Consequently, the Pauline idea of freedom differs in every respect from Seneca's, and it is therefore highly unlikely that the emphasis Paul lays upon freedom has its roots in Stoic thought. [1]

In his conversation with M. de Saci Pascal accuses Epictetus of 'diabolical pride'; this in connection with the many errors committed by the Stoic with respect to human ability. [2] Pascal would probably have been quite prepared to say the same of Seneca. Naturally Epictetus and Seneca would never have thought themselves to be suffering from this, because the particular opinions they held concerning human ability were founded on their anthropology. As soon as one considers the soul to be of divine origin, [3] the possibility of man's acquiring and retaining freedom himself is placed in quite a different light; for Paul sees man, natural man, as a sinner before the holy God, and so deems his self-liberation an impossibility. The only chance of redemption for Paul must lie in God's hands, God Himself must take the initiative. Man could never free himself from the powers, the law, sin, and death; he would be quite helpless; God's power in Christ alone can liberate him. At the end of his discourse on the true situation of Jew and Gentile alike Paul declares that we 'are under the power of sin' and illustrates this by a quotation from Ps. 14: 'No one is righteous, no, not one;' etc. (Rom. 3 : 9-20). There is, however, thanks be to God a means of redemption other than reliance upon our own strength, which is ineffectual. This means is heralded in the 'but now' with which Rom. 3 : 21-26 begins. Accordingly, Paul's and Seneca's views on freedom are divergent right from the start.

The question now arises whether unbridled faith in the possibilities which are inherent in man is always characteristic of Seneca's philosophy. Does not Seneca too sometimes evince a strong sense of sin? Does not he too know that all human beings are sinful? Is the Stoic

---

[1] C. Clemen, op. cit., p. 412, see however p. 308; cf. Max Pohlenz, *Griechische Freiheit*, 1955, p. 182: 'Die griechische Freiheit ist die Selbstbestimmung des natürlichen Menschen, die paulinische ist die gottgewirkte Befreiung von der Macht der Sünde, ist Erlösung'; R. Bultmann, *Glauben und Verstehen*, Vol. 3, 1960, p. 161.

[2] 'une superbe diabolique' in the 'Entretien de Pascal avec M. de Saci' in *Pensées de Pascal*, Librairie Garnier Frères, n.d., p. 40; cf. D. Loenen, *Eusebeia en de cardinale deugden*, 1960, p. 94.

[3] Accordingly Pascal mentions among the errors which Epictetus commits as a result of 'ces principes d'une superbe diabolique', first and foremost: 'que l'âme est une portion de la substance divine.'

philosophers' sense of sin sometimes so pronounced that we may say:

> Dann stammt aus ihr vielleicht zum Teil die Betonung der Allgemeinheit der Sünde und namentlich der Knechtschaft, die sie über den Menschen ausübt. [1]

The basic tenets of the Stoics lead one to expect unbridled optimism. If man is by virtue of his reason, his soul and his spirit related to God, if all that matters is for him to live in accordance with nature, if moral strength is inherent in the autonomous human being, then he may perhaps err from time to time, but it should not be difficult to set him on the right road again by restoring his essentially sound judgment. Such reasoning is indeed to be found in abundance in Seneca, and theoretically at any rate he adheres entirely to this belief. Nevertheless it is impossible to regard him as wholly optimistic. On the contrary, Seneca sometimes strikes such a sombre note on the universal sinfulness of the human race that we are reminded of Paul and would scarcely ascribe such declarations to a Stoic if we did not know they came from Seneca. A notable example of this is the following:

> We have all sinned — some in serious, some in trivial things; some from deliberate intention, some by chance impulse, or because we were led away by the wickedness of others; some of us have not stood strongly enough by good resolutions, and have lost our innocence against our will and though still clinging to it; and not only have we done wrong, but we shall go on doing wrong to the very end of life. Even if there is any one who has so thoroughly cleansed his mind that nothing can any more confound him and betray him, yet it is by sinning that he has reached the sinless state. [2]

If one observes the crowds in the forum, on the Campus Martius, or in the circus where people often display themselves as they are, one may see that there are as many vices as men. What a dissension, what a hatred and envy is rife among men: 'They live as though they were in a gladiatorial school — those with whom they eat, they likewise fight.' Society is like a herd of wild animals, or even worse for animals are gentle and peaceful towards each other and do not molest their own kind, while men delight in harming one another. [3] Wickedness and debauchery has spread and increased to such an extent in the hearts of

---

[1] C. Clemen, op. cit., p. 412; on p. 131 also he claims that it is precisely in the Stoic writers that we find pronouncements on the universality of sin which resemble those expressed in the New Testament.

[2] Clem. i. 6. 3, 4; cf. the beginning: *Peccavimus omnes* with the Latin text of Rom. 3 : 23: *omnes enim peccaverunt.*

[3] *Ira* ii. 8. 1 ff.

men that innocence is not only rare, but non-existent. It is not only the individual here and there or small groups of men who offend against the moral code; nay, it is as if at a prearranged signal the whole of mankind has suddenly risen to exchange right for wrong. If a wise man were to be as angry as the enormity of the crimes demands, he would not merely have to be angry but delirious. [1] But a wise man does not grow angry with sinners; for he knows that vice is universal. He knows that such people are sick and cannot help themselves, and he will look upon the sinful throngs as a doctor does upon his patients. [2] In judging others we must always bear in mind that none of us is blameless, *neminem nostrum esse sine culpa*. Our violent indignation frequently arises from our thinking: ' "I am not to blame," "I have done nothing wrong" ' *nihil peccavi, nihil feci*. We react thus because we will not admit to our faults; if we are up in arms about a reprimand, our very indignation is a sin because we are adding to our misdeeds arrogance and pride. It is a feeble claim to say that we have never broken any law. Those who consider it sufficient to obey the law must have a very restricted interpretation of innocence. The demands of duty extend somewhat further than this:

> How much more comprehensive is the principle of duty than that of law! How many are the demands laid upon us by the sense of duty, humanity, generosity, justice, integrity — all of which lie outside the statute books! [3]

If we see humanity in its true colours, we must conclude that:

> We are all inconsiderate and unthinking, we are all untrustworthy, discontented, ambitious — why should I hide the universal sore by softer words? — We are all wicked [*omnes mali sumus*]. And so each man will find in his own breast, the fault which he censures in another .... And so let us be more kindly toward one another; we being wicked live among the wicked [*mali inter malos vivimus*]. [4]

Thus far quotations concerning the depravity of the humaan race have only been taken from two books, *De Clementia* and *De Ira*. It has been maintained that these are the only writings of Seneca's in which such passages are to be found, and that it is not surprising that they occur here, because Seneca's intention is first to arouse the indulgence of

---

1 *Ira* ii. 9. 1 ff.
2 *Ira* ii. 10. 4, 6, 7.
3 *Ira* ii. 28. 1, 2.
4 *Ira* iii. 26. 4.

masters and secondly to curb man's anger. [1] This is, however, incorrect, since similar sombre declarations on the low moral standards of the human race are to be found elsewhere, and although they do not occur as frequently as in *De Ira* they are scarcely less outspoken:

> Vices do not wait expectantly in just one spot, but are always in movement and, being at variance with each other, are in constant turmoil, they rout and in turn are routed; but the verdict we are obliged to pronounce upon ourselves will always be the same: wicked we are, wicked we have been, and, I regret to add, always shall be. Homicides, tyrants, thieves, adulterers, robbers, sacrilegious men, and traitors there always will be. [2]

Not only are all men ungrateful, but:

> they are also covetous and spiteful and cowardly — especially those who appear to be bold. Besides, all are self-seeking, all are ungodly. But you have no need to be angry with them; pardon them — they are all mad. [3] All the vices exist in all men, yet not all are equally prominent in each individual. This man's nature impels him to greed; this one is a victim of wine, this one of lust, or, if he is not yet a victim, he is so constituted that his natural impulses lead him in this direction. [4]

In order to achieve tranquillity of mind, one must not only quell one's own sorrows, but one must be able to overcome the hatred of the human race, *odium generis humani,* which can sometimes seize one. For what a miserable state humanity is in:

> When you reflect how rare is simplicity, how unknown is innocence, and how good faith scarcely exists, except when it is profitable, and when you think of all the throng of successful crimes and of the gains and losses of lust, both equally hateful, and of ambition that, so far from restraining itself within its own bounds, now gets glory from baseness — when we remember these things, the mind is plunged into night, and as though the virtues, which it is now neither possible to expect nor profitable to possess, had been overthrown, there comes overwhelming gloom.

Seneca's advice in the face of this sombre picture is:

> We ought, therefore, to bring ourselves to believe that all the vices of the crowd are, not hateful, but ridiculous. [5]

When at the end of the third book of the *Naturales Quaestiones* Seneca describes the re-birth of the world out of the ruins of a former

---

1 As de Bovis, op. cit., p. 82.
2 *Ben.* i. 10. 3, 4.
3 *Ben.* v. 17. 3.
4 *Ben.* iv. 27. 3.
5 *Tranqu. an.* 15. 1, 2.

age, he says that there will then be a man who knows nothing of crime and who will be born under the most favourable auspices. But this innocence will only last as long as the souls are new. Evil soon creeps in. Vice is acquired only too easily, even without a tutor. [1]

Accordingly, abundant evidence of Seneca's poor opinion of the moral standards of mankind is to be found in various of his writings. It is incorrect to say that in his letters to Lucilius no mention is made of man's universal wickedness. [2] For even in one of these letters he strikes, after an optimistic passage on man as 'a reasoning animal', *rationale animal*, a sombre note:

> man is a reasoning animal. Therefore, man's highest good is attained, if he has fulfilled the good for which nature designed him at birth. And what is it which this reason demands of him? The easiest thing in the world — to live in accordance with his own nature. But this is turned into a hard task by the general madness of mankind [*communis insania*]; we push one another into vice. [3]

In addition to this Seneca frequently warns his readers that they must not regard him as a wise man, that he does not wish to be considered as an exception to the rule that humanity is imperfect. He confesses:

> I am not a 'wise man,' nor — to feed your malevolence! — shall I ever be. And so require not from me that I should be equal to the best, but that I should be better than the wicked. It is enough for me if every day I reduce the number of my vices, and blame my mistakes .... I am sunk deep in vice of every kind. [4]

When he is reproached for not practising what he preaches, Seneca pleads guilty of this at once. Philosophers of former times too,

> told, not how they themselves were living, but how they ought to live. It is of virtue, not of myself, that I am speaking, and my quarrel is against all vices, more especially against my own. [5]

Spiteful criticism will not hinder him,

> from continuing to vaunt the life, not that I lead, but that I know ought to be led — from worshipping virtue and from following her, albeit a long way behind and with very halting pace. [6]

---

[1] *N.Q.* iii. 30. 8; cf. *N.Q.* iv a, Praef. 19.

[2] De Bovis, op. cit., p. 82: 'Les lettres n'affirment nulle part la culpabilité générale. Elles ne la nient pas non plus.'

[3] *Ep.* 41. 8, 9.

[4] *V.B.* 17. 3, 4; cf. *Helv.* 5. 2.

[5] *V.B.* 18. 1.

[6] *V.B.* 18. 2.

Seneca knows quite well that he needs to be not only reformed, but transformed, *transfigurari*. However, he considers it an advance that he recognizes his own shortcomings:

> And indeed this very fact is proof that my spirit is altered into something better, — that it can see its own faults, of which it was previously ignorant. In certain cases sick men are congratulated because they themselves have perceived that they are sick. [1]

From this it is of course but a step to:

> I am not so shameless as to undertake to cure my fellow-men when I am ill myself. I am, however, discussing with you troubles which concern us both, and sharing the remedy with you, just as if we were lying ill in the same hospital. Listen to me, therefore, as you would if I were talking to myself. [2]

He feels obliged to confess that he has not always been able to maintain the composure of the wise man, [3] that he is often too fearful, too hesitant, that his principles are not yet firmly enough rooted in him, and that he still pays too much attention to the opinions of others. [4] If a man recognizes the imperfect moral state of mankind and knows himself well enough to recognize his own failings, he will realize that it will be wise for him to seek the support of others in his struggle against his own moral weakness and uncertainty. He can do this by choosing someone whose moral perfection is greater than his own. Seneca agrees whole-heartedly with Epicurus's advice to keep always the example of some good man before one's eyes ' "living as if he were watching you, and ordering all your actions as if he beheld them." ' For:

> we can get rid of most sins, if we have a witness who stands near us when we are likely to go wrong. The soul should have someone whom it can respect, — one by whose authority it may make even its inner shrine more hallowed .... Choose a master, whose life, conversation, and soul-expressing face have satisfied you; picture him always to yourself as your protector or your pattern. For we must indeed have someone according to whom we may regulate our characters; you can never straighten that which is crooked unless you use a ruler. [1]

No man is strong enough to liberate himself from his lack of resolution:

---

[1] *Ep.* 6. 1.
[2] *Ep.* 27. 1; cf. *Ep.* 57. 3.
[3] *Ep.* 63. 14.
[4] *Ep.* 87. 4, 5.
[5] *Ep.* 11. 8-10; cf. *Ep.* 25. 6; in both passages the spiritual mentor whom one should choose is referred to as a *custos* and *paedagogus*.

No man by himself has sufficient strength to rise above it; he needs a helping hand, and some one to extricate him. [1]

Seneca had procured for himself just such a support. In a passage where he denies that he is a wise man he tells his mother that in order to alleviate his unhappiness, he has surrendered himself to wise men:

not yet being strong enough to give aid to myself, I have taken refuge in the camp [i.e. the Stoic school] of others — of those, clearly, who can easily defend themselves and their followers. They have ordered me to stand ever watching, like a soldier placed on guard, and to anticipate all the attempts and all the assaults of Fortune long before she strikes [2]

Sometimes Seneca not only appeals to man for aid but also to God. For,

indeed, no man can be good without the help of God. Can one rise superior to fortune unless God helps him to rise? He it is that gives noble und upright counsel. [3]
No mind that has not God, is good. [4]

Even if the road to the happy life is an easy one, Seneca still advises: 'do but enter on it — with good auspices and the good help of the gods themselves!' [5]

When we read Seneca's frequent comments on the sinfulness of the human race and on his own shortcomings, on the necessity of having human examples to encourage us, or even divine aid, we inevitably wonder whether these do not closely resemble what Paul writes. The question is whether apparently related statements are indeed meant to be understood in the same way or whether they are really set in different keys. Let us first consider the help of the gods: what Seneca says on this subject might well be reminiscent of Paul's repeated allusions to man's dependence upon God's grace. But if we examine what Seneca says more closely, we find that he does not contemplate a God who personally offers his merciful help to man in some special way; for him the help of God is identical with the presence of part of the divine spirit in man. God 'helps' by his immanence in man. The passage 'no man can be good without the help of God' from *Ep.* 41. 2 has already been quoted. If we read what precedes this statement, we find that it is by no means meant as a testimony to man's depen-

---

[1] *Ep.* 52. 2.
[2] *Helv.* 5. 2, 3.
[3] *Ep.* 41. 2: *bonus vero vir sine deo nemo est.*
[4] *Ep.* 73. 16; cf. J. van Wageningen, *Seneca's leven en moraal*, 1917, p. 19.
[5] *Ira* ii. 13. 2: *dis bene iuvantibus.*

dence upon God's grace in the Pauline sense. In the first place, it is noteworthy that it is not a question of God's help being necessary because man is such a sinner, but of man not being able to rise superior to fortune without God's aid. Secondly, it is apparent from what immediately precedes that Seneca is most certainly not advocating supplication to the gods; for this is unnecessary, since God is in man's own spirit. *Ep.* 41 begins thus:

> You are doing an excellent thing, one which will be wholesome for you, if, as you write me, you are persisting in your effort to attain sound understanding; it is foolish to pray for this when you can acquire it from yourself. We do not need to uplift our hands towards heaven, or to beg the keeper of a temple to let us approach his idol's ear, as if in this way our prayers were more likely to be heard. God is near you, he is with you, he is within you. This is what I mean, Lucilius: a holy spirit indwells within us, one who marks our good and bad deeds, and is our guardian. As we treat this spirit, so we are treated by it.

This is immediately followed by: 'Indeed, no man can be good without the help of God.' Consequently, it is plain from what has gone before, that what Seneca really means here is that the good man is never without God because God's spirit is in him. In this context *ab illo adiutus,* 'helped by God', means strengthened by the divine spirit in man.

We reach the same conclusions if we consider the expression *nulla sine deo mens bona est* in *Ep.* 73. 16 in its context, which is the following:

> Do you marvel that man goes to the gods? God comes to men; nay, he comes nearer, — he comes into men. No mind that has not God, is good. Divine seeds are scattered throughout our mortal bodies.

Seneca then embroiders upon the image of the divine seeds: if a good gardener tends them they will bear fruit, if, however, he be bad, the seeds will yield nothing, or at most only weeds fit for the dung-hill. It is plain that for Seneca the emphasis here lies, not on the dependence of man upon God, but on the presence of the godhead in every good man, a presence which is to be accounted for by the fact that divine seeds are scattered through mens' bodies. Once again the presence of God means the immanence of God in man, owing to the fact that the good man is part of the godhead.

What Seneca says on the universal sinfulness of the human race is also in a very different key from Rom. 3 : 9 ff. Paul visualizes man standing before the holy God, and he wonders whether man's own

strength can enable him to comply with that God's commandments. [1]
In the presence of that God the moral behaviour of neither Jew nor
Gentile can exist. Naturally enough, Seneca does not see this problem
in the same way, because he does not acknowledge a personal relationship between God and man, and hence has no conception either of
a 'wrath of God' which 'is revealed from heaven against all ungod-
liness and wickedness of men who by their wickedness suppress the
truth' (Rom. 1 : 18). For Seneca the standard by which man's moral
behaviour may be judged is never God's holy law, but the ideal of the
wise man, a certain human perfection, compared with which most
men fall short. It is conspicuous that in spite of his testimony to the
universal sinfulness of mankind Seneca can still refer weak, uncertain
persons to a number of good men whose support they can seek either
in reality or in imagination. How can he refer the man who is not
strong enough in himself to the help of other humans, if he is of the
opinion that all are sinful? Where do these good men get their strength
from? Are there then exceptions to the rule of human weakness?

This arouses our suspicions that Seneca's declarations concerning
the universal sinfulness of mankind are not expressive of man's fundamental sinfulness in the face of the holy God; they are the philosophical
lamentations of a man who understands human beings and contemplates the decadence of his race with a smile, [2] tinged sometimes with
bitterness. Measured against the ideal of the wise man the life of the
individual and society present a dismal picture. After observing men
in those places where they come together and reveal themselves for
what they are, [3] Seneca is forced to conclude that innocence is not
only rare, but that it no longer exists. [4] Mankind is in a sorry state.
Seneca perceives the decadence rife among his contemporaries. Therefore his statements do not really testify to a pessimistic view of man
as such and his possibilities, but they are expressive of his indignation
at the degeneracy of his contemporaries.

Seneca's attitude towards the bustle of living is one of weary,
philosophical resignation. It is for him a reason to warn his readers

---

[1] Hence it is indeed possible to say: 'The word *peccatum* which was in use at
all periods of the Latin language does not acquire its actual meaning, i.e. of sin,
until in the Latin of the Christian era...', H. H. Janssen, *Gedachten over het lijden
in klassieke oudheid en Christendom*, 1949, p. 18.

[2] *Tranqu. an.* 15. 2.

[3] *Ira* ii. 8. 1 ff.; cf. C. C. Grollios, *Seneca's Ad Marciam. Tradition and Originality*,
1956, p. 64 f.

[4] *Ira* ii. 9. 1.

and himself against self-overestimation, and also to remind them that they must not judge their fellow men too harshly. When they see what humanity, themselves included, is like, they should be persuaded to be generous in their criticism of others.

Hence Seneca's lamentations result from his keen observation of the reality around him, rather than from a negative opinion of mankind as such. This pessimistic view of human activity does not mean that he excludes the possibility of man ever achieving a high moral status. He has not renounced his fundamentally optimistic conception of the possibilities that are inherent in man. [1] Despite his lamentations he retains his belief in the essential goodness of human nature and thus remains convinced that virtue may be learned and vice unlearned:

> There is nothing, Lucilius, to hinder you from entertaining good hopes about us, just because we are even now in the grip of evil, or because we have long been possessed thereby. There is no man to whom a good mind comes before an evil one. It is the evil mind that gets first hold on all of us. Learning virtue means unlearning vice [*virtutes discere vitia dediscere est*]. We should therefore proceed to the task of freeing ourselves from faults with all the more courage because, when once committed to us, the good is an everlasting possession; virtue is not unlearned [*non dediscitur virtus*]. For opposites find difficulty in clinging where they do not belong, therefore they can be driven out and hustled away; but qualities that come to a place which is rightfully theirs abide faithfully. Virtue is according to nature; vice is opposed to it and hostile. But although virtues, when admitted, cannot depart and are easy to guard, yet the first steps in the approach to them are toilsome, because it is characteristic of a weak and diseased mind to fear that which is unfamiliar. The mind must, therefore, be forced to make a beginning; from then on, the medicine is not bitter; for just as soon as it is curing us it begins to give pleasure. One enjoys other cures only after health is restored, but a draught of philosophy is at the same moment wholesome and pleasant. [2]

It is philosophy's task to discover the truth about things divine and things human. While it may also be said that:

> From her side religion never departs, nor duty, nor justice, nor any of the whole company of virtues which cling together in close-united fellowship. [3]

---

[1] Cf. H. Preisker. *Das Ethos des Urchristentums,* 1949, p. 159 f.; Georges Pire, op. cit., p. 186 ff.; J. Th. Ubbink, Seneca en Paulus, *Nieuwe theologische studiën,* 1918, p. 280 f.

[2] *Ep.* 50. 7-9.

[3] *Ep.* 90. 3.

The difference between the innocent, guileless, primal man and the philosopher is that the latter has had to fight to achieve his high moral standard. And that is virtue in its true form, 'for nature does not bestow virtue; it is an art to become good. [1] Primal man was innocent by reason of his ignorance of virtue and vice. Hence it is not possible to call him virtuous because 'virtue is not vouchsafed to a soul unless that soul has been trained and taught, and by unremitting practice brought to perfection.' [2]

Consequently virtue is a matter of teaching, training and constant, persistent practical application. It will then most certainly be attained. Why is this never hopeless? Because man only has to bear in mind his divine origin, *originis suae memor*. It is not presumptuous of man to endeavour to ascend to the heights from which he once descended:

> Why should you not believe, that something of divinity exists in one who is a part of God? All this universe which encompasses us is one, and it is God; we are associates of God; we are his members. Our soul has capabilities, and is carried thither [i.e. to participation in the divine existence], if vices do not hold it down. Just as it is the nature of our bodies to stand erect and look upward to the sky, so the soul, which may reach out as far as it will, was framed by nature to this end, that it should desire equality with the gods. And if it makes use of its powers and stretches upward into its proper region it is by no alien path that it struggles toward the heights. It would be a great task to journey heavenwards; the soul but returns thither. [3]

Therefore it is for Seneca incontestable that:

> a noble mind is free to all men; according to this test, we may all gain distinction; [4] we mortals have been endowed with sufficient strength by nature, if only we use this strength, if only we concentrate our powers and rouse them all to help us or at least not to hinder us. The reason is unwillingness, the excuse, inability; [5] nothing is so hard and difficult that it cannot be conquered by the human intellect and be brought through persistent study into intimate acquaintance, and there are no passions so fierce and self-willed that they cannot be subjugated by discipline. Whatever command the mind gives to itself holds its ground; [6] nor, as some think, is the path to the virtues steep and rough; they are reached by a level road. [7]

---

1 *Ep.* 90. 44.
2 *Ep.* 90. 46.
3 *Ep.* 92. 30.
4 *Ep.* 44. 2.
5 *Ep.* 116. 8.
6 *Ira* ii. 12. 3, 4.
7 *Ira* ii. 13. 1.

Seneca knows quite well that he shares this fundamental optimism concerning human ability with the whole school of Stoic philosophers. [1]

If virtue can be taught and acquired, if it is a question of insight, it follows that the source of evil lies in an error of judgment:

> What then is good? The knowledge of things. What is evil? The lack of knowledge of things. [2] Virtue means the knowledge of other things besides herself: if we would learn virtue we must learn all about virtue. Conduct will not be right unless the will to act is right; for this is the source of conduct. Nor, again, can the will be right without a right attitude of mind; for this is the source of the will. Furthermore, such an attitude of mind will not be found even in the best of men unless he has learned the laws of life as a whole and has worked out a proper judgment about everything, and unless he has reduced facts to a standard of truth. Peace of mind is enjoyed only by those who have attained a fixed and unchanging standard of judgment. [3]

Right or wrong, peace or discord, rest or unrest are all a question of purity of judgment, of clear insight. Philosophy is therefore the great liberator, since it releases man from his illusions. [4] It can free man from his false ideas. [5]

To do wrong is an error, and, like a sick man, man may be cured of it. Philosophy can cure him of this error. If this is so a man cannot really be considered guilty, he cannot be blamed for the wrong he has done. A temporary aberration of the mind only calls for a clarification of insight. A wrongdoer has to be taught to realize what he really already knows by virtue of his nature. Hence according to Seneca evil should be treated rationally: every man who errs can be appealed to through his reason.

Does Seneca pursue this line of argument to its logical conclusion? He sometimes uses terms which make this seem doubtful. He is able to speak of the torments and eternal unrest of a bad conscience; he knows:

> that bad deeds are lashed by the whip of conscience, and that conscience is tortured to the greatest degree because unending anxiety drives and whips it on, and it cannot rely upon the guarantors of its own peace of mind. [6]

---

[1] *V.B.* 3. 3.
[2] *Ep.* 31. 6.
[3] *Ep.* 95. 56 f.
[4] Cf. e.g. *Ep.* 71. 4-7; 89. 1-8.
[5] *Ep.* 94. 13.
[6] *Ep.* 97. 15.

Is this remorse, this self-reproach,this constant unrest after a bad deed compatible with Seneca's rationalistic approach towards evil? Do not words like *culpa, turpitudo*, and *peccatum* which repeatedly flow from his pen, point to an attitude towards evil which is not entirely in harmony with his identification of evil with error?

In his *Hercules Furens* the hero declares that his soul is too greatly defiled by his crimes for him to be able to live any longer. Only a self-chosen death can heal these sins and atone for this accumulation of evil: 'No power could purge a tainted spirit; by death must sin be healed'. [1] In the *Agamemnon* Clytemnestra says it is never too late to return to virtue, and if one repents of one's sins, one is almost innocent, *quem paenitet peccasse paene est innocens*. [2] Are these utterances to be taken for Seneca's own opinion or are they merely prompted by the dramatic material which he had passed down to him from the Greeks? If dying can serve as an act of penance, if repentance can make amends for sin, then Seneca is no longer regarding sin as an error alone. For an error can only be remedied by an improvement in the wrongdoer's insight, by his acquiring a more profound knowledge of himself.

Elsewhere too Seneca sometimes — perhaps unconsciously — says things from which it may be concluded that sin is not simply the same as an error which can be rectified by teaching and training. In one of his letters he writes about the difference between the 'diseases of the mind' and 'its passions'. Of the former he says:

> the diseases are hardened and chronic vices, such as greed and ambition; they have enfolded the mind in too close a grip, and have begun to be permanent evils thereof. To give a brief definition: by "disease" we mean a persistent perversion of the judgment. [3]

Here, too Seneca maintains that 'disease of the mind' has its roots in a perversion of the judgment, but it is a persistent perversion, *pertinax*. There is evidently something obstinate in such a perversion which cannot be readily expelled by an improvement in the insight. The use of such a word as 'disease' betrays Seneca's realization that evil is very different from an error.

Hence it may be seen that Seneca occasionally approaches a less rationalistic conception of evil. Nevertheless such passages remain the

---

[1] *Hercules Furens* 1261 f.; cf. *Hercules Oet.* 930 f.: *Interim poena est mori sed saepe donum; in pluribus veniae fuit.* See also *Phoen.* 140 ff.

[2] *Agamemnon* 242 f.

[3] *Ep.* 75. 11.

exception. If he had pursued this line of thought further, his receptivity for what Paul means by sin might have become greater, and his testimony to the universality of sin might have approached that of Paul more closely.

Generally speaking, however, Seneca evinces such an unimpaired faith in man's reason, in the validity of 'trust in oneself', *sibi fidere*, [1] in the possibility of 'a stout and unconquerable soul', *magnus et invictus animus,* [2] in man's 'bravery', *fortitudo,* [3] in the wise man as the pedagogue of the human race', [4] in the 'greatness of the mind,' [5] in reason which does 'everything under its own authority', [6] that his ethical principles must of necessity stem from a different root from Paul's message.

Attention has still to be drawn to two other ways in which Seneca, despite his sometimes pessimistic view of man and the community, differs fundamentally from Paul in his approach to ethics. The first of these is his advocacy of *living in accordance with nature.* Seneca argues repeatedly that what matters is that we should live, judge and act in accordance with nature. *Secundum naturam vivere* must most certainly be called a central notion in Seneca's ethics. He regards it as the highest good. [7] He knows that this belief is shared by all the Stoics:

> I follow the guidance of Nature — a doctrine upon which all Stoics are agreed. Not to stray from Nature and to mould ourselves according to her law and pattern — this is true wisdom. [8]

Although Seneca frequently uses this expression in many of his writings, and in his letters to Lucilius in particular, he never gives an exact definition of it. Various interpretations are possible. What we may ask, does he mean by 'nature': the whole of creation or human nature? In my opinion he means both. For Seneca there is no profound difference between the two. Nature as a whole is governed by a universal reason. Nature is organized along rational lines, and since man too has a share in that reason, or rather since reason constitutes the pure essence of man, living ethically is for him living in accordance

---

[1] *Ep.* 31. 3.
[2] *Ep.* 31. 6.
[3] *Ep.* 67. 6; 85. 28; 88. 29; 113. 27.
[4] *Ep.* 89. 13.
[5] *Marc.* 1. 5.
[6] *V.B.* 8. 6.
[7] *De Otio* 5. 1.
[8] *V.B.* 3. 3.

with reason, that is to say in accordance with nature. Consequently the ethical man is the man who is willing to submit to the laws of the universe. [1] Living according to nature is living according to reason which reveals itself not only in the general course of the universe, but also in man. Therefore in order to keep to the path of virtue and to find his true self again man has only to turn to himself, to the laws of nature and reason within himself. If we are governed by vices, we must always bear in mind that we were not created with them. They have infiltrated into our lives from without. When nature created us, we were pure. If despite this we have strayed, she has nevertheless given us sufficient strength to retrace our steps:

> Nature has brought us forth brave of spirit, and, as she has implanted in certain animals a spirit of ferocity, in others craft, in others terror, so she has gifted us with an aspiring and lofty spirit, which prompts us to seek a life of the greatest honour, and not of the greatest security, that most resembles the soul of the universe, which it follows and imitates as far as our mortal steps permit. [2]

'Virtue is according to nature; vice is opposed to it and hostile.' [3] When nature created us we were good, but unfortunately we have not remained true to our original state. It must be confessed that man is worse when he leaves life than when he enters it:

> we are worse when we die than when we were born; but it is our fault, and not that of Nature. Nature should scold us, saying: "What does this mean? I brought you into the world without desires or fears, free from superstition, treachery and the other curses. Go forth as you were when you entered!" [4]

In another letter Seneca expresses the same idea in slightly different words, but no less plainly:

> you are mistaken if you suppose that our faults are inborn in us; they have come from without, have been heaped upon us . . . . Nature does not ally us with any vice; she produced us in health and freedom. [5]

Hence if we lead wicked lives we are rebelling against nature, and abandoning 'the appointed order', [6] not building on the foundations

---

[1] Cf. E. Vernon Arnold, op. cit., p. 283: 'In the main therefore "life according to nature" means to the Stoics life in accordance with the general movement of the universe, to which the particular strivings of the individual must be subordinated'; Georges Pire, op. cit., p. 113.

[2] *Ep.* 104. 23.

[3] *Ep.* 50. 8.

[4] *Ep.* 22. 15.

[5] *Ep.* 94. 55, 56.

[6] *Ep.* 122. 5.

nature laid in us, and stifling the growth of the seeds of virtue which nature has planted in us. 1

In spite of his pessimistic view of the human scene as it was enacted around him it is abundantly evident, as has already been shown, that Seneca never doubted for a moment that nature has given man the ability to remain on the path of virtue, or to return to it, if he has temporarily strayed. 2 There is in his writings an undercurrent of optimism; there is a conviction that perfect harmony exists between reason and nature, that a division between the two is scarcely conceivable:

> we must use Nature as our guide; she it is that Reason heeds, it is of her that it takes counsel. Therefore to live happily is the same thing as to live according to Nature. 3
> Reason is in accordance with nature. "What, then", you ask, "is reason?" It is copying nature. 4

In reason nature has armed us with adequate weapons for the battle of life. 5 From this it follows that for Seneca straying from the path of virtue may ultimately always be attributed to failure to use the reason with which nature has endowed us. It is up to man himself whether or not he uses his reason. Therefore vice is the result of faulty reasoning, and so in fact a problem pertaining to the intellect. If we think clearly, we act rightly; and this is nothing other than living in accordance with nature. 6

For anyone reasonably familiar with Paul's kerygma it is immediately obvious that such a fundamentally optimistic view of living according to nature is not compatible with Paul's ideas. If we look for verbal parallels, we must consider the word φύσις, which does indeed occur a number of times in Paul. It is , however, sometimes used in such a way that it need scarcely be considered in connection with Seneca. Paul speaks of the 'physically uncircumcised' (Rom. 2 : 27), and elsewhere of the 'Jews by birth' φύσει 'Ιουδαῖοι (Gal. 2 : 15). Or he addresses churches which now know the true God as people who

---

1 *Ep.* 108. 8; in *De Ira* it is said repeatedly of one particular vice, anger, that it is contrary to nature, *Ira* i. 5. 1, 3; i. 6. 4, 5.

2 *Ep.* 44. 2, 3; 31. 9; 116. 8; *Ben* iv. 17. 3.

3 *V.B.* 8. 1, 2; cf. *Ep.* 41. 8, 9; 76. 15.

4 *Ep.* 66. 39.

5 *Ira* i. 17. 2.

6 Cf. H. Preisker, *Nautestamentliche Zeitgeschichte*, 1937, p. 63: 'Sünde hat für die Stoa ihren Sitz im Intellekt, im Denken .... Die Sittlichkeit beruht für die Stoa eben auf richtigem Denken.'

formerly served gods 'that by nature are no gods' (Gal. 4 : 8). He uses the word several times when alluding to the Gentiles and Israel metaphorically as the wild and the cultivated olive: the wild olive is 'grafted, contrary to nature, into a cultivated olive tree' (Rom. 11 : 21, 24). In describing the moral corruption among the Gentiles, he also uses it in connection with the fact that men and women had exchanged natural sexual intercourse for unnatural (Rom. 1 : 26, 27). Paul considers natural intercourse to be normal. Sexual acts committed contrary to nature he looks upon as an expression of 'dishonourable passions', to which God has given up the Gentiles. They are 'shameless acts' and form part of the aberration of the Gentiles (Rom. 1 : 27).

On rare occasions and in connection with a concrete question, he appeals to a universal consciousness innate in man, which he also assumes to be alive in a Christian community. A case in point is when he asks his readers:

> Does not nature itself teach you that for a man to wear long hair is degrading to him. but if a woman has long hair, it is her pride? (1 Cor. 11 : 14, 15). [1]

Paul is best compared with Seneca in the verses discussed above (Rom. 2 : 14-16) on the consciousness of Gentiles who 'do by nature what the law requires'. Right op until the present day opinions have differed greatly as to the interpretation of φύσει in Rom. 2 : 14. [2] Some scholars believe that Paul's words are highly reminiscent of fundamental Stoic principles, [3] others strongly emphasize the difference existing between Paul and the Stoics on the point. [4]

In the first place the great significance of the fact that Paul uses the word φύσει here should be realized. Some writers weaken the meaning of this word in order to accentuate the contrast between the

---

[1] Cf. R. Bultmann, *Glauben und Verstehen*, Vol. 2, 1952, p. 66; Else Kähler, *Die Frau in den paulinischen Briefen*, 1950, p. 65, 234 [280].

[2] Cf. Max Lackmann, *Vom Geheimnis der Schöpfung*, 1952, pp. 96 ff., 103 ff., 217 ff.; F. Flückiger, 'Die Werke des Gesetzes bei den Heiden', *Theol. Zeitschrift*, 1952, pp. 17-42; G. Bornkamm, *Studien zu Antike und Urchristentum*, 1959, p. 101 ff.

[3] Lietzmann, for example, begins his extensive elucidation of this text: 'Dass alles sittliche Handeln die Befolgung der uns von der Natur eingepflanzten Gesetze sei und in der Gottheit wurzele, ist der Fundamentalsatz der stoischen Ethik.' H. Lietzmann, *An die Römer*, [2]1919, p. 39.

[4] E.g. Lackmann, op. cit., p. 217 f.: 'Der Unterschied des paulinischen Gebrauchs zum Sprachgebrauch der Zeit ist deutlich. Beide sagen sie *Physis,* der Hellenist und der Apostel. Aber wo jener statisch, naturrechtlich, naturgesetzlich, ontisch denkt, denkt dieser dynamisch, personalistisch, real-präsentisch aus der Kraft seines israelitischen Schöpferglaubens. Wo jener autonom denkt, denkt dieser glaubend...'

Stoics and Paul as much as possible. This is plain from the way in which Lackmann, for example, paraphrases φύσει:

> Sie [die Heiden] vernehmen ohne den Dekalog zu lesen oder zu hören, seine fordernde Stimme in ihrem natürlichen Zustande als Geschöpfe Gottes, nicht als Besitzer eines ihnen inhärierenden „νόμος τῆς φύσεως", aber als von ihrem Schöpfer unaufhörlich beanspruchte, geleitete, geforderte Gefässe seines Lebenshauches. [1]

Barth, too, translates 'in ihrem natürlichen Zustande als Geschöpfe Gottes' similarly with 'in ihrem Naturzustande'. [2] This is neither quite exact nor strong enough. Such a translation might well suggest that Paul is only saying that the Gentiles still live in their natural state and that even then God speaks to them as His creatures. However, the word φύσει also says something about why they do what the law requires: they obey the law φύσει, by nature. Lackmann's interpretation is justified, inasmuch as he makes it clear that by virtue of the context this passage must be taken to refer to something other than the Stoic law of nature and natural right. But this does not alter the fact that Paul says of some Gentiles (ἔθνη without the article), that they do by nature what the law requires. 'By nature' not 'in their natural state'. Hence Paul wishes to say here that since God has ordained that some Gentiles show plainly that they do by nature what the law requires, it cannot be asserted that the Gentiles who do not know the written law, do not know how they should act either.

If we bear this context in mind it also becomes clear that, despite the use of the word φύσει here, there is still a profound difference between Paul and Seneca on this point. In connection with the conscience it has already been pointed out that Paul is by no means referring to a 'natural revelation', but that he wishes to demonstrate that the Gentiles, too, may be judged according to the standard of the law, since they, too, have the law written on their hearts. Paul does not profess that the highest good or the happy life is to be achieved by living according to nature; a life to which every human being is called and can achieve by using those powers with which nature has endowed him. It has already been seen in the chapter on God that Seneca repeatedly identifies God and nature. This being so, *secundum naturam vivere* must for him possess an entirely different

---

[1] Lackmann, op. cit., p. 217.

[2] K. Barth, *Der Römerbrief*, [6]1933, p. 41; Bornkamm reproaches Flückiger for interpreting φύσει in this passage too 'unterminologisch und unbetont', G. Bornkamm op. cit., p. 103.

meaning from the Pauline φύσει. For Paul φύσει has no decisive significance within the framework of salvation. The meaning he gives
tc φύσει within the framework of the history of salvation is abundantly clear from another passage where he uses exactly the same
phrase in describing the vivid contrast between 'once' and 'now',
between man prior to Christ and man knowing God's grace in Christ.
'Once', Paul says, 'we were by nature children of wrath' (Eph. 2 : 3);
literally children by nature of wrath τέκνα φύσει ὀργῆς, which means
that φύσει and ὀργῆς both receive special emphasis. Do not let us
forget, Paul wishes to say, that we Christians too were once, prior to
Christ, children of wrath. Natural man, man prior to Christ, is subject to God's wrath. Contrasted with this are the riches of God's mercy
now, in Christ. Against the background of once having been children
of wrath this mercy stands out in all its glory. The words 'you have
been saved' and 'grace' which recur repeatedly in this pericope reflect
the glory of the 'now' of salvation. There is indeed reason to be
joyful, Paul says, when we recall that the whole of humanity, both
Jews and Gentiles alike, were once subject to God's wrath. [1]

It is well known that Paul's letters are full of such contrasts between
'once' and 'now', sometimes explicit, [2] and sometimes understood. And
what applies to the churches in this respect, applies also to the individual Christian: there is a sharp distinction between the 'old' man, the
natural man, and the 'new' man in Christ. The 'new' man is put on
like a garment that lies ready when a man puts on Christ. [3] It is
highly significant how differently Paul and Seneca use this same image.
Paul exhorts the Ephesians:

> Put off [ἀποθέσθαι] your old nature which belongs to your former
> manner of life and is corrupt through deceitful lusts, and be renewed in
> the sprit of your minds, and put on [ἐνδύσασθαι] the new nature,
> created after the likeness of God in true righteousness and holiness (Eph.
> 4 : 22-24).

Hence he urges them to cast aside their old nature. The members of
the Church must discard it like an old garment. Seneca, on the other
hand, gains hope from the fact that a man never entirely discards
his original good nature:

---

[1] Eph. 2 : 1-10; cf. R. V. G. Tasker, *The Biblical Doctrine of the Wrath of God.*
1951, p. 15 f.

[2] E.g. Eph. 2 : 11, 12, 13; 5 : 8; Rom. 5 : 10 f.; 11 : 30 f.

[3] Eph. 4 : 24; Gal. 3 : 27; Rom. 13 : 14; cf. Rom. 6 : 4, 5; Col. 3 : 10.

no one has ever so far revolted from Nature's law and put aside humanity [*hominem exuit*] as to be evil for the pleasure of it. 1

Whereas Paul is convinced that a man only becomes a new creature
in Christ, and consequently urges the members of the Church to
'put on [ἐνδύσασθαι] the Lord Jesus Christ' (2 Cor. 5 : 17; Rom.
13 : 14), Seneca has strong faith in the possibilities of the natural
man, as may be seen from *Ep.* 67 where he exhorts Lucilius to clothe
himself with a hero's courage, *indue magni viri animum.* 2 The divergent use of the same image shows clearly how far removed Paul is
from the optimistic view of man as he is, which is implied in Seneca's
glorification of living in accordance with nature.

The second notion to display the basic difference between Seneca
and Paul's approach to ethics is that of *perfection.* It is understandable
that this point is bound up with the previous one. De Bovis is justified
in saying:

> Concluons que les mots 'honestum', 'virtus', 'sapientia', 'vivere secundum
> naturam', 'ratio perfecta' sont des termes interchangeables. Chacun d'entre
> eux désigne la même réalité fondamentale, mais la présente sous un
> aspect particulier. 3

It has already been established that in Seneca's eyes there is perfect
harmony between reason and nature and that a division between the
two is scarcely conceivable. 4 It is in reason that man's chance of perfection lies.

In the following pasage nature, reason and perfection are indissolubly linked with one another in Seneca's mind:

> Praise the quality in him [man] which cannot be given or snatched away,
> that which is the peculiar property of the man. Do you ask what this is?
> It is soul, and reason brought to perfection in the soul [*ratio in animo
> perfecta*]. For man is a reasoning animal. Therefore, man's highest good
> is attained, if he has fulfilled the good for which nature designed him
> at birth. And what is it which this reason demands of him? The easiest
> thing in the world, — to live in accordance with his own nature. 5

This link between reason and perfection is referred to in various other
passages:

> Since reason alone brings man to perfection, reason alone, when perfected,
> makes man happy. 6

---

1 *Ben.* iv. 17. 3.
2 *Ep.* 67. 12.
3 De Bovis, op. cit., p. 37.
4 See above p. 137.
5 *Ep.* 41. 8, 9.
6 *Ep.* 76. 16; cf. 76. 10.

In another letter Seneca asserts,

> that the happy life depends on this and this alone: our attainment of
> perfect reason.

He who lives accordingly relies solely upon his own strength, *nisi sibi
innixus*. [1] It is obvious that the concord between nature and reason
can indeed bring man to perfection, and that this perfection is by no
means beyond his reach. Hence *perfectus* is a notion that frequently
occurs in Seneca's letters and other of his writings.

Virtue may become perfect; for this an even temperament and
utterly harmonious life is necessary: [2]

> The larger part of goodness is the will to become good. You know what
> I mean by a good man? One who is complete, finished [*perfectus,
> absolutus*], — whom no constraint or need can render bad. I see such a
> person in you, if only you go steadily on and bend to your task, and
> see to it that all your actions and words harmonize and correspond with
> each other and are stamped in the same mould. [3]

A man that is perfect in both body and soul has achieved the tranquillity of a clear blue sky:

> When a man takes care of his body and of his soul, weaving the
> texture of his good from both, his condition is perfect .... the absolute
> good of man's nature is satisfied with peace in the body and peace in
> the soul. [4]

Man is composed of two contrasting parts:

> the one part is irrational, — it is this that may be bitten, burned or hurt;
> the other part is rational, — it is this which holds resolutely to opinions,
> is courageous, and unconquerable. In the latter is situated man's Supreme
> Good. Before this is completely attained, the minds waver in uncertainty;
> only when it is fully achieved [*perfectum est*] is the mind fixed and
> steady. [5]

Virtue makes a man absolutely happy:

> It is absurd to say that a man will be happy by virtue alone, and yet not
> absolutely happy. I cannot discover how that may be, since the happy
> life contains in itself a good that is perfect and cannot be excelled. If a
> man has this good, life is completely happy. [6]

---

[1] *Ep*. 92. 2.
[2] *Ep*. 31. 8.
[3] *Ep*. 34. 3, 4.
[4] *Ep*. 66. 45, 46.
[5] *Ep*. 71. 27.
[6] *Ep*. 85. 19.

"What! does virtue alone suffice for living happily?" Perfect and divine as it is, why should it not suffice — nay, suffice to overflowing? 3

Neither does perfection depend upon the length of a man's life. When Lucilius laments upon the death of the philosopher Metronax, and maintains that he should have lived longer, Seneca chastizes him, saying that a man's life ought not to be judged by its length but by whether it has been a full one. Even if a life has not attained its normal span, it can still be perfect and complete:

> Just as one of small stature can be a perfect man, so a life of small compass can be a perfect life. 1

Such a perfect man, full of human and divine virtue, need never fear a loss. 3 Seneca readily admits that he himself is not perfect, not even tolerably so. If one wishes to see a perfect man, one must observe a man over whom fortune has lost her control. 4

Accordingly Seneca gives us in his writings a clear picture of what he understands by the perfect man: a man full of human and divine virtues, whose inner life is completely harmonious and steadfast because his whole being is founded upon reason, a man who has attained the highest good and consequently the highest happiness, and whose state of mind is therefore like a calm blue sky.

Paul too, makes repeated use of the word 'perfect', τέλειος, but it is only natural that the difference between his starting-point and Seneca's should inevitably lead to a different usage of this word. This may be demonstrated first by the fact that it more than once occurs in an eschatological context, the clearest instance of this perhaps being the well known pericope 1 Cor. 13 : 8-13:

> Love never ends; as for prophecy, it will pass away; as for tongues, they will cease; as for knowledge, it will pass away. For our knowledge is imperfect and our prophecy is imperfect; but when the perfect comes, the imperfect will pass away (vv. 8-10).

The perfection of the aeon to come is contrasted with the imperfection, the transitoriness of the present. Likewise, in Col. 1 : 25-29 what is 'perfect' is seen within the framework of the eschatological proclamation. Once the mystery of salvation was hidden for ages and genera-

---

1 *V.B.* 16. 3.
2 *Ep.* 93. 4, 7.
3 *Const.* 6. 8.
4 *Ep.* 57. 3.

tions, but now it has been revealed to the saints, the Church. Paul can now proclaim Christ, in whom the glory of this mystery has been revealed. He proclaims Him too when he corrects and teaches every man in all wisdom, in order that every man may be made perfect in Christ, τέλειον ἐν Χριστῷ (Col. 1 : 28). So, too, perfection can only be attained by living in obedience to God's will which can be discerned by the man who no longer lives in conformity with this age but is transformed by the renewal of his mind (Rom. 12 : 1, 2). Perfection belongs to the coming age, but this age is no longer merely a time still awaited, since it is already present in Christ. Hence what is perfect can already invade this age as a sign that in Christ the old age has been pervaded by the new.

Likewise, in those passages where the eschatological situation is not so clearly indicated, perfection is placed against the background of Christ's work of salvation. [1] One of the most disputed pericopes dealing with this subject is 1 Cor. 2 : 6-3 : 4. [2] The main point with which the exegetes are concerned is whether Paul considers he has two gospels, one for τέλειοι and one for νήπιοι which would mean that the simple preaching of Christ crucified would only be for the latter, or whether he means that the preaching of Christ crucified is the wisdom of God for the whole of mankind, but that the Corinthians are not able to grasp it because they have not yet seriously given themselves up to the Spirit and are still of the flesh. The latter interpretation is the most satisfying. [3] The perfect are then the spiritual men. [4] In writing 1 Cor. 3 : 1-4 Paul is not really departing from his fundamental belief that all the members of the Church are in possession of the Spirit (3 : 16 f.; cf. Gal. 3 : 2, 5; Rom. 8 : 9, 15, 26). But in Corinth they have not been allowing themselves to be completely guided by the Spirit who has been granted them; their thoughts and their deeds are not yet determined by the Spirit. Proof of this is the 'jealousy and strife' that reigns among them (3 : 3).

---

[1] e.g. Phil. 3 : 12-16; 1 Cor. 14 : 20; Col. 4 : 12; Eph. 4 : 12, 13; cf. B. Rigaux, 'Révélation des Mystères et Perfection à Qumran et dans le Nouveau Testament', *NTS*, July 1958, p. 237 ff., especially p. 248 ff.

[2] See K. Deissner, *Paulus und die Mystik seiner Zeit*, 1921, pp. 26 ff., 39-47, who counters R. Reitzenstein, *Hellenistische Mysterienreligionen;* cf. also Joh. Weiss, *Das Urchristentum*, 1917, p. 492; id., *1 Kor.*, 1925, xix, 73 f.; E. B. Allo, *St. Paul, Première Épître aux Corinthiens*, 1956, p. 89 ff.; Ulrich Wilckens, *Weisheit und Torheit, Eine exegetisch-religionsgeschichtliche Untersuchung zu 1 Kor. 1 und 2*, 1959, p. 52 ff.; R. Bultmann, *Glauben und Verstehen*, 1933, p. 42 ff.

[3] Cf. e.g. 1 : 24, 30; 2 : 6.

[4] Cf. 1Cor. 2 : 6 with 3 : 1.

Herein lies the second difference between Paul and Seneca in this respect: in Paul all members of the Church are fundamentally perfect, not primarily because of what they do themselves, but because of what they are in Christ. They are all 'spiritual men'. The Church has received the Spirit, who as the first fruits, as a pledge, in this age already points towards the full harvest, towards the sum total of the age to come. Hence perfection is an integral part of belonging to the Church, belonging to Christ. Paul never for an instant expects perfection of the natural man, of man as he is; neither does he assume the possibility of every man attaining perfection, but he knows of it as a reality in the life of the 'new' man in Christ. Of the natural man who has not been renewed by the Spirit of God in fellowship with Christ Paul expects little or nothing, but he sees great possibilities and realities in the 'new' man in Christ, and hence also in the Church. This may also be seen from those passages where he does not use the word 'perfect', but nevertheless employs very similar expressions. By virtue of what he has said in the whole chapter 1 Cor. 15 on salvation through Christ's resurrection and the resurrection of the dead he can end with an exhortation to the Church which knows this salvation and bases its life upon it:

> Therefore, my beloved brethren, be steadfast, immovable, always abounding in the work of the Lord, knowing that in the Lord your labor is not in vain (1 Cor. 15 : 58).

For those who by their baptism were buried with Christ and will rise with Him it automatically applies that: 'sin will have no dominion over you, since you are not under law but under grace' (Rom. 6 : 14). Time and again Paul assumes a radical change in those who live in fellowship with Christ and in the salvation granted in Him. He need not urge his followers to bring about this change, since it has already taken place. The imperative quite justifiably has its roots in the indicative. 'Those who belong to Christ Jesus have crucified the flesh with its passions and desires. If we live by the Spirit, let us also walk by the Spirit' (Gal. 5 : 24 f.). He ventures to speak of the members of the Church being 'unblamable in holiness' (1 Thess. 3 : 13), 'guiltless in the day of our Lord Jesus Christ' (1 Cor. 1 : 8), as being so, that nobody could bring a charge against them (cf. Rom. 8 : 33 f.), as being 'holy and blameless and irreproachable' (Col. 1 : 22). In a Christian community the works of the flesh are not done; there the fruit of the Spirit is to be seen (Gal. 5 : 19 ff., 22). Full of confidence in the effect of the salvation granted them Paul ventures to appeal to a church to:

> Do all things without grumbling or questioning, that you may be blameless and innocent, children of God without blemish in the midst of a crooked and perverse generation, among whom you shine as lights in the world (Phil. 2 : 14, 15).

'Steadfast,' 'unmovable' (1 Cor. 15 : 58), 'unblamable' (1 Thess. 3 : 13), 'guiltless' (1 Cor. 1 : 8), 'blameless', 'irreproachable' (Col. 1 : 22) are all words that would not be out of place in Seneca's definition of the life of the perfect man. In Seneca, however, such words are descriptive of qualities which arise from the heart of a man who relies upon his own strength,[1] in Paul they are rooted as the fruit of the Spirit in 'what no eye has seen, nor ear heard, nor the heart of man conceived, what God has prepared for those who love him.'[2]

Proof of the ultimate anthropocentricity of Seneca's ethics may also be found in the frequency with which Seneca uses the word *virtue*, and more especially in the way in which he uses it. For the use of this word is inevitably bound up with notions of human excellence, human merits, or human achievements. When 'virtue' occupies a central position in an ethical system, as it does in Seneca, interest must automatically be focussed on the virtuous man.

The question arises whether 'virtue' is always the most suitable translation for the word *virtus* as Seneca uses it. What Pohlenz says of the Stoic school in general also applies to Seneca:

> Die Virtus hat für die Römer immer etwas vom kraftvollen Mannestum behalten. Aber dieses Mannestum bewährt sich für das neue Geschlecht nicht mehr durch Einsatz für den Staat im Krieg und öffentlichen Leben, sondern als die feste, unerschütterliche Haltung, die gewiss auch den Dienst an der Gemeinschaft zur Pflicht macht, aber zunächst dem Einzelmenschen zur Erfüllung seiner Bestimmung und zur Eudämonie verhilft. Sie ist die Vollendung des Logos, den der Einzelne in sich trägt, und damit der Inbegriff individueller Vollkommenheit, eine einheitliche Gesamthaltung, der gegenüber die einzelnen virtutes zurücktreten; sie ist so wenig wie die Eudämonie einer Steigerung fähig, und dieses 'Mannestum' ist allen Menschen, ob Frau oder Mann, ob Sklave oder Bürger, gleich zugänglich.[3]

---

[1] *Ep.* 92. 2.
[2] Gal. 5 : 22; 1 Cor. 2 : 9.
[3] Pohlenz, *Stoa* I, p. 314; cf. Karl Büchner, *Humanitas romana*, 1957, p. 211: 'Was ist *virtus*? In erster Linie „männliche Kraft" und „männliches Wesen" ', cf. pp. 310-13; in ἀρετή, too, various shades of meaning were already hidden. W. Nestle

It is indeed notable that in Seneca, too, the individual virtues remain unstressed, despite the fact that the word *virtus* occurs quite frequently in the plural. [1] It is true that individual virtues are sometimes enumerated [2] — friendship is for example mentioned as a particular virtue [3] — but *virtus* in the singular occurs far more frequently and where it does, it indeed denotes a 'Gesamthaltung', an 'Inbegriff individueller Volkommenheit'. The word denotes the attitude towards life of the man of strong character who has attained spiritual inviolability and consequently inner peace, harmony and happiness. Hence *virtus* may be deemed to be one of the principal notions around which Seneca's ethics revolve. He never tires of singing the praises of *virtus* in all keys.

Virtue is the crowning glory of man's inner life; its light is never extinguished:

> Virtue alone affords everlasting and peace-giving joy; even if some obstacle arise, it is but like an intervening could, which floats beneath the sun but never prevails against it. [4]

Man himself possesses all that is necessary for happiness. There is no need for him to call upon the gods, he can make himself happy, and he will succeed in this if he understands that whatever is blended with virtue is good. [5] Virtue is its own reward. When asked what it is he seeks in virtue, Seneca replies: 'Only herself. For she offers nothing better — she herself is her own reward.' [6]

Let virtue go first, proudly bearing the standard. A virtuous life is one that differs radically from the life of those who

> do not possess pleasure, but are possessed by it. [7] Virtue does not exist if it is possible for her to follow; hers is the first place, she must lead, must command, must have the supreme position; you bid her ask for the watchword! [8]

---

says, for example, of the sophists who travelled the country for their education: 'Alle diese Männer sind darin einig, dass sie die „areté" lehren wollen, was man gewöhnlich mit „Tugend" übersetzt, was aber hier mehr die praktische Tüchtigkeit bedeutet', W. Nestle, op cit., p. 321.

[1] e.g. *Ep.* 14. 11; 50. 7; 59. 7; 66. 41; 90. 46; *Ira* ii. 12. 2; 13. 1, 2; iii. 8. 2; *Ben.* iv. 30. 1, 3; *V.B.* 8. 6; *Const.* 6. 8; *Brev.* 19. 2; *Marc.* 24. 1; *Helv.* 8. 1; 9. 3; *Otio* 3. 4; *Clem.* i. 5. 3.

[2] *Helv.* 9. 3.

[3] *Ep.* 9. 8.

[4] *Ep.* 27. 3.

[5] *Ep.* 31. 5.

[6] *V.B.* 9. 4.

[7] *V.B.* 14. 1.

[8] *Ben.* iv. 2. 2.

The question whether a virtuous life is possible has already been encountered elsewhere in another connection. Of great importance for the answer is Seneca's belief that virtue is part and parcel of living according to nature and that it is born of reason. The truly noble man is he who is by nature fitted for virtue, and not the man who can point to a gallery full of smoke-begrimed ancestors. [1]

Seneca repeatedly argues, as has already been seen, that there is a link between virtue and reason, [3] and that therefore virtue can be acquired. [4] However, even though virtue is according to nature this does not mean it is to be had for the asking. Nature does not hand it to man on a silver platter. The acquisition of virtue requires constant training, it is an art and as such demands instruction and practice. The raw material for virtue is in everyone's possession, but virtue itself is not. [5] If a man is willing to pay the price of instruction, training, effort and practice, a life of virtue is within his grasp. Seneca protests emphatically against a pessimistic view of man's capacity to lead a good life:

> since we are born to do right, nature herself helps us if we desire to be improved. Nor, as some think, is the path to the virtues steep and rough; they are reached by a level road .... In short, the maintenance of all the virtues is easy .... [6]

We are fortunate that there are men who show us the grandeur of the happy life without making us despair of ever attaining it. [7]

Accordingly it is not to be wondered at that virtue may be found everywhere, in all classes of society. It is neither dependent upon rank or station, nor upon physical beauty. Virtue has its own splendour; even if it inhabits a misshapen body;

> virtue needs nothing to set it off; it is its own great glory, and it hallows the body in which it dwells .... A great man can spring from a hovel; so can a beautiful and great soul from an ugly and insignificant body. For this reason Nature seems to me to breed certain men of this stamp with the idea of proving that virtue springs into birth in any place whatever .... virtue is just as praiseworthy if it dwells in a sound and free body, as in one which is sickly or in bondage. [8]

---

[1] *Ep.* 44. 5.
[2] *Ep.* 50. 8; 66. 41.
[3] *Ep.* 76. 10, 16.
[4] *Ep.* 88. 32; cf. *Ep.* 31. 6; 123. 16.
[5] *Ep.* 90. 44, 46; cf. *Ep.* 94. 47.
[6] *Ira* ii. 13. 1, 2.
[7] *Ep.* 64. 5, 6.
[8] *Ep.* 66. 2, 3, 22.

So Seneca is convinced that:

> Virtue closes the door to no man; it is open to all, admits all, invites all, the freeborn and the freedman, the slave and the king, and the exile; neither family nor fortune determines its choice — it is satisfied with the naked human being. [1]

Hence men of perfect character, who are content in themselves and have by their virtue attained an exalted harmony, whose balance can in no way be disturbed, and who find perfect happiness in themselves, are to be found in all walks of life. Behind all the particular virtues of such men there is a single one — 'that which renders the soul straight and unswerving.' [2] In such a harmonious life in which 'all the works of virtue are in harmony and agreement with virtue itself' [3] every form of torment and grief has been overcome:

> Just as the brightness of the sun dims all lesser lights, so virtue, by its own greatness, shatters and overwhelms all pains, annoyances, and wrongs; and wherever its radiance reaches, all lights which shine without the help of virtue are extinguished; and inconveniences, when they come in contact with virtue, play no more important a part than does a storm-cloud at sea. [4]

For the truly harmonious character, suffering of any kind is only an opportunity to display his inner strength, his *virtus*. Therefore we must not shrink in fear 'from those things which the immortal gods apply like spurs to our souls.. Disaster is Virtue's opportunity.' [5] Naturally no one desires the miseries and discomforts of life. No one is so foolish as to wish to be ill, but, says Seneca,

> if I must suffer illness, I shall desire that I may do nothing which shows lack of restraint and nothing that is unmanly. The conclusion is, not that hardships are desirable, but that virtue is desirable, which enables us patiently to endure hardships .... it is not mere endurance of torture, but brave endurance, that is desirable. I therefore desire that "brave" endurance; and this is virtue. [6]

A man may display his virtue in times of great danger, in prison, in war, but he can also do so in his bed. There, too, proof may be given of a powerful, unflinching spirit. [7]

---

1 *Ben.* iii. 18. 2.
2 *Ep.* 66. 13.
3 *Ep.* 74. 30.
4 *Ep.* 66. 20; cf. *Ep.* 82. 18; 120. 11; *V.B.* 8. 6.
5 *Prov.* 4. 6.
6 *Ep.* 67. 4, 6; cf. *Ep.* 87. 16, 17.
7 *Tranqu. an..* 5. 4; *Ep.* 78. 21.

Such a man is entirely content in himself, rejoicing in his own virtue. *Virtute contentus* is a favourite expression of Seneca's, [1] and so it goes without saying that one of his favourite themes is that true happiness is to be found in virtue. Virtue alone is enough for a happy life. Nothing else, no external trappings are necessary:

> If a man has been placed beyond the reach of any desire, what can he possibly lack? If a man has gathered into himself all that is his, what need does he have of any outside thing? [2]

Virtue is constant and permanent:

> Every virtue and every work of virtue abides uncorrupted. [3] I do not know whether this Aetna of yours can collapse and fall in ruins, whether this lofty summit, visible for many miles over the deep sea, is wasted by the incessant power of the flames; but I do know that virtue will not be brought down to a lower plane either by flames or by ruins. Hers is the only greatness that knows no lowering; there can be for her no further rising or sinking. Her stature, like that of the stars in the heavens, is fixed. [4]

There is no abiding good other than that which the soul finds in itself. 'Virtue alone affords everlasting and peace-giving joy.' [5] A virtuous life is indestructible. [6] We may always have virtue at our side. It accompanies us everywhere and so also into exile. This thought was of great comfort to Seneca in his own exile. Both his mother and himself he comforted from his place of exile with the reminder that:

> Wherever we betake ourselves, two things that are most admirable will go with us — universal Nature and our own virtue .... When virtue has once steeled your mind, it guarantees to make it invulnerable from every quarter. [7]

Such an extreme comment on virtue as 'her stature, like that of the stars in heaven, is fixed', [8] is boldly repeated by Seneca in a variety of ways:

> Nothing is more excellent or more beautiful than virtue. [9] Virtue is something lofty, exalted and regal, unconquerable, and unwearied. [10]

---

1 *V.B.* 4. 2; *Const.* 5. 4; cf. *Ira* i. 9. 1; *virtute laetus V.B.* 4. 2.
2 *V.B.* 16. 1, 3; cf. *Ep.* 85. 1; 71. 16.
3 *Ep.* 74. 24; cf. *Ep.* 76. 20.
4 *Ep.* 79. 10.
5 *Ep.* 27. 3.
6 *Ep.* 82. 23.
7 *Helv.* 8. 1, 2; 13. 2.
8 See above, *Ep.* 79. 10.
9 *Ep.* 67. 16.
10 *V.B.* 7. 3.

Virtue, the *aeterna virtus*, [1] brings man very close to the gods. It attains the highest peaks. [2] Virtue puts a man in a position where he no longer has anything in common with ordinary mortals. [3] It makes a man worthy of the company of the gods, [4] it lays a bond of friendship between good men and the gods. [5] Hence virtue is worthy of being honoured like the gods:

> Have respect for virtue, give credence to those who, having long pursued her, proclaim that they themselves are pursuing something that is great and that every day seems greater, and do you reverence her as you do the gods, and her exponents as the priests of the gods. [6]

The prominence in Seneca's thoughts of virtue, his own included, is underlined by his death, as it is described by Tacitus. Even death, if it is voluntarily accepted and this acceptance is a fully conscious decision, is, as a final act of heroism, part of the virtuous life. The attitude of the Stoics in general towards virtue makes this readily comprehensible. [7] In his death Seneca practised what he had once preached to Lucilius in connection with what he considered to be the praiseworthy conduct of a man who sacrificed his life because he regarded

> a noble death as a thing to be desired. Do you doubt, then, whether it is best te die glorious and performing some deed of valour? When one endures torture bravely, one is using all the virtues. Endurance may perhaps be the only virtue that is on view and most manifest; but bravery is there too, and endurance and resignation and long-suffering are its branches. There, too, is foresight; for without foresight no plan can be undertaken; it is foresight that advises one to bear as bravely as possible the things one cannot avoid. There also is stead-fastness, which cannot be dislodged from its position, which the wrench of no force can cause to abandon its purpose. There is the whole inseparable company of virtues; every honourable act is the work of one single virtue, but it is in accordance with the judgment of the whole council. [8]

Seneca might well have applied and wished to apply, these words to his own life.

Moreover, from the vantage point of a manly death he could look

---

[1] *Herc. Oet.* 1835.
[2] *Prov.* 5. 10; *Ep.* 76. 17; *Ira* i. 21. 4.
[3] *Const.* 15. 2.
[4] *N.Q.* i Praef. 6.
[5] *Prov.* 1. 5.
[6] *V.B.* 26. 7.
[7] Cf. E. Benz, op cit., p. 85 f.
[8] *Ep.* 67. 9, 10.

back with satisfaction and pride on his life, which, according to Tacitus, he was capable of referring to as the finest possession he would leave behind him. When the centurion, who had notified him of his duty to depart this life, refused him permission to make a will, he turned to his friends and declared that now he was forbidden to express his thanks for their services he would leave them his one remaining possession, which was at the same time his finest, the image of his life, *imago vitae suae.*

> ... if they kept the remembrance of that always before their minds, they would gain a reputation for virtuous conduct, as well as for faithful friendship. When they burst into tears, he restored their composure, by alternately soothing and, as it were, rebuking them. 'Where' he asked, 'were their precepts of philosophy. Where were the rules prescribing conduct in misfortune which they had studied for so many years?' ...
> ... After speaking in this manner to one and all of those around him, he embraced his wife, and abating for a moment a little of the stern fortitude which sustained him, tenderly begged and prayed her to abstain from the indulgence of everlasting grief, and to try to find in the contemplation of a virtuous life, a noble consolation which might mitigate her poignant sorrow for the loss of her husband. 1

Anyone who can refer to the *imago vitae suae* as the *unum pulcherrimum,* anyone who can recommend the contemplation of his *vita per virtutem acta* as a source of consolation must be highly aware of his own virtue.

When we turn to Paul after reading Seneca's clamorous glorification of human virtue, we are struck by a strange silence surrounding this word, a silence which is only once broken by the mention of the word ἀρετή in Phil. 4 : 8. However, this silence is not really so strange as it first seems if we bear in mind the fundamental anthropocentricity of the word 'virtue', which focusses attention upon the excellence, merits and achievements of mankind rather than upon God's deeds, with which the Bible is primarily concerned. We may indeed say the whole Bible. For it is not only in the Pauline epistles that we remark the almost complete absence of the word 'virtue' but throughout the whole of the New Testament. While it is noteworthy that the Old Testament has no equivalent for the Greek word ἀρετή. 2 It is only Hellenisticly influenced Judaism that adopts the word. Philo's writings, for example,

---

1 Tacitus, *Ann.* 15. 62, 63.
2 Bultmann points this out repeatedly: R. Bultmann, *Glauben und Verstehen,* 1933, p. 232; *Theologie des N.T.,* 1948, p. 72; *Das Urchristentum im Rahmen der antiken Religionen,* 1949, p. 48 f.

are full of it. He is, however, never able to derive it from Old Testament texts, but introduces it by way of his lengthy allegories, with the aid of which he transplants Biblical words into quite a different climate of ideas. 1 The mere fact that 'virtue' is a central ethical notion in Philo proves that he was estranged from the essential message of the books of the Old Testament, in spite of his obvious familiarity with them and the sincerity of his desire to point out to his contemporaries the significance of the Old Testament for them. 2

As is known the word ἀρετή occurs very rarely in the New Testament, to be precise four times, and in two of these cases it refers to God. In both these places it is better not to translate it with 'virtue' but with 'wonderful deeds' (1 Pet. 2 : 9) and with 'excellence' (2 Pet. 1 : 3). It is only used twice in connection with human virtue (Phil. 4 : 8; 2 Pet. 1 : 5). This is indeed extremely little. In the gospels it does not occur at all, in the Pauline epistles once. Its absence is exceptionally striking if one approaches the New Testament with Seneca's writings in mind, which we have seen to abound in lengthy commentaries on *virtus*.

Of course it may be argued that the absence of the word does not necessarily imply the absence of the notion. This is indeed so, as has been pointed out repeatedly. In the case of Paul Gal. 5 : 22 ff. has for instance been mentioned side by side with Phil. 4 : 8. However, if one is going to discuss Gal. 5 : 22 ff. under the heading "virtue', which word is taken as comprising various virtues, one must certainly not forget that one is using a word which does not occur in the text itself. If one wishes to deal with what Paul terms 'the fruit of the Spirit' under the heading 'virtues and virtue' one must bear in mind that his choice of words is by no means insignificant and that by employing other words one can easily be misled. For it is indisputable that 'virtue' has an anthropocentric connotation of human excellence and achievement. In Paul the term 'the Spirit' is most certainly devoid of this, indicative as it is of the whole salvation-occurrence and eschatological background. 3 Anyone who places Paul's words: 'If we live by the

1 E.g. *Fuga inv.* 58 (Deut. 30 : 15); *Det. pot.* 70 (Gen. 4 : 10). In neither of these texts themselves does the word 'virtue' occur.

2 Hence Philo frequently makes statements about virtue which are strongly reminiscent of Seneca, e.g. when he emphasizes, as he does repeatedly, that a virtuous life is possible, and that virtue and happiness belong together, cf. J. N. Sevenster, *Het verlossingsbegrip bij Philo*, 1936, p. 51 ff.

3 Gerard Brom, *Gesprek over de eenheid van de kerk*, 1946, p. 104, mentions Phil. 4 : 8 and Gal. 5 : 22 ff. as texts where the concept 'virtue' occurs. Likewise

Spirit, let us also walk by the Spirit' (Gal. 5 : 25), on well-nigh equal
footing with *vita per virtutem acta* about which Seneca wrote so pro-
lificly during his life and which when about to die he was bold enough
to point out to his wife as a source of consolation, does not realize that
he is transposing Paul's words into quite a different key, and one which
will form a jarring discord in his preaching as a whole.

Is the view expressed here one which will demand alteration after
careful reading of the only passage in which Paul does use the word
ἀρετή:

> Finally, brethren, whatever is true, whatever is honorable, whatever is
> just, whatever is pure, whatever is lovely, whatever is gracious, if there
> is any excellence [ἀρετή], if there is anything worthy of praise, think
> about these things (Phil. 4 : 8).

Is it possible to say on the strength of this verse:

> The Apostle has not only availed himself of a notion inherent in the
> culture of his day. He has also commended it to his Christians. 1

That this is the only time Paul uses the word ἀρετή is not the only
remarkable feature of this passage. By Paul the word σεμνός is used
only here and in the Pastoral Epistles, while the words προσφιλής and
εὔφημος occur nowhere else in the New Testament. 2 Neither are 'true'
ἀληθής and 'just' δίκαιος used in the sense in which Paul almost always
uses them. It is probable that he has here taken these words over from
popular moral philosophy, and also used ἀρετή because it was a notion
familiar to his contemporaries. 3

The question now suggests itself whether, together with these words,

---

G. Brillenburg Wurth, *Eerherstel van de deugd*, 1958, p. 61, deals with Gal. 5 : 22
under the heading 'virtue', even though he is fully conscious of the fact that the word
'virtue' had a very specific meaning and connotation in the non-Biblical world: in the
Stoic school p. 21 f., in connection with the Old Testament p. 44, in the N.T. pp. 82,
98-101. This being so, why one may ask does not the writer preserve the Biblical
terminology, and why does he plead so emphatically for 'the rehabilitation of
virtue'?

1 W. K. M. Grossouw, *Sint Paulus en de beschaving van zijn tijd*, 1947, p. 15; on
p. 22, note 66, he records that the commentators differ in their appreciation, and
he does not consider it so surprising that the Protestant writers are, on the whole,
more reluctant to recognize this positive acceptance of Hellenistic culture.

2 εὐφημία occurs in 2 Cor. 6 : 8.

3 E. Haupt, *Die Gefangenschaftsbriefe*, 81902, p. 166; S. Greydanus, *De brief van
de apostel Paulus aan de gemeente te Philippi*, 1937, p. 323; R. Bultmann, *Theologie
des N.T.*, 1948, pp. 72, 117; id., *Glauben und Verstehen*, Vol. 3, 1960, p. 160;
S. Wibbing, *Die Tugend- und Lasterkataloge im Neuen Testament*, 1959, p. 80. 83 f.,
101 ff., 118 f.

Paul has also taken from Hellenism part of the contemporary moral code. Some scholars answer this question in the affirmative. 1 And it would indeed seem from the choice of words that Paul is here recommending to his readers a moral principle which was also esteemed as an ideal in their Graeco-heathen environment; he does not, however, place such a principle on a completely equal level with the life in Christ, and according to the Spirit. It has sometimes been thought that the way in which Paul expresses himself here is indicative of the relative inferiority which he attributes to this common moral principle. (1) 'Finally', τὸ λοιπόν would indicate that after the climax in verse 7 he is about to descend to something of lesser importance. 2 However, this is unlikely. Paul is fond of using this expression when concluding a section, and particularly when this is close to the end of the entire letter. 3 (2) In verse 8 the appeal is worded differently from in vers 9: in verse 8 he urges his readers to 'think about these things', in verse 9 he commands them: 'What you have learned and received and heard and seen in me, do'. Although the difference in phraseology, ταῦτα λογίζεσθε (v. 8) and ταῦτα πράσσετε (v. 9) is indeed notable, too great a significance ought not to be attached to it. After all, verse 8 is not intended as an incitement to reflection without deeds. 4 What may be gathered from the fact that this is followed immediately by verse 9 is that obedience to 'what you have learned and received and heard and seen in me' is what is ultimately of most importance for the Church. This also means that the action-provoking meditation of verse 8 should always be viewed in the light of verse 9. As Christians, instructed by Paul in the life and fellowship in Christ, the Philippians must of course remain critical towards heathen culture and morality as this is described here. This is perhaps also implied in the λογίζεσθε of verse 8. In this we hear 'an appeal to an independent moral judgment, to thoughtfully estimate the value of things'. 5 From Paul they will

---

1 M. Dibelius in Lietzmann's *Handbuch zum Neuen Testament, Die neun kleinen Briefe*, 1913, p. 62 f.: 'Es liegt nahe, hier ein Stück populärer Moralphilosophie zu finden'; E. Haupt, op. cit., p. 166: 'Wie nach Röm 13,9 die christliche Sittlichkeit sämtliche Forderungen des A.T. einschliesst, so auch nach unserer Stelle sämtliche Forderungen der natürlichen Moral.'

2 Cf. K. Barth, *Erklärung des Philipperbriefes*, ⁵1947, p. 122.

3 Phil 3 : 1; 2 Cor. 13 : 11; 1 Thess. 4 : 1; 2 Thess. 3 : 1; cf. E. Lohmeyer, *Die Briefe an die Philipper, Kolosser und Philemon*, 1956, p. 172.

4 'Es ist nicht die Art des Paulus, seine Gemeinden — am wenigsten am Briefschluss — nur zum Nachdenken aufzufordern. Die Gemeinde soll nachdenken, wie sie Gutes *tut*', Heidland, art. λογίζεσθαι *Th. W.* IV, p. 291 f.

5 M. R. Vincent, *Epistles to the Philippians and to Philemon*, ³1922, p. 139.

doubtless also have learnt that for Christians that life and fellowship, as it is here formulated with the aid of terms taken from Greek moral philosophy, entails obedience to God's commandments, an obedience which in them proceeds from belonging to Christ and from the possession of the Spirit which is at work in the Church. And so it is that there is something rather provisional about verse 8: in appealing to the Philippians Paul takes into account their environment in order to obtain every possible support and understanding for what he wishes to say in verse 9. The interpretation of this verse given in Lightfoot's old commentary is not unjustified:

> 'Whatever value may reside in your old heathen conception of virtue, whatever consideration is due to the praise of men'; as if the Apostle were anxious not to omit any possible ground of appeal. Thus Beza's remark on ἀρετή seems to be just; 'Verbum nimis humile, si cum donis Spiritus Sancti comparetur.' [1]

Paul is indeed seeking to add strength to his ethical exhortation — his readers should be mindful of the world in which they live (Phil. 2 : 15, 16) — by reminding the Philippians of the ideals of their fellowmen, ideals which were theirs too before they were converted to Christianity. In all events they should not fail to live up to these. Hence ἀρετή is not a word which Paul uses to describe the evangelical ethics which he himself preaches, but a word by means of which he alludes to 'your old heathen conception of virtue', to what his followers once called virtue, or what the world around them still calls virtue. Thus only can be explained the sudden and unique appearance of this word here, since otherwise: 'St Paul seems studiously to avoid this common heathen term for moral excellence, for it occurs in this passage only'. [2] Therefore an undue burden is being placed on this verse by those who wish to read in it the Apostle's estimation of the culture and morality of his time. It is furthermore not without significance for an assessment of the value attached to 'virtue' in this passage that it is not mentioned as *the* central notion but as one among many. [3] All acclaim of virtue as the basis of the perfect and happy life, such as is repeatedly encountered in Seneca, is utterly foreign to Paul.

Just as virtue itself is essentially an anthropocentric notion, so also are the individual virtues that are frequently deemed by the Stoic

---

[1] J. B. Lightfoot, *Saint Paul's Epistle to the Philippians*, ²1956, p. 162.
[2] J. B. Lightfoot, op. cit., p. 162.
[3] This is pointed out by E. Lohmeyer, op. cit., p. 175.

philosophers to be the principal virtues. These too — wisdom, bravery, equanimity, and justice — centre primarily around man. One of them, *bravery,* is quite often mentioned by Seneca; while in Paul it, or rather the word denoting it, never once occurs. That Seneca makes frequent use of the word *fortitudo* is to be expected. It is appropriate to his moral philosophy as a whole, and it is not difficult to visualize what he understands by *fortitudo.* A few passages from his writings are sufficient illustration of it:

> Bravery is the virtue that scorns legitimate dangers, or knowing how to ward off, to meet and to court dangers. [1] Bravery despises and challenges danger. The most beautiful and the most admirable part of bravery is that it does not shrink from the stake, advances to meet wounds, and sometimes does not even avoid the spear, but meets it with opposing brest. [2]
>
> Bravery is a scorner of things which inspire fear; it looks down upon, challenges, and crushes the powers of terror and all that would drive our freedom under the yoke. [3]
>
> Teach me, not whether Bravery be a living thing, but prove that no living thing is happy without bravery, that is unless it has grown strong to oppose hazards and has overcome all the strokes of chance by rehearsing and anticipating their attack. And what is Bravery? It is the impregnable fortress for our mortal weakness; when a man has surrounded himself therewith, he can hold out free from anxiety during life's siege; for he is using his own strength and his own weapons. At this point I would quote you a saying of our philosopher Posidonius: "There are never any occasions when you need think yourself safe because you wield the weapons of Fortune; fight with your own! Fortune does not furnish arms against herself; hence men equipped against their foes are unarmed against Fortune herself." [4]

These quotations are sufficient to conjure up for us the picture of the life inspired by bravery: it is the picture of the man who is intrepid in the face of all of life's contingencies, who is unmoved by his experiences, sometimes even proudly challenging fate, who safe in the strong fortress of his own *fortitudo* calmly awaits all attacks from without, since his fortress is impregnable. He does not fight with the weapons provided by fate, but with his own, with which he has furnished himself. Thus is he able to look down upon the repeated attacks of fate with self-confident contempt.

Notable but not surprising is the fact that the Greek equivalent for

---

[1] *Ben.* ii. 34. 3.
[2] *Ep.* 67. 6.
[3] *Ep.* 88. 29.
[4] *Ep.* 113. 27, 28.

fortitudo, ἀνδρεία, does not occur in Paul or in the whole of the New Testament. It was not until later that the word or one of its derivatives was introduced into Christian writings; in some it is only encountered once (1 *Clem.* 55. 3), in others several times, as for example in the *Pastor Hermae*. In Paul not only the notion is lacking, but also its basis. For bravery is a human quality which places a man and his relationship to himself in the centre of interest, confronting him with his fellow men and fate; it is founded upon unwavering self-confidence and the belief that one's own strength will prevail, and therefore upon the premise of human greatness.

Nevertheless we are more than justified in saying that, from an anthropocentric viewpoint Paul's letters tell of heroic struggles, bravery and incredible courage. But even when these qualities manifest themselves most clearly and as a matter of course, Paul never seeks to express them in terms of the Stoic doctrine of virtue, because his attention is never focussed upon man, but upon the salvation in Christ. Therefore where Seneca would speak of *fortitudo*, we find in Paul's letters those expressions which refer pointedly to the salvation-occurrence, and which for this reason do not revolve around man: to take up the cross, to be crucified, to die and rise again with Christ, [1] endurance and steadfastness in afflictions, the afflictions which are a constant reminder to the Church that it is living in the decisive era of time. For the Stoic, endurance, which is comparable with Seneca's *pati*, would be part of that inner strength striven after by the brave man. A strong soul accepts suffering unmoved, bearing it with its own strength. In Paul ὑπομονή is used in a different sense; it is closely connected with hope; suffering may be endured, because one has hope and a fixed belief in the last things. It is the 'steadfastness of hope in our Lord Jesus Christ' (1 Thess. 1 : 3), 'the steadfastness of Christ' (2 Thess. 3 : 5). Christians have still to endure suffering in an often hostile world, in an atmosphere of disbelief, not, however, in passive acquiescence, but in the certain knowledge of what has already been seen and therefore also of the coming salvation. This certain knowledge gives birth to unheard of bravery, but this is never referred to as such because it is never man's greatness which Paul admires, instead he marvels at God's great deeds.

If Paul speaks of being 'always of good courage', it is clear from the context that he is convinced that he need never lose courage because he

---

[1] Gal. 2 : 19; 5 : 24; 6 : 14; Rom. 6.

is completely sure of salvation in Christ in the present and future, and not because he can place his trust in something in himself. Those who already have the Spirit as a 'guarantee', and the prospect of being 'at home with the Lord', need never lose courage (2 Cor. 5 : 5-10).

Accordingly, the sufferings experienced by the Apostles and the members of the Church are never described in order to honour the courageous man. The individual can never be of prime importance to anyone for whom the history of salvation in Christ is central. Hence it is incorrect to compare Paul's words, 'We are afflicted in every way, but not crushed; perplexed, but not driven to despair; persecuted, but not forsaken; struck down, but not destroyed' (2 Cor. 4 : 8, 9) with those of a wise man who is impervious to insult and undaunted by ordeals. To do so is to lose sight of the difference between the mental climate of the Stoa and the foundation upon which Paul's message lies.[1]

Paul knows that he shares in the sufferings of the Apostles and of the entire Church.[2] But in addition — and this is of prime importance — these sufferings are endured in fellowship with Christ, and this is why they are accepted gladly and courageously. Paul knows that he belongs to a very special generation, the generation of those 'upon whom the end of the ages has come' (1 Cor. 10 : 11). It is characteristic of the close of the age that it offers many trials and afflictions to those who belong to Christ, whose life, death and resurrection form a decisive turning-point in the close of the age (Col. 1 : 26). Now that the end of time has been ushered in, the suffering that is an attribute of that time has also begun. Thus this suffering assumes a definite meaning. This eschatological suffering which was inaugurated by the suffering and death of Jesus Christ is continued in the suffering of those who belong to Him.[3]

The certain knowledge that all the sufferings, that he has voluntarily taken upon himself, are precisely what unites him with Christ in the close of the age, gives to the Apostle the incredible courage which he displays in the face of afliction; from this it also becomes understandable why he never does and never can use the word ἀνδρεία, bravery, namely because this word inevitably draws attention to something which Paul never contemplates: the magnificence of suffering and struggling man.

---

[1] As e.g. Dom Jacques Dupont O.S.B., op. cit., p. 117 ff.
[2] 1 Cor. 4 : 9; 2 Cor. 1 : 6 f.; Phil. 1 : 29, 30.
[3] 2 Cor. 4 : 17, 18; 1 Thess. 3 : 3, 4; Rom. 14 : 7, 8; 8 : 17; Phil. 3 : 10 f.; Gal. 6 : 17; Col. 1 : 24; 2 Cor. 1 : 3-7.

This may be more fully illustrated by the contrasting ways in which the same image is used by Seneca and Paul. It has already been seen how Seneca uses the image of the warrior in connection with his ideas on *fortitudo*. [1] This image recurs frequently both in his letters and in his other writings:

> Life, Lucilius, is really a battle. For this reason those who are tossed about at sea, who proceed uphill and downhill over toilsome crags and heights, who go on campaigns that bring the greatest danger, are heroes and front-rank fighters; but persons who live in rotten luxury and ease while others toil, are mere turtle-doves — safe only because men despise them. [2]

In the opening lines of another letter he reminds Lucilius that by solemnly promising to be a good man, he has sworn an oath of allegiance which is the strongest chain between himself and 'a sound understanding', *bona mens*. A little further on Seneca goes on to elaborate the image by saying that, while there are men who lower their weapons and plead for mercy, the brave man does not do this; instead he dies erect and unyielding. [3]

Comfortable winter-quarters were Hannibal's ruin:

> his pampering in Campania took the vigour out of that hero who had triumphed over Alpine snows. He conquered with his weapons, but was conquered by his vices. We too have a war to wage, a type of warfare in which there is allowed no rest or furlough. To be conquered, in the first place, are pleasures, which, as you see, have carried off even the sternest characters.

Hence, unlike Hannibal, we should never give up the struggle temporarily, and surrender to physical comfort, for by doing so we endanger the victory. [4]

A man must use his reason both in order to endure prosperity well and in order to face adversity bravely. In both situations he should behave like a soldier:

> That man may be just as brave who sleeps in front of the ramparts without fear of danger when no enemy attacks the camp, as the man, who, when the tendons of his legs have been severed, holds himself up on his knees and does not let fall his weapons; but it is to the blood-stained soldier returning from the front that men cry: "Well done, thou hero!" [5]

---

[1] *Ep.* 67. 6; 113. 27, 28.
[2] *Ep.* 96. 5.
[3] *Ep.* 37. 1, 2, oath of allegiance, *sacramento rogatus*, Ep. 65. 18 also.
[4] *Ep.* 51. 6, 7.
[5] *Ep.* 66. 50.

We must arm ourselves against the vicissitudes of fate; our inner lives must be transformed into an impregnable fortress. The only weapon strong enough to resist the enemy, fate, is reason. [1] Therefore:

> gird yourself about with philosophy, an impregnable wall. Though it be assaulted by many engines, Fortune can find no passage into it. The soul stands on unassailable ground, if it has abandoned external things; it is independent in its own fortress; and every weapon that is hurled falls short of the mark. [2]

Sometimes it is the good soldier's obedience to duty which is held up as an example:

> That which you cannot reform, it is best to endure, and to attend un-complainingly upon the God under whose guidance everything progresses; for it is a bad soldier who grumbles when following his commander. [3]

The realization that he himself is not strong enough and must therefore seek the support of wise men causes Seneca to compare himself with a soldier who has sought and found refuge in a well-armed camp. Of these wise men he can say:

> They have ordered me to stand ever watching, like a soldier placed on guard and to anticipate all the attempts and all the assaults of Fortune long before she strikes. [4]
> Great men rejoice oft-times in adversity, as do brave soldiers in warfare. [5]
> It is for the common good to have the best men become soldiers, so to speak, and do service. [6]

Sometimes virtue too is forced to retreat before fate, but this should be a gradual retreat without surrendering the standards or the honour of a soldier. [7]

The wise man is accordingly sufficiently well-armed for life's battle:

> Nature has given to us an adequate equipment in reason; we need no other implements. This is the weapon she has bestowed; it is strong, enduring, obedient, not double-edged or capable of being turned against its owner. Reason is all-sufficient in itself, serving not merely for counsel, but for action as well. [8]

---

[1] *Ep.* 74. 19, 21.
[2] *Ep.* 82. 5.
[3] *Ep.* 107. 9; cf. *Ep.* 120. 12; *V.B.* 15. 5.
[4] *Helv.* 5. 2, 3.
[5] *Prov.* 4. 4.
[6] *Prov.* 5. 1.
[7] *Tranqu. an.* 4. 1; cf. 8. 9.
[8] *Ira* i. 17. 2.

We are indeed justified in saying: 'von militärischen Wörtern und Bildern sind alle Schriften Senecas durchzogen'. [1]

Seneca's frequent use of images drawn from military life has often given rise to comparison with Paul. [2] It is indeed true that such images occur in Paul as well, not only in the Pastoral Epistles, [3] but also in those letters generally accepted as genuine. Sometimes they are only in the form of brief allusions, but now and then they are elaborated in some detail. [4]

There is, however, not the slightest reason to assume that Paul has derived this imagery from the Stoic school. On the contrary, it is made clear by Eph. 6 that if there is a source to which he is endebted, it is the Old Testament. The allusion to Isa. 11 : 5; 59 : 16 f.; 52 : 7 is so obvious that the derivation at least of Eph. 6 may be considered as proven. As far as the choice of words is concerned Paul could also have been influenced by Wisd. of Sol. 5 : 17 ff., but since the allusions to Deutero-Isaiah are numerous elsewhere in Paul it is unnecessary to think of the Wisdom of Solomon in particular. In all events the similarity to passages in Deutero-Isaiah is so striking that Stoic influence need not be contemplated. Furthermore the use of this image is so natural and so widespread in the works of many writers that there is no reason to doubt the spontaneity with which it occurs in different places and entirely different mental climates.

But even though we may reject the possibility of influence it is nevertheless worthwhile determining whether there is an analogy between Seneca's and Paul's application of this imagery. It soon becomes apparent that this is not the case. In Seneca the image of the soldier is used in connection with the man who bears all the vicissitudes of fate

---

[1] Pohlenz, *Stoa* I, p. 314; cf. C. C. Grollios, op. cit., p. 46 f.

[2] F. C. Baur quotes, for example, Fleury who compares Paul's exhortation to Timothy: 1 Tim. 1 : 18; 2 Tim. 2 : 3 f. with *Ep.* 96. 5. (*vivere militare est*) and *Ep.* 61. 6 (*Ep.* 51. 6 is meant), *Zeitschrift für wissenschaftliche Theologie*, 1858, p. 443. Kreyher, too, p. 93 f., partly in imitation of Fleury, mentions *Ep.* 51. 6; 65. 18; 37. 1 side by side with 2 Tim. 2 : 3, 1 Tim. 6 : 12 (Heb. 12 : 1, 4), 2 Tim. 4 : 7. Lightfoot, p. 287, lists among the 'coincidences with St. Paul': 'that Seneca, like the Apostle to the Gentiles, compares life to a warfare (*Ep.* 96; 51; 65; 120. 12) or describes the struggle after good as a "contest with the flesh" (*Marc.* 24).' Carl Clemen, op. cit., p. 412, includes the similes from army life among the possible borrowings from the Stoics. Dibelius also mentions in his excursus to Eph. 6 : 10 ff.: 'Das Bild von der Waffenrüstung des Frommen', a parallel from Seneca's writings: Ep. 107. 9: *malus miles est, qui imperatorem gemens sequitur, Handbuch zum Neuen Testament, Die neun kleinen Briefe*, 1913, p. 123.

[3] 1 Tim. 1 : 18; 6 : 12; 2 Tim. 2 : 3 f.; 4 : 7.

[4] Rom. 6 : 23; 13 : 12; 1 Cor. 9 : 7; 2 Cor. 10 : 4, 5; 1 Thess. 5 : 8; Eph. 6 : 10-20.

in a manly fashion, who wages war with his own passions resolutely, who even rejoices in misfortune like a soldier in war, who accepts all ordeals as orders, who bears all set-backs as a soldier does his wounds, and who is capable of such conduct because he has made his inner life an impregnable fortress, and has surrounded himself by the love of reason and philosophy as by a wall which no enemy can successfully storm. Nature herself has provided him with the weapon of reason, so that it is his own weapon with which he can attack all his enemies.

If we compare this with Eph. 6 : 10-18 where Paul elaborates the image of a battle most fully, we see that a deep gulf exists between the two ways in which the image is applied. In the first place Paul's battle is not against the vicissitudes of fate or human passions but 'against the principalities, against the powers, against the world rulers of this present darkness, against the spiritual hosts of wickedness in the heavenly places' (Eph. 6 : 12). Even if this struggle assumes the form of a tangible struggle against human beings, or sometimes perhaps against what Seneca terms the vicissitudes of fate or the passions, Paul sees this solely as an outward manifestation of the struggle against the 'powers'. It is in this struggle that the Christian has a part to play, but there would be no question of his being able to hold his ground if his only source of power were his own human strength of will. No, he can only be strong, gain strength (ἐνδυναμοῦσθε v. 10) 'in the Lord and in the strength of his might.' It is only this strength which can bestow upon the believer a complete set of armour (πανοπλία vv. 11 and 13). It is only in this sense that the armour lies ready for use, and only has to be taken up (ἀναλάβετε v. 13) 'that you may be able to withstand in the evil day, and having done all, to stand.' All the weapons are, without exception, weapons which man *receives*, not ones he has by nature: his girdle is truth, his breastplate righteousness, his feet are shod for battle in the gospel of peace, his shield is faith, his helmet salvation, his sword which is handed to him by the Spirit, the word of God (Eph. 6 : 14-17).

It has occasionally been pointed out that the type of weapons mentioned here would indicate that Paul envisages the believers to be on the defensive rather than the offensive:

Although the believer must put up a conscious resistance against the powers, there is no other way for him to do so than by simply being strong in faith. He does not need to do more than he is thus able to do. He does not have to defeat the powers. That is the work of Jesus Christ Himself. He has provided for that and will continue to do so. We have merely been called to play a defensive role, because Christ will take care of the offensive. 1

This is reasoned from the very heart of Paul's preaching of the Gospel; it is surely not accidental that the stress here lies completely upon defensive weapons such as girdles, breastplates, footwear, shields and helmets and not upon weapons of attack such as lances, spears, bows and arrows. If 'sword' is taken to refer to the short sword, a defence weapon, in contrast to the broadsword, a weapon of attack, then Eph. 6 could be said to list defence weapons solely. It is, however, incorrect to say that μάχαιρα which is used in Eph. 6, only applies to the former and ῥομφαία only to the latter. Such an assertion by no means holds good in the Septuagint. 2

But be this as it may, it is clear that Paul and Seneca do not attach the same meaning to this image. Seneca uses it in connection with the self-reliant warrior, while Paul applies it to the man who in Christ and in the Spirit receives everything from God. 3

Whereas the word denoting the first mentioned of the four principal Stoic virtues, bravery, occurs frequently in Seneca and not at all in Paul, the word for one of the other virtues, *wisdom*, is used by both writers. It will now be clear what Seneca chiefly means by wisdom: it is a notion that he for the most part uses in a practical ethical sense in order to indicate a particular attitude towards life. Hence it is to be expected that it is frequently linked with the other principal notions familiar to us from Seneca's writings. Wisdom is living in accordance with nature:

> Not to stray from Nature and to mould ourselves according to her law and pattern — this is true wisdom. 4 This is wisdom — a return to Nature and a restoration to the condition from which man's errors have driven us. 5 Wisdom is the perfect good of the human mind. 6

Wisdom is the virtue which leads to the imperturbable, inwardly inviolable life which places its trust in reason, and finds support therein. 7 The wise man, the perfect man who is full of human and

---

1 H. Berkhof, *Christus en de machten*, p. 51.

2 Cf. *Th. W.* IV. 530 f.

3 The same contrast emerges if we compare Seneca and Paul with each other in their use of metaphors pertaining to athletics; cf. e.g. *Ep.* 15. 5; 78. 16; 80. 3; *Tranqu. an.* 3. 1; 9. 3; *Const.* 9. 5; *Ira* ii. 14. 2 with 1 Cor. 9 : 24-27; Phil. 3 : 14; 1 Tim. 6 : 12; 2 Tim. 4: 7.

4 *V.B.* 3.3.

5 *Ep.* 94. 68.

6 *Ep.* 89. 4.

7 *Const.* 8. 2, 3.

divine virtues [1] is 'the pedagogue of the human race.' [2] Hence wisdom is something constant, because the wise man always remains the same. [3] Like the gods, the wise man reigns over the whole world without recourse to weapons, and is raised far above the world in serene unassailability. [4] 'The wise man is next-door neighbour to the gods and like a god in all save his mortality.' [5]

Wisdom has, accordingly, a practical application. It is innate in the perfect man who unites in himself all virtues, whose own excellence always fills him with serene joy [6] and who is like the gods in his inner inviolability. Seneca indeed lauds the wise man to the skies. He takes a continual delight in glorifying this ideal man and describing him in lyrical terms. Of Seneca too we are justified in saying that the wise man is, as it were, the sole subject and true aim of his philosophy. [7]

Paul would doubtless have considered the wisdom of the self-sufficient man to be that of the natural man, which he condemns harshly and repeatedly as carnal, human wisdom, wisdom of this age and world. [8] It is precisely this wisdom, according to the flesh that is put to shame by God. [9]

Opposed to the carnal wisdom of this world is the true wisdom. This has its roots in the wisdom of God Himself. This wisdom of God's is to be seen in God's revelation for man's salvation, and in God's ways with His people and His Church. [10] Thus Christ may be called the wisdom of God (1 Cor. 1 : 24).

By virtue of this Paul is able to speak of the wisdom which has been given to the Church, because God has revealed His wisdom to it. Members of the Church are therefore able to instruct each other in that wisdom. [11] It has a bearing upon God's will for salvation, [12] and upon Christ 'whom God made our wisdom' (1 Cor. 1 : 30), 'in whom are hid all the treasures of wisdom and knowledge' (Col. 2 : 3). It is in this sense that a church can be exhorted to conduct itself wisely

---

[1] *Const.* 6. 8.
[2] *Ep.* 89. 13.
[3] *Ep.* 20. 5.
[4] *Ben.* vii. 3. 2.
[5] *Const.* 8. 2.
[6] *Ep.* 59. 16.
[7] Ulrich Wilckens, op. cit., p. 257, says this of the Stoic philosophy in general.
[8] 2 Cor. 1 : 12; 1 Cor. 2 : 5, 6, 13; 3 : 19.
[9] 1 Cor. 1 : 26, 27; cf. 3 : 18-20; Rom. 1 : 22, 28.
[10] Rom. 11 : 33; 1 Cor. 2 : 7; Eph. 3 : 10.
[11] Col. 1 : 28; 3 : 16.
[12] Eph. 1 : 8, 9; Col. 1 : 9.

(Col. 4 : 5). This wisdom is the gift which is given to the Church with God's works of salvation and the possession of the Spirit. [1]

Being wise is only praised in Paul if it springs from this wisdom. It has already been seen that he frequently uses the word unfavourably. And it is remarkable, though scarcely surprising, that in the only place where the word 'philosophy' occurs in his letters, it is used unfavourably (Col. 2 : 8). Occasionally the word σοφός is rather neutral in tone, [2] while in Eph. 5 : 15 it is decidedly favourable. But of one thing the Apostle is certain: a man must first surrender what he looks upon as wisdom and become foolish, before he can become truly wise (1 Cor. 3 : 18). If a man is not wise by virtue of the wisdom granted by the only wise God (Rom. 16 : 27), then his wisdom extends no further than carnal, human wisdom, the wisdom of this world.

Hence the true wisdom is indissolubly linked with the deeds of the self-revealing God. Upon this God man is utterly dependent as far as his true wisdom is concerned. He has no wisdom in himself. Therefore this wisdom is diametrically opposed to the wisdom of the perfect man who unites all virtues within him, the wisdom which is founded upon reason, upon living according to nature, as it is proclaimed in the writings of Seneca.

---

[1] 1 Cor. 12 : 8; Eph. 1 : 8, 17; Col. 1 : 9.
[2] Rom. 1 : 14; 1 Cor. 3 : 10; 6 : 5; Rom. 16 : 19.

CHAPTER FIVE

SOCIAL RELATIONS

As is the case with Paul and Seneca's ethics concerning the individual one finds, when one compares their social ethics, that so much depends upon the backgrounds against which they write. First the question arises as to what they each consider to be the basis of human society. Seneca sees the individual as part of a vast community, of an organic whole of cosmic dimensions. By means of his reason man is in touch with nature in all its vastness, and by his spirit, which is of divine origin, with a heavenly world which embraces gods and man alike in one great organic whole. For this reason man ought to respect and help his fellows.

Of great importance here is what Seneca says concerning the divine origin of the spirit, which has already been mentioned in our discussion on the relationship between the body and the spirit. Into 'this petty body', *corpusculum*, a 'divine power', *vis divina,* has descended. The soul is moved by 'a force from heaven', *caelestis potentia.*

> Just as the rays of the sun do indeed touch the earth, but still abide at the source from which they are sent; even so the great and hallowed soul, which has come down in order that we may have a nearer knowledge of divinity, does indeed associate with us, but still cleaves to its origin; on that source it depends, thither it turns its gaze and strives to go, and it concerns itself with our doings only as a being superior to ourselves. [1]

Our spirit will have reason to rejoice when it is finally liberated from the darkness in which it finds itself here, and has returned to heaven where it belongs, *redditus caelo suo*, when it has once again assumed the place which is its birth-right. Its origin summons it upward. Even before it is released from its earthly prison it can attain this goal, 'as soon as it has cast off sin and, in purity and lightness, has leaped up into celestial realms of thought.' [2]

It is axiomatic that it is for Seneca but a short step from this belief in the relationship between God and man to the idea of one great coherent whole, a cosmos embracing both the gods and man. In some places his line of thought may be clearly observed:

---

[1] *Ep.* 41. 4, 5.
[2] *Ep.* 79. 12.

"He in whose body virtue dwells, and spirit e'er present", is equal to the gods; mindful of his origin, he strives to return thither. No man does wrong in attempting to regain the heights from which he once came down. And why should you not believe that something of divinity exists in one who is a part of God? All this universe which encompasses us is one, and it is God; we are associates of God; we are his members. 1 All that you behold, that which comprises both god and man, is one — we are the parts of one great body. Nature produced us related to one another, since she created us from the same source and to the same end. She engendered in us mutual affection, and made us prone to friendships [*haec nobis amorem indidit mutuum et sociabiles fecit*]. She established fairness and justice; according to her ruling, it is more wretched to commit than to suffer injury. Through her orders, let our hands be ready for all that needs to be helped. Let this verse be in your heart and on your lips: "I am a man; and nothing in man's lot do I deem foreign to me." Let us possess things in common; for birth is ours in common. Our relations with one another are like a stone arch, which would collapse if the stones did not mutually support each other, and which is upheld in this very way. 2

The work of nature has accordingly made each of us part of one vast community. By nature we are social beings. It goes without saying that all those who belong to that vast harmonious cosmic body help each other. Just as stones in an arch need each other to remain in place, so are we human beings unable to do without one another. Seneca makes use of various images to illustrate this idea: we are all citizens of an even greater fatherland than our earthly one; we are members of one body:

To injure one's country is a crime; consequently, also, to injure a fellow-citizen — for he is a part of the country, and if we reverence the whole, the parts are sacred — consequently to injure any man is a crime, for he is your fellow-citizen in the greater commonwealth. What if the hands should desire to harm the feet, or the eyes the hands? As all the members of the body are in harmony one with another because it is to the advantage of the whole that the individual members be unharmed, so mankind should spare the individual man, because all are born for a life of fellowship, and society can be kept unharmed only by the mutual protection and love of its parts. 3

This image of the world being the wise man's fatherland, the real state of which a human being is a citizen, recurs repeatedly in Seneca.

---

1 *Ep.* 92. 30; Seneca is quoting Virgil, *Aeneid* 5. 363 here.

2 *Ep.* 95. 52, 53; *homo sum, humani nihil a me alienum puto* is a quotation from Terence, *Heautontimorumenos*.

3 *Ira* ii. 31. 7.

There is a *res publica generis humani*. [1] It is the prime endeavour of the Stoics to establish the *societas generis humani*, [2] to promote intercourse with the whole earth, *totius orbis commercium*. Man can claim the *mundus* as his *patria*. [3] The wise man knows himself to be a 'citizen and soldier of the universe'. [4] The universe is the *res publica* which is worthy of the wise man. [5] Hence Seneca exhorts Lucilius: 'Live in this belief: "I am not born for any one corner of the universe; this whole world is my country." ' [6]

Seneca's basic conception of society is clear: it is founded on the bonds existing between all human beings because they are all part of a vast organic whole. They belong together by nature. Accordingly they will help each other by nature: 'What is more loving to others than man? — Man is born for mutual help.' [7] This help should of course be rendered to all without exception:

> Nature bids me do good to all mankind — whether slaves or freemen, freeborn or freed-men, whether the laws gave them freedom or a grant in the presence of friends — what difference does it make? Wherever there is a human being there is the opportunity for a kindness. [8]

Because all are *homines,* members of the same great whole, all are by nature worthy of help, even complete strangers. [9]

If the emphasis thus lies on a *totius orbis commercium* (*Tranqu.* 4. 4), on the *societas generis humani* (*Ben.* i. 15. 2), the *res publica generis humani* (*Const.* 19. 4) on the *unitas generis humani* (*Ben.* iv. 18. 4), if a human being is *in adiutorium mutuum genitus* (*Ira* i. 5. 2), if he like the *sociale animal et in commune genitus mundum ut unam omnium domum spectat* (*Ben.* vii. 1. 7), if an appeal is made to being *civis universi* (*Ep.* 120. 12) it is clear that humanity, *humanitas,* must occupy an important place in Seneca's writing, even if the word itself does not occur very frequently. At the end of the three books on anger Seneca uses the word in a sentence summing up how he thinks a human being should conduct himself: 'so long as we draw breath, so long as

---

1 *Const.* 19. 4.
2 *Ben.* i. 15. 2.
3 *Tranqu an.* 4. 4.
4 *Ep.* 120. 12.
5 *Ep.* 68. 2.
6 *Ep.* 28. 4.
7 *Ira* i. 5. 2: *homo in adiutorium mutuum genitus est.*
8 *V.B.* 24. 3.
9 *Ira* i. 5. 2.

we live among men, let us cherish humanity.' [1] If this is done *humanitas* will inspire human beings in their conduct towards each other. A man acts humanly, and that is to say in a very special, sublime manner, if he feels himself to be a part of that vast whole with whose harmony he then reconciles his own deeds. Once again: since all human beings are part of that whole, they should all be respected not for other qualities or for their rank or class, but because they are members of that great *societas,* the *res publica generis humani.* Whatever else a man may be is unimportant. He remains a man and therefore must be helped. It is in this sense that we must understand 'man, object of reverence in the eyes of man.' [2] Seneca may indeed be looked upon as a representative of the Roman school of Stoic philosophers of whom it has justly been said that they gave the world something which has had a lasting influence. [3]

A suitable starting point for a comparison between Seneca and Paul in this respect is the metaphor of the body used by both of them. It has already been encountered in Seneca: 'all that you behold, that which comprises both god and man, is one — we are the parts of one great body.' [4] While his words are even more strongly reminiscent of Paul's when he holds up the harmony of the limbs of the body as an example to humanity: 'What if the hands should desire to harm the feet, or the eyes the hands?' [5]

It seems no more than natural to recall Paul's frequent use of the same metaphor. [6] Kreyher, for example, places 1 Cor. 12 : 20 ff. and *Ira* ii. 31. 7 side by side as parallels in his section on 'Biblische Anklänge in Seneca's Schriften'. [7] Joh. Weiss feels entitled to say of 1 Cor. 12 : 12 ff.: 'Benützt ist hier ein in der griechisch-römischen

---

[1] *Ira* iii. 43. 5: *colamus humanitatem.* For the word *humanitas* see also *Ep.* 5. 4; 81. 26; 88. 30; 115. 3; *N.Q.* iv. Praef. 18; *humana societas* Ben. i. 4. 2.

[2] *Homo, sacra res homini, Ep.* 95. 33.

[3] H. Wagenvoort in an article on Roman culture in: W. Banning-J. D. Bierens de Haan, *Europeesche geest,* 1939, p. 109; for the notion *humanitas* see also: Max Mühl, *Die antike Menschheitsidee in ihrer geschichtlichen Entwicklung,* 1928; Joh. Mewaldt, 'Das Weltbürgertum in der Antike' in *Die Antike,* 1926, pp. 177-89; the article 'Humanitas' in Pauly's *Real-Encyclopädie der classischen Altertumswissenschaft,* Supplementband, 1931, p. 282 ff.; Karl Büchner, *Humanitas romana,* 1957, especially pp. 271-5; J. L. Koole on the contrast between Christian and Stoic fellowship in *Cultuurgeschiedenis van het Christendom,* I, 1948, p. 423 ff.; Jean Laloup, op. cit., p. 223.

[4] *Ep.* 95. 52.

[5] *Ira* ii. 31. 7.

[6] E.g. Rom. 12 : 3-8; 1 Cor. 12 : 4-27; Eph. 4 : 1-7.

[7] Kreyher, p. 88.

Literatur, besonders in der stoischen Diatribe ungemein häufiger Gemeinplatz', and he makes a reference to *Ira* ii. 31 and *Ep.* 95. 52, passages which he also mentions in his commentary on 1 Cor. 12. [1] Clemen too states in connection with 1 Cor. 12 : 12 ff. that the metaphor of the body 'bei den Stoikern besonders beliebt war', and refers *inter alia* to *Ep.* 95. 52. [2] F. C. Baur already pointed out the coincidence, although he apparently also appreciated the difference in application as he writes:

> Wie also in der christlichen Anschauung Christus das Haupt ist, dessen Leib die Gläubigen sind, oder der Leib, dessen Glieder sie sind, so betrachtet Seneca die Menschheit als einen Leib, in welchem die Einzelnen als Glieder desselben organischen Ganzen begriffen sind, und hier wie dort ist die Liebe das Band, das das Ganze zusammenhält und die Einzelnen im Interesse des Ganzen mit ihm verknüpft. [3]

Joh. Weiss likewise realizes that the fact that they both use the same metaphor by no means necessitates a more fundamental agreement. In discussing 'love' in the Pauline epistles he for instance remarks:

> Wort und Begriff der Menschheit fehlen überhaupt im Neuen Testament. Dies ist vielmehr die Basis der stoischen Menschenliebe.

He then quotes *Ep.* 95. 52 and goes on to say:

> Die christliche Liebespflicht wird von Paulus auch nicht auf natürliche Anlage begründet; sie ist, wie gesagt, eine Auswirkung der erfahrenen Gottesliebe. [4]

Indeed, the very notion Seneca seeks to demonstrate with the aid of this metaphor is completely lacking in Paul. Hence it would apparently seem that the use of this image does not in itself mean so very much; while it is so obvious and in such general use that it is by no means certain that Paul derived it from the Stoics. Seneca too sometimes uses it in a very diferent context, one which is more essentially reminiscent of Paul than *Ep.* 95. 52 and *Ira* ii. 31. 7: if the emperor is kind, he says in his *De Clementia,* this kindness will gradually extend further and further:

---

[1] Joh. Weiss, *Das Urchristentum*, 1917, p. 487; id., *1 Kor.* in Meyer, [10]1925, p. 302.

[2] Carl Clemen, op. cit., p. 326; cf. also E. Käsemann, *Leib und Leib Christi,* 1933, p. 46; John A. T. Robinson, op. cit., p. 59[1].

[3] F. C. von Baur, 'Seneca und Paulus'. *Zeitschrift für wissenschaftliche Theologie,* 1858, p. 211. He quotes *Ira* ii. 31. 7 in this connection.

[4] Joh. Weiss, *Das Urchristentum,* 1917, p. 444 f., note 3; cf. G. A. van den Bergh van Eysinga, *De wereld van het Nieuwe Testament,* 1929, p. 212: 'This idea of humanity is not a motive for love in the New Testament: the notion 'humanity' does not even occur there.'

> That kindness of your heart will be recounted, will be diffused little by
> little throughout the whole body of the empire, and all things will be
> moulded into your likeness. It is from the head that comes the health of
> the body; it is through it that all the parts are lively and alert or languid
> and drooping according as their animating spirit has life or withers. [1]

Here, in the metaphor of the body the head acquires a special significance, such as it has in Paul's letters where Christ is the head. [2]
What is so striking about Paul's use of this metaphor is that he always
applies it to the Church. The Church is the body of Christ or the body
whose head is Christ. Of Him Paul might well have said: 'It is from
the head that comes the health of the body; it is through it that all
the parts are lively and alert', since he too believes that the true life
does not spring from the limbs but that Christ, the head, grants it to
them. He alone can make them grow and give them unity, salvation and
life. He,

> from whom the whole body, joined and knit together by every joint with
> which it is supplied, when each part is working properly, makes bodily
> growth and upbuilds itself in love (Eph. 4 : 16).

The way Paul uses this metaphor is entirely in keeping with his
ideas of fellowship. For him fellowship between men is based upon their
fellowship with Christ. Hence it is characteristic of his conception of
fellowship that he should use the word κοινωνία both for fellowship
with Christ, the faithful partaking in Christ and all his gifts, and for
the fellowship of the faithful among one another. A church is called
into fellowship with the Son (1 Cor. 1 : 9). This fellowship already
exists, although it will not be fully realized until the close of the age.
It is particularly intense at the Lord's Supper (1 Cor. 10 : 16 ff.).
The link between Christ and the Church is most profound at the Lord's
table. And it is axiomatic that those who have experienced this fellowship with Christ are also in mutual fellowship with one another. Col-
lective participation in spiritual goods leads naturally to a willingness
to share earthly ones (Rom. 15 : 26 f.; cf. Phil. 4 : 14). It is not in
human feelings and sympathies that fellowship has its foundations
but in the central event in the life of man. Salvation binds the members of the Church together: the Church is the fellowship of 'those
consecrated in Christ Jesus, called to be saints together with all those
who in every place call on the name of our Lord, both their Lord and

---

[1] *Clem.* ii. 2. 1; *Clem.* i. 5. 1: *tu animus rei publicae tuae es, illa corpus tuum*;
cf. Spanneut, op. cit., p. 388 ff.

[2] 1 Cor. 11: 3; Eph. 1: 22; 4: 15; 5: 23; Col. 2: 10.

ours' (1 Cor. 1 : 2). As 'God's elect' (Rom. 8 : 33), as 'God's chosen ones, holy and beloved' (Col. 3 : 12) they are bound one to another. Their mutual relations are founded upon this fellowship. The love they bear each other has its roots in God's love in Christ (Eph. 4 : 32-5 : 1; 2 Cor. 8 : 9; 1 Cor. 8 : 11).[1]

Seneca's notion of fellowship being based upon such very different premises from Paul's deprives the fact that they both use the same metaphor of much of its significance. It is scarcely worthwhile enumerating those places where Paul uses σῶμα and Seneca *corpus* when their meaning is so disparate. A catalogue of verbal similarities will not contribute to the exegesis of the Pauline epistles.

A question that now arises is whether Paul's conception of fellowship does not differ from Seneca's in that it is more restricted. For Paul continually, or at all events primarily, has in mind the Church, while Seneca is thinking of that vast organic whole in which men are united not as believers but as human beings. Is not fellowship in Paul restricted in a way that is alien to Seneca's broad cosmopolitanism? A comparison along these lines sometimes seems justified. 'Through love be servants of one another' (Gal. 5 : 13) might be understood as an exhortation to love only those within the small compass of the Church. The phrase 'those who are of the household of faith' conjures up the picture of one large family, but when Paul declares 'let us do good to all men, and especially to those who are of the household of faith' (Gal. 6 : 10), visions of the egoism of a closed family circle may be provoked.

Nevertheless it would be incorrect to contrast Seneca's universalism in this respect with narrowness on the part of Paul. If love has its roots in God's work of salvation, it is out of the question that its realization should be confined within narrow bounds. For one whose life is inspired by the belief that 'God was in Christ reconciling the world to himself' (2 Cor. 5 : 19), who sees the work of salvation in a worldwide perspective (Col. 1 : 15 ff.), who knows that it embraces all human beings, the emphasis which is indeed frequently placed upon relations within the Church can never be intended as a fundamental restriction. Proof of this are those passages where Paul declares emphatically that love of one's neighbour — how could it be otherwise using the word 'neighbour' — ought not to be extended to members of the Church only, but to all:

---

[1] Cf. R. Bultmann, *Theologie des Neuen Testaments*, 1948, p. 306.

> May the Lord make you increase and abound in love to one another and
> to all men, as we do to you (1 Thess. 3 : 12). See that none of you
> repays evil for evil, but always seek to do good to one another and to all
> (1 Thess. 5 : 15; cf. Rom. 12 : 17). .

That relations within the Church are usually uppermost in Paul's mind
may be explained first by the fact that his letters are those of an
Apostle to groups for which he holds himself particularly responsible,
and secondly by his belief that this love will and must find its inception and be revealed in the concrete relations in the small Christian
communities within which the love of Christ has to overcome all kinds
of opposition. Paul moreover avoids the pitfall which frequently threatens the superficially broader universalism of Seneca and other Stoics,
namely that 'in its theorizing it remains confined to generalities.' [1]
Of the love of which Paul speaks, it may be said:

> This *caritas* may entail various risks, but one that it avoids is that of
> becoming a "Seid umschungen, Millionen'. For the purely Stoic idea of
> humanity, uninfluenced by Christianity this danger is a real one.' [2]

In addition we repeatedly witness the fact that in Seneca a more
powerful motive for moral conduct breaks through those feelings
which have their roots in *humanitas*. It is often plain that this *humanitas* is ultimately in the service of the ego that wishes at all events
to preserve its inner imperturbability and harmony of life. For this is
the only way of attaining the greatest happiness. Hence every contact
with other human beings, every attachment, every sympathy and love
is bounded by the hallowed egoism of the wise man. If feelings for
others interfere with the almost sacred inner life of the wise man,
they must be repressed. They are only acceptable, if they can contribute to the edification of the life of the wise man.

This is most clearly exemplified by those passages in which Seneca
writes about *friendship*. He has often devoted himself to the theme
of true friendship. He esteems it highly. It forms a bond between fine
minds, between sensible people. If a man chooses his friends carefully
his spiritual life can profit greatly by them:

> Nothing gives the mind so much pleasure as fond and faithful friendship.
> What a blessing it is to have those to whose waiting hearts every secret

---

[1] J. L. Koole, *Cultuurgeschiedenis van het Christendom,* I, 1948, p. 429.

[2] H. Wagenvoort, *Europeesche geest,* 1939 (see p. 170 note 3), p. 109; cf. A.
Juncker, *Die Ethik des Apostels Paulus,* II, 1919, p. 233: '.... immer droht sie [die
stoische Liebe] in der Stimmung jenes allgemeinen ziel- und inhaltlosen Wohlwollens
„Seid umschlungen Millionen" stecken zu bleiben.'

may be committed with safety, whose knowledge of you you fear less than your knowledge of yourself, whose conversation soothes your anxiety, whose opinion assists your decision, whose cheerfulness scatters your sorrow, the very sight of whom gives you joy! 1

But in choosing friends a man must endeavour to choose those free of vices, 'for vices spread unnoticed, and quickly pass to those nearest and do harm by their contact.' As in an epidemic when one must always be on guard against coming into contact with those already infected with a disease, their very breath being dangerous, so also in choosing friends one must take care to choose those 'who are marked with fewest stains; to combine the sick with the sound is to spread disease.' 2 Elsewhere too Seneca uses the same metaphor in order to underline how desirable fastidiousness is in the choice of friends:

Since we do not know how to bear injury, let us endeavour not to receive one. We should live with a very calm and good-natured person — one that is never worried or captious; we adopt our habits from those with whom we associate, and as certain diseases of the body spread to others from contact, so the mind transmits its faults to those nearby. The drunkard lures his boon companions into love of wine; shameless company corrupts even the strong man and, perchance, the hero; avarice transfers its poison to its neighbours. The same principle holds good of the virtues, but with the opposite result — that they ameliorate whatever comes into contact with them; an invalid does not benefit so much from a suitable location or a more healthful climate as does the mind which lacks strength from association with a better company. You will understand what a powerful factor this is if you observe that even wild animals grow tame from intercourse with us, and that all beasts, no matter how savage, after enduring long companionship with man cease to be violent; all their fierceness is blunted and gradually amid peaceful conditions is forgotten. 3

Lucilius is therefore advised:

Withdraw into yourself, as far as you can. Associate with those who will make a better man of you. Welcome those whom you yourself can improve. The process is mutual; for men learn while they teach. 4

Only after due deliberation should someone be accepted as a friend:

Ponder for a long time whether you shall admit a given person to your friendship; but when you have decided to admit him, welcome him witr all your heart and soul. Speak as boldly with him as with yourself. 5

1 *Tranqu. an.* 7. 3.
2 *Tranqu. an.* 7. 3, 4.
3 *Ira* iii. 8. 1-3.
4 *Ep.* 7. 8.
5 *Ep.* 3. 2.

He who recognizes the spiritual blessings of friendship 'will seek either
the perfect wise man or one who has progressed to a point bordering
on perfection.' [1]

It is clear that the pros and cons in human relations are weighed up
carefully. The chances whether a friendship will yield spiritual profit
are precisely calculated. A man must bear in mind the fact that mankind is divided into the wicked, who are infected with vice and consequently easily infect others, and the virtuous who raise everyone
with whom they come into contact to their own spiritual level. It goes
without saying that a man should seek contact only with the latter,
for they alone contribute to the shaping and growth of his personality.
Accordingly Seneca contemplates friendship anthropocentrically, and
even — though with great refinement — egocentrically. Discoursing
on friendship Seneca can give the advice: 'you must live for your
neighbour, if you would live for yourself.' [2] A man's own spiritual
life cannot develop fully if living for others has no part in it.

On the other hand too great an attachment to his fellow men can
at times form a threat to the peace of mind of the wise man. For a man
ought to be able to part from his friends with cheerful acquiescence:

> In this sense the wise man is self-sufficient, that he can do without
> friends, not that he desires to do without them. When I say "can", I
> mean this: he endures the loss of a friend with equanimity. [3]

To be sure, the wise man

> craves as many friends as possible, not, however, that he may live hap-
> pily; for he will live happily even without friends. The Supreme Good
> calls for no practical aids from outside; it is developed at home, and
> arises entirely within itself. If the good seeks any portion of itself
> from without, it begins to be subject to the play of Fortune. [4]

A wise man deems nothing good that can be taken away from him.
He follows the example of Stilbo who lost his wife and children during
the capture of his birthplace and, when asked if he had lost anything,
replied: 'I have all my goods with me, I have lost nothing.' [5]

Seneca knows that true friendship which can be destroyed neither
by hope nor fear nor self-interest, that friendship in which and for
the sake of which men die, in which 'souls are drawn together by

---

[1] *Ep.* 109. 15.
[2] *Ep.* 48. 2.
[3] *Ep.* 9. 5.
[4] *Ep.* 9. 15; cf. *Ep.* 78. 3, 4.
[5] *Ep.* 9. 18, 19.

identical inclinations into an alliance of honourable desires', and in which men 'have all things in common, especially their troubles.' 1 But even this friendship appears to be a relationship between noble, like-minded souls who thus shape each other's spiritual life — 'this community of goods can exist between wise men only' —, 2 and who may not in the last resort be dependent upon the support of such a friendship.

Hence when Seneca seeks to form a clear idea of what friendship is or ought to be, the shaping and perfection of the personality is always uppermost in his thoughts. In a relationship like this regard for one's own personality prevails over going out towards one's fellow man. 3

If one wishes to compare Paul and Seneca on this point it is in the first place significant that Paul never uses the word φίλος or φιλία in his letters. In the introduction to his commentary on First Corinthians James Moffatt says in connection with Paul's arrival in Corinth from Athens: 'There he, who happens never to mention the word "friend", made one of his closest friendships.' 4 He is hereby referring to Paul's sojourn in the house of Aquila and Priscilla in Corinth (Acts 18 : 1-3), who are also mentioned in the list of those to whom the Apostle sends his greetings in Rom. 16 : 3 ff. Paul does not, however, call them 'friends', although he was assuredly closely connected with them for many years of his life. However richly varied the words of praise which he accords to all whom he greets in Rom. 16 may be, the word 'friends' is not among them. And the same may be said of all the Pauline epistles. Outside Paul's letters the word φιλία only once occurs in the New Testament, and then in a figurative sense, and not in connection with a relationship between people (Jas. 4 : 4). Only in Acts is mention once made of the fact that Paul had friends in a church somewhere. 5 It is most striking that Paul himself never uses the word to describe the bond between him and members of the Church, not even when, as in Rom. 16, he is obviously alluding to a

---

1 *Ep.* 6. 2, 3.

2 *Ben.* vii. 12. 2.

3 Cf. de Bovis, op. cit., p. 118: 'L'inspiration générale est nettement égocentrique. La valeur de l'amitié ne semble pas résider dans l'ami lui-même, mais uniquement dans le sage qui exerce la vertu d'amité'; cf. H. Greeven, *Das Hauptproblem der Sozialethik in der neueren Stoa und im Urchristentum,* 1935, p. 150 ff.; Th. Schreiner, op. cit., pp. 106 f., 113 f.

4 James Moffatt, *The First Epistle of Paul to the Corinthians,* 1947, p. xiii.

5 Acts 27 : 3; in Acts 19 : 31 it has another meaning: well-disposed.

very personal relationship. In connection with a number of those persons to whom he there sends his greetings, Phoebe, Prisca and Aquila, Andronicus and Junias, and the mother of Rufus, allusions are made which the recipients of the letter will probably have understood instantly, while we often have to guess at what is referred to. [1] But nowhere does Paul say that, by reason of these apparently very close ties between them, they are his friends, not even where it would be most natural for him to testify to their firm friendship. [2]

It is hard to maintain that this is fortuitous, if one considers that in Rom. 16, as in so many other places, he mentions details concerning his relationship to certain persons which would have automatically occasioned Seneca to eulogize friends and friendship. Even if Paul has not intentionally avoided these words, it is remarkable that he does not use them automatically when he is dealing with such intimate relationships.

Those persons with whom Paul knows himself to have personal ties, are fellow workers, who have come into contact with him through their common task in the service of Jesus Christ. When choosing them he never first investigates their virtuousness, never wonders whether their vices could be detrimental to his spiritual life. He sees all relationships that bind him in some particular way to others in the light of the salvation which has manifested itself in Christ and which has been granted also to him personally. This salvation must be preached. Churches are made up of persons who have received that salvation in faith. Those who belong to these churches are in this capacity saints, called to be saints, consecrated in Christ Jesus (1 Cor. 1 : 2). They are not united on account of their virtues, they have not selected each other in order to profit as much as possible by each other in their spiritual life, but they are 'God's elect' (Rom. 8 : 33), 'God's chosen ones, holy and beloved' (Col. 3 : 12). Therefore Paul can greet one of those mentioned in Rom. 16 as τὸν ἐκλεκτὸν ἐν κυρίῳ (Rom. 16 : 13), and another as 'the first convert in Asia for Christ' (Rom. 16 : 5). He further recalls in this list of greetings work shared by him and his fellow workers in Christ (Rom. 16 : 3, 9). And when he speaks of 'fellow workers' he constantly has in mind his fellow workers in Christ. [3] They are always men and women who 'have labored side by

---

[1] Rom. 16 : 2, 3, 4, 7, 13.
[2] For Prisca and Aquila see e.g. 1 Cor. 16 : 19; 2 Tim. 4 : 19.
[3] Rom. 16 : 21; Phil. 2 : 25; 4 : 3; Philem. 24.

side with [him] in the gospel' (Phil. 4 : 3), who have often also
suffered with him in the service of Christ, sometimes been imprisoned
with him on this account, and who have therefore given evidence of
being proven in Christ. Paul was united with them because they had
consciously taken this common suffering upon themselves for Christ's
sake, because by preaching the Gospel in word and deed, by sacrifice,
suffering, indignity and persecution they are orientated towards salvation in Christ.

This is in my opinion the underlying reason why Paul never speaks
of friends and friendship. He may not have avoided these words
consciously, but his attitude towards his fellow men was such that it
did not occur to him to use these words to indicate the bonds which
tied him to them. If he chose other words it was not because he felt
himself obliged to describe the relationship which men like Seneca call
friendship, in more edifying terms, but because this word was not
sufficiently expressive of what he felt to be of fundamental importance
in his relationship to others. For Paul this relationship was not anthropocentric, still less egocentric, but Christocentric. Friendship and
friends are words whose meaning is too greatly restricted to the human
plane alone. But in the situation in which Paul realizes himself to be,
it is ultimately unimportant whether men and women support and help
each other, whether they gain by each other spiritually, whether they
can get on well with one another as virtuous and like-minded human
beings, what does matter is whether they are united by faith with
Christ, and hence with each other, whether they know themselves
virtuous or wicked, — it has already been observed that Paul only uses
the word ἀρετή once, in Phil. 4 : 8 — to be collectively atoned for,
redeemed and consecrated in Christ, whether they collectively preach
the salvation which has been revealed in Christ and will one day be
brought to fulfilment. If they do, then they are united as men who
speak and live towards the day of Jesus Christ. Then the relationship
qualified as συνεργοί εἰς τὴν βασιλείαν τοῦ θεοῦ (Col. 4 : 11)
arises. What precisely does Paul mean by the preposition εἰς ? In my
opinion this text should in this respect be compared with places like
Eph. 4 : 30 ('sealed for the day of redemption'), Phil. 1 : 10 ('pure
and blameless for the day of Christ', cf. Phil. 2 : 16) and translated
by 'auf das Reich Gottes hin'. [1] For Paul wishes to say of these Christ-

---

[1] E. Lohmeyer, *Die Briefe an die Philipper, Kolosser und an Philemon,* [10]1954,
Kol., p. 167.

ians that, like him, and working together with him, their whole lives and all their labours are orientated towards the coming of God's kingdom.

Words like 'friends' and 'friendship' are inadequate to describe such relationships. They simply do not cover what matters. And so it is not by chance that Paul never uses these words. It was not possible for him to belong to those 'Virtuosen der Freundschaft'. [1]

A distinct difference between the motives behind Paul's *attitude towards enemies* and Seneca's may also be observed. Seneca emphatically insists that we should help our enemies. He deems it to be common knowledge that the Stoics say:

> We shall engage in affairs to the very end of life, we shall never cease to work for the common good, to help each and all, to give aid even to our enemies when our hand is feeble with age. [2]

Here the motive for helping one's enemies is not mentioned explicitly. Perhaps it is implied in 'the work for the common good,' and thus bound up with the idea of that vast harmonious body of which man is a part. This same motive is perhaps in evidence when Seneca calls the 'power of injury', *vis nocendi,* 'vile and detestable and most unnatural for man, by whose kindness even fierce beasts are tamed', [3] or when after declaring that he will always be gentle and lenient towards enemies, that he will grant forgiveness before it is asked and will yield to all honourable requests, he immediately professes, as he does elsewhere also, that the whole world is his fatherland, that the gods who abide above him and around him are his rulers, the censors of his words and deeds. [4]

But this is not Seneca's principal motive. We approach that more closely when we read how foolish it is to devote oneself with such fervour to quarrels and enmity when this life is so fleeting:

> Why do we, forgetting our weakness, take up the huge burden of hate, and, easily broken as we are, rise up to break? Soon a fever or some other bodily ill will stay that war of hatred, which we now wage with such unrelenting purpose. Soon death wil step in and part the fiercest

---

[1] The name given to the Hellenes by F. Heiler, *Das Gebet,* [3]1921, p. 200.

[2] *De Otio* 1. 4. Reference has frequently been made to this passage when what Seneca says about loving one's enemies is compared with what is written in the gospels; cf. Baur, p. 209; Kreyher, p. 75 f.; G. A. van den Bergh van Eysinga, op. cit., p. 211; G. Sevenster, *Nieuw Theologisch Tijdschrift,* 1932, p. 32 f.; R. Bultmann, *Jesus,* p. 102 f.; id., *Glauben und Verstehen,* 1933, p. 236.

[3] *Ira* ii. 31. 6.

[4] *V.B.* 20. 5.

pair of fighters .... Fate looms above our heads .... That hour which you appoint for the death of another is perchance near your own. Why do you not rather gather up your brief life and render it a peaceful one to yourself and all others? Why do you not rather make yourself beloved by all while you live, and regretted by all when you die .... Wait a little. Behold, death comes, who will make you equals. [1]

Our fate is often like that of those animals, for example, a bull and a bear, which, bound together in the arena, wound and molest each other until they are put to death by an appointed slayer:

Their fate is ours; we harass some one bound closely to us, and yet the end, all too soon, threatens the victor and the vanquished. Rather let us spend the little time that is left in repose and peace! Let no man loathe us when we lie a corpse! .... Can you wish for the victim of your wrath a greater ill than death? Even though you do not move a finger, he will die. You waste your pains if you wish to do what needs must be .... Whether your thoughts run on tortures severe or slight, how short is the time in which either your victim can writhe under your torments, or you derive a wicked joy from another's pain-! Soon shall we spew forth this frail spirit. [2]

All this points towards the principal motive, mentioned repeatedly by Seneca, behind the way one should behave towards one's enemies: the wise man who sees the bustle of living as it really is, will never allow himself to be disturbed by the behaviour of others, even if it is hostile, churlish or insulting. He will ignore it completely. Indeed it cannot even reach him, it never penetrates that sphere of serene tranquillity in which the wise man always lives. It may accordingly be said that the wise man cannot suffer an injustice or insult, since he is untouched by it. He is raised far above it.

Here too, as in connection with suicide, Cato is for Seneca the great example. The conduct of this hero from the past is evidence that 'no wise man can receive either injury or insult.' [3] 'The wise man is safe, and no injury or insult can touch him.' [4] Some may say: 'But of course there is some pleasure in anger'. 'Not at all', replies Seneca,

for it is not honourable, as in acts of kindness to requite benefits with benefits, so to requite injuries with injuries. In the one case it is shameful to be outdone, in the other not to be outdone.

Cato's conduct proves this:

---

1 *Ira* iii. 42. 3, 4; 43. 1, 2.
2 *Ira* iii. 43. 2-4.
3 *Const.* 2. 1.
4 *Const.* 2. 3.

Once when Marcus Cato was in the public bath, a certain man, not knowing him, struck him unwittingly; for who would knowingly have done injury to that great man? Later, when the man was making apology, Cato said, "I do not recall that I received a blow." It was better, he thought, to ignore the incident than to resent it. "Then the fellow," you ask, "got no punishment for such an act of rudeness?" No, but much good — he began to know Cato. Only a great soul can be superior to injury; the most humiliating kind of revenge is to have it appear that the man was not worth taking revenge upon. Many have taken slight injuries too deeply to heart in the act of revenging them. He is a great and noble man who acts as does the lordly wild beast that listens unconcernedly to the baying of tiny dogs. [1]

Once again Cato displayed the same imperturbable attitude towards insult:

when he was pleading a case, Lentulus, that factious and unruly man who lingers in the memory of our fathers, gathering as much thick saliva as he could, spat it full upon the middle of Cato's forehead. But he wiped it off his face and said, "To all who affirm that you have no cheek, Lentulus, I'll swear that they are mistaken." [2]

Hence Cato was one of those wise men of whom it might be said:

He despises the wrongs done him; he forgets them, not accidentally, but voluntarily. He does not put a wrong construction upon everything, or seek for someone whom he may hold responsible for each happening; he rather ascribes even the sins of men to chance. He will not misinterpret a word or a look; he makes light of all mishaps by interpreting in a generous way. He does not remember an injury rather than a service. [3]

The conduct of such a wise man is proof that, 'The invulnerable thing is not that which is not struck, but that which is not hurt'. [4] Injustice simply does not touch the wise man:

"What then?" you say; "will there be no one who will attempt to do the wise man injury?" Yes, the attempt will be made, but the injury will not reach him. For the distance which separates him from contact with his inferiors is so great that no baneful force can extend its power all the way to him. Even when the mighty, exalted by authority and powerful in the support of their servitors, strive to injure him, all their assaults

---

[1] *Ira* ii. 32. 1-3. This anecdote about Cato is also recorded in *Const.* 14. 3.

[2] *Ira* iii. 38. 1, 2. Cato's remark contains a pun: *Adfirmabo omnibus, Lentule, falli eos qui te negant os habere*. To the Loeb translation: 'you have no cheek', a footnote is appended: 'To reproduce the pun in the Latin the word must suggest also its vulgar use in the sense of effrontery.' It is likewise noted in a French translation: 'nier que tu aies une bouche': 'Jeu de mots: ou "que tu sois effronté"'; *Sénèque, Dialogues, De Ira*, texte établi et traduit par A. Bourgery, 1951, p. 104[3].

[3] *Ep.* 81. 24, 25.

[4] *Const.* 3. 3.

on wisdom will fall as short of their mark as do the missiles shot on high by bowstring or catapult, which though they leap beyond our vision, yet curve downwards this side of heaven. [1]

Seneca thus argues repeatedly that it is not possible to insult a wise man, since the insult cannot touch him. [2] Therefore in a conflict a wise man is always the victor, even though he may often appear to be the vanquished. [3] Such a wise man is raised far above the jostling throng; his true greatness is revealed by the fact that he does not feel any blow. [4] As arrows rebound against something hard, as a man injures himself when he strikes such an object, so too does ill treatment leave the wise man unaffected. [5] The wise man is capable of taking all abuse as a joke. He treats his adversaries like children. He sometimes punishes them, not because he has felt their insults, but simply because they have offered them and in order that they may not do so again. The trainer does not get angry with animals he is training with a whip. A doctor does not loose his temper with a lunatic, and does not take seriously the curses of a feverish patient, whom he has denied a drink of cold water. Hence when asked: "Why, if the wise man cannot receive either injury or insult, does he punish those who have offered them?" Seneca naturally replies: 'he is not avenging himself, but correcting them.' [6]

However frequently Seneca may discuss how a man should behave towards his enemies, what he is really interested in is individual and not social ethics. The principal motive behind the conduct he advocates is always the keeping intact of the wise man's inner imperturbability. In Seneca every description of the wise man's conduct towards those who abuse, insult or do him an injustice only serves to magnify the inviolate wise man who is raised far above common mortals, who takes no notice of the bustle of living, and who is left untouched by wrongs and injustice.

It is plain that the love of one's enemies which Paul repeatedly enjoins in his letters, springs from a very different source. Now and then Paul has been accused of falling short of the love to be shown towards enemies, as this is preached by Jesus in the Sermon on the Mount and elsewhere in the gospels. This has been said in connection

---

[1] *Const.* 4. 1.
[2] *Const.* 5. 3, 5; 7. 2.
[3] *Ira* ii. 34. 5.
[4] *Ira* iii. 25. 3.
[5] *Ira* iii. 5. 7, 8.
[6] *Const.* 12. 3; 13. 1, 2.

with Rom. 12 : 19-21 in particular. 1 There the question arises as to
the meaning of the words 'leave it to the wrath of God; for it is
written, "Vengeance is mine, I will repay, says the Lord" ' (Rom.
12 : 19), and ' "by so doing you will heap burning coals upon his
head" ' (v. 20). The first of these two verses might be thought to
mean that even if man does not take vengeance, God will; therefore
those who do not avenge misdeeds done to them may still know to
their satisfaction that the wrongdoer will not evade richteous punishment. The question, however, is whether the latter part of the verse
may be interpreted thus. It is far more probable that Paul intends to
say that even if human retribution is not inflicted, this does not mean
that evil and injustice will triumph. But it is not up to us human beings
to play the judge. We can leave that to God, who will pass judgment
on all misdeeds on the Judgment Day. These words are therefore by
no means intended to satisfy a certain natural desire for retribution,
but to confront men with the holy God, who calls man to account
for his deeds. Moreover, the words 'vengeance' and 'repay', which
are derived from Deut. 32 : 35, have for Paul a particular significance,
since he considers God's justice to be closely bound up with His love,
which excludes the possibility of it being on a par with human vengeance.

The 'heaping of burning coals' in the latter part of verse 20 is sometimes read as a consolation for those who repay evil with good, insofar
as the evildoer will eventually be punished for his misdeeds. This interpretation is, however, unsound in view of the context, particularly
verse 21: 'Do not be overcome by evil, but overcome evil with good.'
A malevolent motive is hereby excluded. We may therefore be well-
nigh certain that the expression is meant metaphorically for the painful
shame the enemy will feel when the evil he has done to another is
repaid by good. It is clear from the whole context that this love of
one's enemies belongs within the framework of that love which is the

---

1 Preisker remarks in connection with these verses: 'Nicht mehr die grenzenlose,
gottgegebene Gewalt der Verpflichtung des Ich dem Du gegenüber zwingt zur Liebes-
tat, sondern klügelnder Sinn und kleinliche Rache diktieren eine Haltung, die nach
Liebe aussehen soll und doch alles andere als Liebe ist. Ganz offensichtlich ist ein
völlig anderer Geist in die christliche Liebe eingedrungen.' H. Preisker, *Das Ethos
des Urchristentums*, 1949, p. 184; cf. E. Stauffer, *Die Botschaft Jesu*, 1959, p. 133.
Juncker on the other hand disputes those who maintain that Paul falls short of
Jesus' command, by saying: 'unzweifelhaft sind vielmehr die im Rechte, die gerade
in dieser Perikope nicht bloss den ältesten, sondern auch den besten Kommentar zu
Mt. 5, 43 ff und Lc. 6, 27 ff. sehen.' A. Juncker, op. cit., p. 230 f.; cf. W. C. van
Unnik in his review of Preisker's book, *Ned. T.T.*, 1950-1, p. 49.

fulfilment of the law (Rom. 13 : 8-10), and which is the subject of Paul's discourse from Rom. 12 : 9 onwards. Even before the concluding verses of this chapter he urges those to whom he is writing to show this love:

> Bless those who persecute you; bless and do not curse them. Repay no one evil for evil, but take thought for what is noble in the sight of all (Rom. 12 : 14, 17).

Elsewhere too it is obvious that he considers that the refusal to repay evil with evil should be an unwritten law in a Christian community (1 Thess. 5 : 15). When he briefly but significantly describes his own life and that of the other Apostles, he finds it only natural that they should give their blessing when reviled (1 Cor. 4 : 12, 13).

No doubt exists as to the source of this love. Paul does not need to write to Christians on this subject. For they have been taught by God Himself to love one another (1 Thess. 4 : 9). God's love has been poured into their hearts through the Holy Spirit, and this love is such that, while they were enemies, they were reconciled with God by the death of his Son (Rom. 5 : 5-11). The Apostle ventures to say of himself that it is no longer he who lives, but Christ who lives in him; 'and the life I now live in the flesh I live by the faith in the Son of God, who loved me and gave himself for me' (Gal. 2 : 20). Christ's love impels him, and it goes without saying that those who live, no longer live for themselves, but for Him who died for them and was raised (2 Cor. 4 : 14, 15). Human forgiveness is of course built upon the foundations of God's forgiveness in Christ (Eph. 4 : 32; 5 : 1, 2).

So we see that Seneca and Paul also have very different motives for enjoining men to love their enemies. For the former the principal motive is the preservation of the inner imperturbability of the wise man, for the latter the love which answers God's love in Christ. [1]

A problem which came up repeatedly in antiquity was that of the treatment of *slaves*, and it is by no means only in the New Testament that the question as to how they should be regarded arises. Seneca

---

[1] Cf. Joh. Weiss, *Das Urchristentum*, 1917, p. 452, who also points out the difference between what Seneca says in *Const.* and 1 Cor. 4 : 12 f. Hence what Paul preaches about loving one's enemies is just as far removed from Stoic doctrine as Jesus' command. For the relationship between Jesus and the Stoics in this respect, see Kreyher, p. 75 f.; R. Bultmann, *Jesus*, n.d., p. 102 ff.; id., *Glauben und Verstehen*, 1933, p. 236 ff.; G. A. van den Bergh van Eysinga, op. cit., p. 211 ff.; G. Sevenster 'Evangelie en Stoa', *Nieuw Theol. T.*, 1932, p. 30 ff. For the difference between Plato and Matt. 5. 44 see W. J. Verdenius, 'Plato-interpretatie', *Ned. Theol. T.*, 1953-4, p. 142.

devoted a great deal of attention to it. Of his forty-seventh letter to
Lucilius in which he discourses at length on how to treat slaves, we
are still able to say with Baur:

> der ganze Inhalt des Briefs ist so wahr und trefflich, dass ihm wohl
> Weniges in gleichem Sinne aus den Schriften des klassischen Alterthums
> wird zur Seite gestellt werden können. 1

Seneca does not, it is true, urge the manumission of slaves, he does not
discuss slavery as a social phenomenon, he does not condemn it as
such, on the contrary he accepts it as something natural, but he nevertheless feels great pity for slaves, and expresses keen censure of the
way they are treated, condemning the misuse of slaves for all kinds
of contemptible tasks.

Seneca knows quite well that some slaves are far from faultless.
After Lucilius has apparently complained to him that some slaves had
taken advantage of the fact that he was absorbed in business and had
run away, Seneca reminds him that other masters have suffered far
worse things at the hands of their slaves:

> Other men have been robbed, blackmailed, slain, betrayed, stamped under
> foot, attacked by poison or by slander; no matter what trouble you men-
> tion, it has happened to many. 2

The manifestation of virtue in slaves is all the more praiseworthy
because it is so rare. 3

Occasionally Seneca makes a remark which attests to his profound
contempt for slaves, as for example when he speaks of persons 'whose
shops are packed with a throng of the meanest slaves', 4 or elsewhere,
when he declares how foolish it is to become angry with a porter who
throws out an unwelcome guest. It is wrong to lose one's temper with
'that lowest kind of slave'.

> Will you then become angry with a chained watchdog? He, too, after all
> his barking, will become gentle if you toss him food. Retire a little way
> and laugh! 5

However, despite this, he pleads repeatedly for better treatment of
slaves, even advocating intercourse with them as equals. Such a plea
is of course based upon the notion of *humanitas*. A slave too is a
human being. Nothing more need be added. Seneca is therefore pleased

---

1 Baur, p. 217.
2 *Ep.* 107. 1, 5.
3 *Ben.* iii. 19. 4.
4 *Const.* 13. 4.
5 *Ira* iii. 37. 2.

to hear from visitors that Lucilius lives on friendly terms with his slaves: "They are slaves," people declare. Nay, rather they are men. "Slaves!" No, comrades. "Slaves!" No, they are unpretentious friends.' [1] It is our own fault that the saying "As many enemies as you have slaves," is so often borne out, for:

> They are not enemies when we acquire them; we make them enemies ... we maltreat them, not as if they were men, but as if they were beasts of burden. [2]

Slaves are human, just as we are:

> Kindly remember that he whom you call your slave sprang from the same stock, is smiled upon by the same skies, and on equal terms with yourself breathes, lives, and dies. [3]
> We all spring from the same source, have the same origin; no man is more noble than another except in so far as the nature of one man is more upright and more capable of good actions. [4]

It is one of the good things about philosophy that it does not examine a man's pedigree. For: 'All men, if traced back to their original source, spring from the gods.' [5] There is a 'soul that is upright, good and great' in every man:

> What else could you call such a soul than a god dwelling as a guest in a human body? A soul like this may descend into a Roman knight just as well as into a freedman's son or a slave. For what is a Roman knight, or a freedman's son or a slave? They are mere titles, born of ambition or of wrong. One may leap to heaven from the very slums. Only rise "And mould thyself to kinship with my God." [6]

In doing good the rank or station of those one benefits is immaterial:

> Nature bids me do good to all mankind — whether slaves or freemen, freeborn or freed-men, whether the laws gave them freedom or a grant in the presence of friends — what difference does it make? Wherever there is a human being there is the opportunity for a kindness. [7]

Naturally a slave too may confer a benefit upon his master. Those who deny the possibility of this are apparently ignorant of 'the rights of man', *ius humanum*:

> for, not the status, but the intention, of the one who bestows is what counts. Virtue closes the door to no man; it is open to all, admits all,

---

[1] *Ep.* 47. 1.
[2] *Ep.* 47. 5.
[3] *Ep.* 47. 10.
[4] *Ben.* iii. 28. 1.
[5] *Ep.* 44. 1.
[6] *Ep.* 31. 11, quotation from Virgil, *Aeneid,* viii. 364 f.
[7] *V.B.* 24. 3.

invites all, the freeborn and the freedman, the slave and the king, and
the exile; neither family nor fortune determines its choice — it is satisfied with the naked human being. 1
What, then, is the case? Does a master receive a benefit from a slave?
No, but a human being from a human being [*homo ab homine*]. 2

Therefore, although in the eyes of the law everything is permissible
in dealing with a slave, there are extremes which 'the right common
to all living creatures [*commune ius animantium*] refuses to allow' 3.
Therefore like every other human being a slave ought to be judged not
according to his duties, but according to his character. 4

The condition of slavery never affects the whole of a man's being:

> It is a mistake for anyone to believe that the condition of slavery pene-
> trates into the whole being of a man. The better part of him is exempt.
> Only the body is at the mercy and disposition of a master; but the mind
> is its own master [*sui iuris*], and is so free and unshackled that not even
> this prison of the body, in which it is confined, can restrain it from using
> its own powers, following mighty aims, and escaping into the infinite
> to keep company with the stars. It is, therefore, the body that Fortune
> hands over to a master; it is this that he buys, it is this that he sells; that
> inner part cannot be delivered into bondage. All that issues from this is
> free. 5

In death the fact emerges that all men are, and really always have
been, essentially equal. However different men's circumstances may
have been in life, death makes an end to these differences, whether
we like it or not:

> Death frees the slave though his master is unwilling . . . . If Fortune has
> apportioned unjustly the common goods, and has given over one man to
> another though they were born with equal rights, death levels all things. 6
> We are unequal at birth, but are equal in death. 7
> Death is not an evil; why need you ask? Death alone is the equal privilege
> of mankind. 8

Hence it may be seen that in Seneca certain themes recur repeatedly
in diverse variations: slaves too are human beings; they spring from
the same source as everyone else, and must therefore be judged by the
same standards. There are spiritual distinctions between men, but these

---

1 *Ben.* iii. 18. 2; cf. 18. 4.
2 *Ben.* iii. 22. 3.
3 *Clem.* i. 18. 2.
4 *Ep.* 47. 15.
5 *Ben.* iii. 20. 1, 2.
6 *Marc.* 20. 2.
7 *Ep.* 91. 16.
8 *Ep.* 123. 16.

transcend all ranks and classes of society. A noble spirit and virtue may just as well dwell in a slave as in any well-born Roman. In his spiritual life a slave is as free as any other man. True equality is revealed in death. He who recognizes the fundamental equality of men, of masters and slaves, will treat slaves with respect and will see nothing strange in behaving towards them as an equal.

Some scholars believe that this attitude towards slaves is very similar to Paul's. It has for example been said:

> The notion that all men are brothers, which we unjustly consider to be specifically Christian, already found complete expression in the Stoic school. [1]

However, as in other cases, the motives behind Seneca's attitude towards slaves are very different from those governing Paul's notions. Again, this is perhaps to be seen most clearly where they apparently have most in common. Like Seneca, Paul does not urge the abolition of slavery as a social institution. What he has to say is based upon the assumption of its existence. He enjoins slaves to be obedient to their masters, albeit in a particular way, namely as servants of Christ. [2] He does not ask Philemon to give the runaway slave who is to return to him his freedom. He exhorts the slave, like all others, to remain in the state in which he was called (1 Cor. 7 : 20). He probably even urges him not to make use of an opportunity to gain his freedom, should one arise, but to show, in his chosen state as a slave, that he makes use of his position for the sake of his own salvation and that of others. Whether this is indeed the case depends upon the interpretation of 1 Cor. 7 : 21. What should be inserted after μᾶλλον χρῆσαι ? Ελεύθερος γενέσθαι or δοῦλος εἶναι ? Opinions are still divided on this point. To my mind the latter interpretation is for the following reasons the most promising: (1) the αἰ is placed before δύναται and not before ἐλεύθερος γενέσθαι. This in my opinion excludes the translation: furthermore if you can gain your freedom. (2) μᾶλλον would be virtually meaningless if Paul were advising: then make use of that opportunity to become free; but it fits in very well if he is advising those who are slaves to do instead the unexpected, namely to remain in bondage despite the fact that there is an opportunity of their gaining their freedom. (3) The train of

---

[1] Otto Seeck, *Geschichte des Untergangs der antiken Welt*, Vol. III, 1909, p. 89, quoted with approval by G. A. van den Bergh van Eysinga, op. cit., p. 205; cf. Baur, p. 214; Max Pohlenz, *Der hellenische Mensch*, 1947, p. 395 f.; C. Clemen, *Religionsgeschichtliche Erklärung des Neuen Testaments*, 1924, p. 322.

[2] *Eph.* 6 : 5-9; Col. 3 : 22-4 : 1.

thought in verses 20-24; the central idea is expressed in verses 20
and 24: a Christian should remain in the state in which he was called.
For Paul this also applies with respect to marriage. If a man is married,
he should remain so; if unmarried, he should not marry. By acting thus,
even when there is the possibility of changing his social status, a
Christian has all the more chance of proving that, since being called,
he no longer need be concerned about the external situation in which
he was called. [1]

Accordingly Seneca and Paul think alike in that they do not condemn slavery as such, but simply take its existence for granted. Both
of them consider that it is not of vital importance whether in the eyes
of society a man is a slave. Both of them are convinced that a man's
attitude towards slaves and the way he conducts himself towards them
undergoes a radical change, if he becomes aware of the true relationship
between masters and slaves. However, although they seem to share the
same beliefs, the motives behind these beliefs are very different. Both
say that a slave may be free and a free man a slave, but each says it in
his own way. At the beginning of the aforementioned forty-seventh
letter it is not only said of slaves that they are 'men', 'comrades',
'unpretentious friends', but also that 'they are our fellow-slaves, if one
reflects that Fortune has equal rights over slaves and free men alike.' [2]
Free men are slaves because they, too, are subjected to fate.

Furthermore what right have we to look down upon a slave? Who
dares to do so, if he realizes what he is himself:

> You who are a slave of lust, of gluttony, of a harlot — nay, who are
> the common property of harlots — do you call any other man a slave?
> *You* call any other man a slave? [3]

Who is then not a slave?

> Show me a man who is not a slave; one is a slave to lust, another to
> greed, another to ambition, and all men are slaves to fear. I will name

---

[1] This interpretation is also given in the commentary by C. F. G. Heinrici (Meyer
81896); J. Weiss (Meyer 101925); Ph. Bachmann (Zahn 31921); W. Bousset
(*Schriften des N.T.*, 31917); H. D. Wendland (*N.T.D.* 51948); H. Lietzmann 31933;
also in A. Juncker, op. cit., p. 176-81; H. Greeven, op. cit., p. 48 ff. The opposing
view, namely, that in Paul's opinion a slave ought to make use of any opportunity
to obtain his freedom is to be found in e.g. the commentaries of A. Robertson-A.
Plummer (*I.C.C.* 21950) and James Moffatt, 1947; also in W. Bienert, *Die Arbeit
nach der Lehre der Bibel*, 1954, p. 338; *Th. W.* II, p. 274 ff.; 1 Cor. 7 : 20-25 is
dealt with at length in J. J. Koopmans, *De servitute antiqua et religione christiana
capita selecta*, 1920, p. 119-29.

[2] *Ep.* 47. 1.

[3] *Ben.* iii. 28. 4.

you an ex-consul who is slave to an old hag, a millionaire who is slave
to a serving-maid; I will show you youths of the noblest birth in serfdom
to pantomime players! No servitude is more disgraceful than that which
is self-imposed. 1

Accordingly as masters may be slaves, so too may slaves be free.
' "He is a slave." His soul, however, may be that of a freeman.' 2 Even
though the body may be at the disposal of a master:

> the mind is its own master, and is free and unshackled .... that inner
> part cannot be delivered into bondage. All that issues from this is free. 3

The same paradox, but with a very different background, is to be
found in Paul. But instead of saying that a free man *may* be a slave,
and a slave *may* be a free man, Paul says that a free man *is* a slave, and
a slave *is* free, namely in Christ. 'He who was called in the Lord as a
slave is a freedman of the Lord. Likewise he who was free when called
is a slave of Christ' (1 Cor. 7 : 22). After Onesimus has accepted the
Gospel preached by Paul in prison, he is, when he returns to his master
Philemon, no longer a slave but a beloved brother (Philem. 16). After
baptism a unity exists between slaves and free men, a unity in Christ
which makes a radical change in their relationship. For then they both
belong to the body of Christ. 4 Hence all that has been said above on
freedom also applies to slaves. They too have been liberated by Christ,
they are now freedmen of the Lord.

On the other hand all the members of the Church who 'were bought
with a price' (1 Cor. 6 : 20; 7 : 23) by Christ, are now slaves, slaves
of Christ. 5 That they are slaves is no disgrace, as Seneca suggests in
connection with free men who are slaves to their passions; therein lies
the glory of the members of the Church. In the opening sentence of
many of his letters Paul calls himself 'a slave of Jesus Christ', before
going on to say that he has been 'called to be an apostle'. 6 He does
not feel this as a disgrace, it is a title of honour, of which he is proud.

Accordingly it may be said of the whole of Christ's Church: all are
free in Him, all are His slaves. Thereby all differences in social status
are in principle removed. If this is so, external differences are no longer
of such importance. Everyone should remain in the state in which he

---

1 *Ep.* 47. 17.
2 *Ep.* 47. 17.
3 *Ben.* iii. 20. 2.
4 Gal. 3 : 28; 1 Cor. 12 : 13; Col. 3 : 11.
5 Cf. Rom. 6 : 16-22; 2 Cor. 4 : 5; 2 Tim. 2 : 24; δουλεύειν Rom. 7 : 6;
12 : 11; 14 : 18; 16 : 18.
6 Rom. 1 : 1; cf. Phil. 1 : 1; Titus 1 : 1; Philem. 1; Gal. 1 : 10.

was called. Slaves ought not to demonstrate the freedom for which Christ has liberated them by acting rebelliously towards their masters. On the contrary, they should be as obedient to their masters 'as to Christ; not in the way of eyeservice, as men-pleasers, but as slaves of Christ, doing the will of God from the heart, rendering service with a good will as to the Lord and not to men' (Eph. 6 : 5-7; cf. Col. 3 : 22-24). In this way their labours gain a new significance. For although they may seem to serve an earthly master, they are in fact servants of Christ. Even when carrying out the most contemptible tasks they may now know themselves to be in the service of Christ. It would be a very faulty conception of brotherhood in Christ, if slaves were to be rebellious and insolent towards their masters who are their brothers in Christ, and display a lack of respect for them (1 Tim. 6 : 1, 2; cf. Titus 2 : 9, 10).

The master is reminded that both he and his slave have to account for themselves before God, who is Master of both of them, and in whose sight they are equal (Eph. 6 : 9). Therefore he must not threaten his slaves. Therefore he must behave justly and fairly towards them (Eph. 6 : 9; Col. 4 : 1).

Hence Christ also determines the whole relationship between slaves and masters. In Him the relationship has radically changed, so much so that it matters little or nothing whether the social barriers between them are raised. For in this new fellowship in Christ this relationship no longer plays any part, not because both slaves and masters belong to one vast cosmos, and bear in themselves the same divine seed, as Seneca suggests, but because they are both brothers in Christ, brothers, for whose sake Christ died, who have been redeemed by Him and are now His property, His slaves, living in Him by God's gift of grace.

Likewise remarkable is the diference between Paul and Seneca's attitude towards *women*. In principle Seneca is quite ready to acknowledge the possibility of a woman leading a virtuous life. He sometimes states this explicitly. When he imagines that he can hear Marcia objecting: ' "You forget that you are giving comfort to a woman; the examples you cite are of men" ', he answers thus:

> who has asserted that Nature has dealt grudgingly with women's natures and has narrowly restricted their virtues? Believe me, they have just as much force, just as much capacity, if they like, for virtuous action; they are just as able to endure suffering and toil when they are accustomed to them. [1]

[1] *Marc.* 16. 1.

Although he does not mention her in so many words, he is certainly also thinking of woman, when he writes: 'Virtue closes the door to no man; is it open to all, admits all, invites all', [1] or elsewhere: 'virtue is accessible to all; she deems no man unworthy if only he deems himself worthy of her', [2] or when he argues that nature proves repeatedly 'that virtue springs into birth in any place whatever.' [3]

Seneca thinks of the lives of some women with great respect and gratitude. For his mother he briefly describes the life of her *soror* (a sister, perhaps a sister-in-law), since she is Helvia's greatest source of comfort. [4] In his desire to cheer her he reminds her of 'the wisdom of this most perfect woman'. [5] When one thinks of lives such as hers, one realizes how many noble deeds of women are done without ceremony, and remain concealed. A woman too can display nobility of character and greatness of spirit. [6]

His own mother, Helvia, he praises more than any other woman. There is, Seneca declares, no reason why she should in her sadness make use of 'the excuse of being a woman'. [7] He praises her at length for her modesty and simplicity which formed such a marked contrast with the conduct of most of the women of her class. Of her he may say: 'your very virtues set you apart'. [8] When wishing to strengthen her in her sorrow, he is confident of being able to appeal to her reason. He ventures to recommend to her philosophic studies, in which all who fly from Fortune must take refuge. He regrets that his father had not given her more opportunity to acquire a thorough knowledge of philosophy, and begs her now to resume these studies, since they will give her security in her life. They will cheer her and comfort her in all her sorrow. Then her heart will be closed to sorrow, anxiety, useless distress or futile suffering, as it has long been closed to all other weaknesses. [9]

Seneca also records with obvious gratitude the tender cares of his wife Paulina. When on account of an attack of fever he flees to his villa at Nomentum, Paulina endeavours to stop him. She always urges

---

1 *Ben.* iii. 18. 2.
2 *Pol.* 17. 2.
3 *Ep.* 66. 3.
4 *Helv.* 19. 1 ff.; cf. P. Faider, *Études sur Sénèque,* 1921, pp. 156, 167, 171.
5 *Helv.* 19. 4.
6 *Helv.* 19. 5, 7.
7 *Helv.* 16. 1, 2.
8 *Helv.* 16. 5.
9 *Helv.* 17. 2-5.

him to take care of his health and knowing that her life depends on his own he is beginning for her sake to pay more attention to his well-being. [1] It is a great joy to him to know that he is dear to his wife:

> for what is sweeter than to be so valued by one's wife that one becomes more valuable to oneself for this reason? Hence my dear Paulina is able to make me responsible, not only for her fears, but also for my own. [2]

With the passing of the years his wife has grown familiar with all his habits, including that of examining all his words and deeds at the end of each day. Then his wife keeps silent. [3]

Accordingly Seneca had no reason to be contemptuous of women on account of his own experience of those close to him. Nevertheless he often judges women very unfavourably. There have certainly been others in history like Helvia and her *soror,* whose excellence has often remained hidden. But they are exceptions. Seneca's opinion of women in general is implied in the already quoted passage where he obviously lauds the excellence of Helvia, in whose life all female vices are absent, as something unique; where he praises her for her chastity thus: 'unchastity, the greatest evil of our time, has never classed you with the great majority of women', [4] or where he comments that Helvia's sister's modesty seems old-fashioned amid the great boldness of her contemporaries. [5]

A woman is usually a weak creature. When Seneca urges Lucilius to bear pain like a man, it is clear that for him the opposite of this is to bear it like a woman, *muliebriter ferre.* [6] It is feminine to rage in anger. [7] The anger of women and children alike is more violent than serious. [8] Generally speaking: 'anger is a most womanish and childish weakness.' [9] A child is excused by its age, a woman by her sex. [10] When insulted one should always investigate the character and purpose of the offender: 'Does a child offend? Excuse should be made for his age — he does not know what is wrong .... A woman? It was a

[1] *Ep.* 104. 1, 2.
[2] *Ep.* 104. 5.
[3] *Ira* iii. 36. 3.
[4] *Helv.* 16. 3.
[5] *Helv.* 19. 2.
[6] *Ep.* 78. 17.
[7] *Clem.* i. 5. 5.
[8] *Ira* ii. 19. 4.
[9] *Ira* i. 20. 3.
[10] *Ira* iii. 24. 3.

blunder.' [1] Seneca presupposes a lack of self-control in women. [2] It is truly base and womanish to give oneself over to be utterly consumed by sorrow. [3]

Seneca stresses the fact that infidelity is as much a masculine failing as a feminine one, but he lays the greater part of the blame for the terrible conditions which according to him prevail in his day upon woman. He obviously finds it wrong that a man should demand conjugal fidelity of his wife, while he does not live up to this himself. A man must constantly be reminded of the injustice of such behaviour. [4] He ought to realize that keeping a mistress is the worst insult to his wife. [5] And it may indeed be said in praise of a woman that by admonition she sometimes brings back her erring husband. [6]

Hence although Seneca is convinced that the infidelity of a man must be condemned just as strongly as that of a woman — and this notion is by no means usual in antiquity —, it is the woman in particular against whom he rails, when describing the moral deterioration of his time as reflected in marital relations:

> Is there any woman that blushes at divorce now that certain illustrations and noble ladies reckon their years, not by the number of consuls, but by the number of their husbands, and leave home in order to marry, and marry in order to be divorced? They shrank from this scandal as long as it was rare; now, since every gazette has a divorce case, they have learned to do what they used to hear so much about. Is there any shame at all for adultery now that matters have come to such a pass that no woman has any use for a husband except to inflame her paramour? Chastity is simply a proof of ugliness. Where will you find any woman so wretched, so unattractive, as to be content with a couple of paramours — without having each hour assigned to a different one? And the day is not long enough for them all, but she must be caried in her litter to the house of one, and spend the night with another. She is simple and behind the times who is not aware that living with one paramour is called "marriage". [7]

Even married women look upon a man as boorish and old-fashioned, if he tries to forbid his wife appearing in public in a sedan-chair,

---

[1] *Ira* ii. 30. 1.
[2] *Helv.* 14. 2.
[3] *Pol.* 6. 2; cf. *muliebris mollitia Tranqu. an.* 17. 4; in *Pol.* 17. 2 'effeminate' is automatically placed on a par with *molliter*; *Ira* i. 12. 1.
[4] *Ep.* 94. 26.
[5] *Ep.* 95. 37.
[6] *Ben.* v. 22. 4.
[7] *Ben.* iii. 16. 2, 3.

exposed for all to see. If he has no mistress they suspect him of carrying on secret affairs with slave girls. [1]

As far as marital relations are concerned woman is rarely treated with much respect by Seneca, but sometimes he bursts out against her with all the profound contempt he feels for her. Some men are so foolish as to imagine that even a woman can insult them. To such men Seneca exclaims indignantly:

> What matters it how they regard her, how many lackeys she has for her litter, how heavily weighted her ears, how roomy her sedan? She is just the same unthinking creature — wild, and unrestrained in her passions — unless she has gained knowledge and had much instruction. [2]

To Marcia he praises her dead son because, although a very handsome young man, and

> surrounded by such a great horde of women, the corruptors of men, he lent himself to the hopes of none, and when some of them in their effrontery went so far as to make advances to him, he blushed with shame as if he had sinned even by pleasing them. [3]

Accordingly, although Seneca is convinced that nature has given woman the capacity for virtue, although for her, too, the path to philosophic wisdom is open, although there are examples of excellent women, she is, on the whole, a weak, inferior creature, afflicted with many vices. Some fairly extensive descriptions, and more frequently still, recurrent casual remarks prove that Seneca's estimation of woman springs from a highly developed sense of masculine superiority. He may in principle consider woman, as she is created by nature, capable of great things, but he usually displays great contempt for her, as she is in reality. [4]

Such an opinion of women as Seneca's is in vivid contrast with certain sayings of Paul's concerning women. Within the Church there is a fundamental equality between men and women. When they have been baptized, men and women are one in Christ, as are Jews and Greeks, slaves and free men (Gal. 3 : 26-29). For then they belong to the one body of Christ (1 Cor. 12 : 13; cf. Col. 3 : 9-11). This also means that women assist in the churches in various ways. It is striking how often Paul refers to women as his fellow workers. He does so, however, quite unobtrusively. Apparently he finds it so natural

---

[1] *Ben.* i. 9. 3, 4.

[2] *Const.* 14. 1.

[3] *Marc.* 24. 3.

[4] In my opinion too little weight is sometimes placed upon such statements of Seneca's, e.g. E. Vernon Arnold, op. cit., p. 270 f.

that he does not deem it necessary to make special mention of the fact that these fellow workers are women. Man and wife sometimes also work side by side. This is the case with Prisca and Aquila (Prisca is mentioned first!), whom Paul calls his 'fellow workers in Christ Jesus'. Not only Paul is indebted to them for personal reasons, but all the churches of the Gentiles have reason to be grateful to them. They have regularly had a church in their house (Rom. 16 : 3-5). Paul's personal bond with them and that of the churches apparently dates back a considerable time. [1] Hence Paul does not hesitate to include a woman in the term 'fellow workers', which is elsewhere often used to indicate male helpers. [2] Therefore he can also say of women that 'they have labored side by side with me in the gospel' (Phil. 4 : 2 f.). Elsewhere too Paul repeatedly mentions women, by no means pointedly, but purely as a matter of course, who have distinguished themselves in one way or another in work in the service of Christ. [3] The fact in itself that women are repeatedly mentioned within the framework of the work in the churches, is evidence of the influence of a very different estimation of them from Seneca's. In Christ a fundamental change in the relationship between man and woman has been made: 'In the Lord woman is not independent of man nor man of woman.' Even the order of creation points in this direction: 'as woman was made from man, so man is now born of woman' (1 Cor. 11 : 11 f.).

In the Pauline epistles it is sometimes also taken for granted that women are called to do special work in the Church, either by preaching or in other ways. Women, too, took part in prophesying and praying at church-gatherings (1 Cor. 11 : 5). The use of the word διάκονος in Rom. 16 : 1 f. probably also indicates that Phoebe occupied a particular place in the church of Cenchreae, though we are left in doubt whether she fulfilled a specific office. It is uncertain whether 1 Tim. 3 : 11 is an allusion to deaconesses, but it is highly likely that in 1 Tim. 5 : 9-16 a reference is made to a particular office held by widows in the Church, perhaps in connection with certain work for women in the community or the care of the sick.

When Paul does admonish women, he does so almost always primarily, because he wishes to discourage what he thinks to be a too extreme tendency towards emancipation. In the same pericope in which

---

[1] Acts18 : 1-3; 1 Cor. 16 : 19; 2 Tim. 4 : 19.
[2] Rom. 16 : 21; 2 Cor. 8 : 23; Phil. 2 : 25; 4 : 3; Col. 4 : 11; Philem. 24.
[3] Rom. 16 : 6, 12, 13, 15; 1 Cor. 1 : 11; Col. 4 : 15; Philem. 2.

he takes for granted that women prophesy and pray together with the other members of the Church, he cautions them not to do this unveiled. Just as he does not wish to see the existing relationship between slaves and their masters imperilled, exhorting them to remain in the state in which they were called, so too is he opposed to a deliberate and conspicuous outward display of the equality between men and women. However difficult the exegesis of 1 Cor. 11 : 2-16 may be, it is in the main concerned with the fact that the relationship between man and woman, which is founded upon the order of creation, may not be severed by a desire for emancipation. Likewise in 1 Cor. 14 : 34, 35 Paul is probably alluding in the first place to a passion for discussion which could give rise to heated argument between a wife and husband. If this text were to mean that no women should be permitted to speak in church, it would be in direct contradiction to 1 Cor. 11 : 5 where a woman's right to prophesy and pray is taken for granted. It may be so that it is considered αἰσχρὸν (1 Cor. 14 : 35) for women to join in avid discussion because this was only done in the ancient world by hetaerae. Paul does not wish women to draw the conclusion that because men and women are one in the Church they should assert themselves by behaving as they please. It is most likely that 1 Tim. 2 : 8-15 also wants to warn against this. The right attitude of a married woman towards her husband may not be undermined by her conduct at church-gatherings, which could apparently be very lively and animated in those days. [1]

With respect to conjugal relations Paul is convinced that a wife should to a certain extent remain subservient to her husband. If this is not acknowledged, freedom may easily degenerate into illicit libertinism. However, if one takes note of the context in which this is said it becomes plain that this 'subjection' of the wife to her husband also has a distinct character. If, for example, the words 'to be subject' contained in Eph. 5 : 21 should also be inserted in Eph. 5 : 22, as is very probable, (the R.S.V. does indeed repeat them, as do many other translations), this would prove that the subjection of the wife to the husband is not seen as anything but the voluntary subordination of one human being to another, which is also characteristic of all services rendered to one another by members of the Church. Neither does the attitude of the man whose aim in marriage is domination fulfil these

---

[1] Cf. G. Huls, *De dienst der vrouw in de kerk,* 1951, pp. 46-49; N. J. Hommes, 'Taceat mulier in ecclesia' in *Arcana revelata,* 1951, pp. 33-43; Else Kähler, op. cit., p. 53 f., 74 ff., 225 f., 238 ff.

requirements: a husband must love his wife as Christ loved the Church (Eph. 5 : 25 ff.). If this is so, subordination can never mean slavish subjection. 1 For the Church never feels her relation to Christ to be such. And when Paul compares the husband as the head of the wife with Christ as the head of the Church, his body, it is plain that the emphasis does not lie on man's dominion over woman, but upon their belonging together, as Christ and the Church belong together like head and body. The φοβεῖσθαι for her husband which befits a wife (Eph. 5 : 33) must also be seen in the light of the φόβος which all members of the Church should feel for Christ (v. 21).

So although Paul fully accepts a subordination on the part of a wife towards her husband, which in Paul's eyes has its foundations in creation, 2 this assumes new dimensions if it is seen against the background of being 'in Christ'. When the order of creation, which Paul wishes to see perpetuated and not destroyed by what he considers to be an unwarrantable urge for emancipation, comes into contact with the new order which is founded upon salvation in Christ, it acquires new meaning. Woman's ὑποτάσσεσθαι and φοβεῖσθαι are no longer answered by masculine lust for power or contempt for woman as an inferior being but by love (Eph. 5 : 25 ff.; cf. Col. 3 : 18, 19). 3

The contrast with Seneca strikes one immediately. First, the fact that a fundamental contempt for woman is out of the question here. Secondly — and this is a positive quality: by virtue of the new aeon of salvation in Christ not only does a radical change take place in the relations between man and wife, 4 but a woman's place in the community is also fundamentally altered, as is perhaps to be seen most plainly in those passages in which Paul refers in passing, but nevertheless clearly, to the fact that women participate in the work of the Church in various ways. It is no exaggeration on the part of one writer, when after quoting Gal. 3 : 28, he says:

> It is necessary to realize how acute the contrasts were in the ancient world, in order to feel the dynamite behind these words which sound so simple and natural to us. 5

From the very beginning this dynamite lay concealed in the coming of the new aeon which has had its inception in Christ.

---

1 Cf. Seneca, Const. 1. 1: altera pars ad obsequendum, altera imperio nata.
2 1 Cor. 11 : 8 f.; 1 Cor. 11 : 3, 7; 2 Cor. 11 : 3; Th. W. I, p. 785.
3 Cf. Else Kähler, op. cit., 99 ff., 134 ff., 138 ff., 172-202.
4 Gal. 3 : 28; 1 Cor. 12 : 13; Col. 3 : 11.
5 G. Huls, op. cit., p. 31; the equalization alluded to here is not only 'das Postulat für den Zustand der Vollendung', it is already applicable; cf. Th. Schreiner, p. 85.

Also revealing of the difference between their starting-points is the way in which Seneca and Paul speak of *wealth and poverty*. Seneca writes repeatedly and at some length about questions concerning the possession of earthly goods. It was a problem which he had of course frequently encountered in his private life. One often has the impression that he is writing an apologia of his own conduct. At all events it is evident that personal experiences have led him to discuss various facets of this question. But they have also induced him to posit these problems in a more universal way, and to ask what the attitude of the wise man should be to earthly goods in general.

On the one hand we find in Seneca a frequently recurring glorification of the simplicity of the life without riches. Fabricius, the proverbial model of a man of integrity who despite his extreme poverty allowed himself to be bribed neither by Pyrrhus nor by the Samnite ambassadors, is praised by Seneca for waging war both on Pyrrhus and on riches, for eating by his hearth only the roots and herbs which he, an old man and honoured by a triumph, had taken from the ground when cleaning off his land. [1]

One must remember, philosophizes Seneca, how much easier it is to have no money than to lose it; and the less we have to lose, the less chance there is of our being tormented by poverty. [2] If anyone doubts Diogenes' happiness, he may just as well doubt the condition of the immortal gods. For they too have none of all the earthly splendours of a rich man:

> Come, turn your eyes upon heaven; you will see the gods quite needy, giving all and having nothing. Do you think that he who stripped himself of al the gifts of Fortune is a poor man or simply like the immortal gods? [3]

Riches bring numerous burdens to a man:

> A household of slaves requires clothes and food; so many bellies of creatures that are always hungry have to be filled, we have to buy clothing for them, and watch their most thievish hands, and use the services of people weeping and cursing. How much happier is he whose only obligation is to one whom he can most easily refuse — himself! [4]
> To how many are riches a burden! [5]

---

[1] *Prov.* 3. 6; cf. however *Ep.* 94. 69.
[2] *Tranqu. an.* 8. 2.
[3] *Tranqu. an.* 8. 5.
[4] *Tranqu. an.* 8. 8.
[5] *Brev.* 2. 4.

By far the greater number of men are poor, and yet they are no more sorrowful and burdened with cares than the rich. On the contrary, 'they are happier because they have fewer things to harass their minds.' [1]

Nature is soon satisfied, she demands but little. However, when the luxury of riches is poured out over a man, he usually only learns from those riches to desire even greater ones, while natural desires are really so limited. [2] The glory of poverty is that it is 'unburdened and free from care.' [3] This is reflected in the faces of the poor: they smile more often and more genuinely and their troubles never go deep down. Even if they are beset by worries, these pass like light clouds. The cheerfulness of those whom men call happy is artificial. Sometimes they can scarcely conceal their misery in public, 'but must act the part of happiness in the midst of sorrows. [4]

In Seneca's tragedies too we find a glorification of the imperturbable peace of the simple life of the poor man who is not tormented by all the cares which never leave a rich man in peace. [5]

Hence there is not the least reason to be afraid of poverty. Inwardly a man may remain completely unmoved by it. Therefore Seneca can exhort his readers: 'Scorn poverty; no one lives as poor as he was born.' [6] Even if one is rich one must always be mentally prepared for poverty:

> We shall be rich with all the more comfort, if we once learn how far poverty is from being a burden. [7]
> He who has arranged his affairs according to nature's demands, is free from the fear, as well as from the sensation, of poverty. [8]

All the luxuriously living gourmands of Rome — 'they vomit that they may eat, they eat that they may vomit' — who have all the delicacies for their orgies fetched from the farthest corners of the earth may well go in mortal fear of poverty, but 'if a man despises such things, what harm can poverty do him?' [9] Hence Seneca is able to

---

[1] *Helv.* 12. 1.
[2] *Ep.* 16. 8, 9.
[3] *Ep.* 17. 3.
[4] *Ep.* 80. 6.
[5] E.g. *Hercules Furens* 159 ff., *Herc. Oet.* 640 ff.; cf. own simplicity *Ep.* 108. 13-23.
[6] *Prov.* 6. 6.
[7] *Ep.* 18. 8.
[8] *Ep.* 119. 10.
[9] *Helv.* 10. 3.

inform his mother from exile that the poverty of exile is no hardship to him. [1]

Poverty can be of great educative value in a man's life. It is often those whom he wishes to achieve perfection whom God puts most rigorously to the test in order to see how much strength and courage they possess. 'You learn to know a pilot in a storm, a soldier in the battle-line.' [2] Poverty can also clarify a man's relationships, insofar as it teaches him who his true friends are. As long as a man is wealthy there is the chance that his friends only seek him out for his riches:

> Is it not true that you should love poverty, if only for this single reason, — that it will show you those by whom you are loved? [3]

Seneca regards poverty, like sickness, pain, exile and death, as one of those things the Greeks call ἀδιάφορα, and he himself the *indifferentia,* the indifferent things. [4] Wealth is not a good either. [5] This is apparent from the fact that it has a different effect from the true *bona*:

> all goods ought properly to be free from blame; they are pure, they do not corrupt the spirit, and they do not tempt us. They do, indeed, uplift and broaden the spirit, but without puffing it up. Those things which are goods produce confidence, but riches produce shamelessness. The things which are goods give us greatness of soul, but riches give us arrogance. And arrogance is nothing else than a false show of greatness. [6] I deny that riches are a good; for if they were, they would make men good. As it is, since that which is found in the hands of the wicked cannot be called a good, I refuse to apply the term to riches. [7]

What Seneca goes on to say subsequent to this passage is, however, noteworthy: 'Nevertheless I admit that they [riches] are desirable, that they are useful, and that they add great comforts to living.' Evidently he has not always automatically reckoned wealth among the 'indifferent things', as he would sometimes like to suggest. It cannot be denied, he says earlier in the same essay, that the 'indifferent things' may also be of value in themselves, and that some of them are more desirable than others: 'Do not, therefore, make a mistake — riches are among the more desirable things.' [8]

---

[1] *Helv.* 10. 11; cf. *Ep.* 123. 16.
[2] *Prov.* 4. 5; cf. *Ep.* 20. 11.
[3] *Ep.* 20. 7.
[4] *Ep.* 82. 10.
[5] *Prov.* 5. 2.
[6] *Ep.* 87. 32; cf. *Helv.* 9. 2.
[7] *V.B.* 24. 5.
[8] *V.B.* 22. 4.

It sometimes seems as if Seneca is not really so indifferent to poverty
as he would like to appear. Perhaps, he argues, it is better to endeavour
to strike a happy medium between wealth and poverty:

> In the case of money, an amount that does not descend to poverty, and
> yet is not far removed from poverty, is the most desirable. 1
> Do you ask what is the proper limit to wealth? It is, first to have what
> is necessary, and second, to have what is enough. 2

Indeed, even wealth should not be condemned out of hand. Much
depends upon the sort of person who possesses it and uses it. The
wise man is equal to wealth. He is proof against it. But there is of
course a great difference between the wise and the others:

> Yes, a very great one; let men find that we are unlike the common
> herd, if they look closely. If they visit us at home, they should admire
> us, rather than our household appointments. He is a great man who uses
> earthenware dishes as if they were silver; but he is equally great who
> uses silver as if it were earthenware. It is the sign of an unstable mind
> not to be able to endure riches. 3
> [A wise man] will not thrust aside the generosity of Fortune, and an
> inheritance that has been honourably acquired will give him no cause
> either to blush or to boast. 4

The wealth of a wise man is always 'honourably acquired'. Therefore men should cease denying a philosopher the right to possess money,
and condemning a wise man to poverty. For he has acquired his wealth
honestly; it has not been extorted from others, it is not stained with
another man's blood:

> ... wealth acquired without harm to any man, without base dealing,
> and the outlay of it will be not less honourable than was its acquisition;
> it will make no man groan except the spiteful.

The wise man will be prepared to invite the whole city to his house
and can say: 'If any one recognizes anything as his own, let him take
it.' He who can without risk allow anyone to make a search of his
house is a great man! If no one finds in a wise man's possession
'a single thing to lay his hands upon, then he can be rich boldly and
in all openness.'

> Not a penny will a wise man admit within his threshold that makes a
> dishonest entry; yet he wil not repulse or exclude great wealth that is

---

1 *Tranqu. an.* 8. 9.
2 *Ep.* 2. 6.
3 *Ep.* 5. 6.
4 *V.B.* 23. 2.

the gift of Fortune and the fruit of virtue. For what reason has he to grudge it good quarters? Let it come, let it be welcomed. [1]

Such honourably acquired riches can present the wise man with ample material for the practice of virtue. Naturally it can happen and has happened that riches have stood in the way of the search for wisdom. 'Riches have shut off many a man from the attainment of wisdom.' [2] But how much more opportunity do riches often give the wise man to make the splendour of his virtue shine more brightly. He thinks himself wholly worthy of the gifts of Fortune.

> He does not love riches, but he would rather have them .... he keeps them and wishes them to supply ampler material for exercising his virtue. [3]

For wealth gives a man more chance of developing his powers. 'In poverty there is room for only one kind of virtue — not to be bowed down and crushed by it' — while riches can bring to light so many more virtues: 'moderation and liberality and diligence and orderliness and grandeur all have a wide field.' [4] In giving to others he will use his discretion. He will not give of his wealth at random, but:

> he will give of it either to good men or to those whom he will be able to make good men .... he will give of it only for a reason that is just and defensible, for wrong giving is no other than a shameful waste. [5]

It is no easy matter to give wisely, but wealth presents ample opportunity for good works. [6]

If wealth is thus honestly acquired and regarded as a means of exercising particular virtues, a man may be both wealthy and spiritually independent of his wealth, preserving his peace of mind in all situations. Seneca continually emphasizes the fact that a wise man, even if he is wealthy, has a different attitude towards riches from others. He is at all times prepared to renounce them. If he suddenly loses his wealth, it leaves him unmoved, he remains inwardly the same. He who is dependent upon wealth, must always live in fear:

> No man enjoys a blessing that brings anxiety. [7]

He alone is in kinship with God who has scorned wealth. Of course I

---

[1] *V.B.* 23. 1-3.
[2] *Ep.* 17. 3.
[3] *V.B.* 21. 4.
[4] *V.B.* 22. 1.
[5] *V.B.* 23. 5.
[6] *V.B.* 24. 1, 2.
[7] *Ep.* 14. 18.

do not forbid you to possess it, but I would have you reach the point
at which you possess it dauntlessly; this can be accomplished only by
persuading yourself that you can live happily without it as well as with
it, and by regarding riches always as likely to elude you. 1
We must spurn wealth: wealth is the diploma of slavery .... Liberty
cannot be gained for nothing. If you set a high value on liberty, you
must set a low value on everything else. 2

When Seneca had to do without his wealth while in exile, it left him
spiritually unmoved. For 'the mind has no concern with money'. 3
What an outcry there is in the world over money! The wise man
contemplating all the lawsuits, quarrels and wars over money can only
deem them ridiculous and unworthy. All the treasures of the earth
do not move him. Seneca even ventures to say that all the treasures
of the earth are not worth a good man's frown.' 4

Seneca is probably answering reproaches which have been levelled
at him personally, when he opens the well known chapters of the *De
Vita Beata,* in which he discusses at some length the wise man's attitude
towards his wealth, with a question posed by an imaginary opponent:

Why does that man espouse philosophy and yet live in such opulence?
Why does he say that riches ought to be despised and yet have them?
Seneca replies:

He says these things ought to be despised, not to keep him from having
them, but to keep him from being worried about having them. 5

Even if a wise man enjoys being wealthy, he is not in love with his
riches: 'He does not admit them to his heart, but to his house'. 6 Again
the imaginary opponent is put in his place when he ventures the
opinion that wealth is the same for Seneca as for himself. Seneca
replies:

Do you want to know what a different place they occupy? In my case,
if riches slip away, they will take from me nothing but themselves, while
if they leave you, you will be dumb-founded, and you will feel that you
have been robbed of your real self; in my eyes riches have a certain place,
in yours they have the highest; in fine, I own my riches, yours own you. 7

He would never look up to himself on account of his wealth, however
great it might be, but neither would he look down upon himself,

---

1 *Ep.* 18. 13.
2 *Ep.* 104. 34.
3 *Helv.* 11. 5, 6.
4 *Ira* iii. 33. 1, 4.
5 *V.B.* 21. 1, 2.
6 *V.B.* 21. 4.
7 *V.B.* 22. 5.

were he to end up among the beggars who stretch out their hands for alms. [1] Accordingly there is a vast difference between the wise man's attitude towards wealth and the fool's: 'in the eyes of a wise man riches are a slave, in the eyes of fools a master'. The wise man always bears in mind that riches are never a permanent possession. He

> never reflects so much upon poverty as when he abides in the midst of riches. [2]
>
> .... the wise man — whoever steals away his riches will still leave to him all that is his own; for he ever lives happy in the present and unconcerned about the future. [3]

Thus also when discussing riches Seneca focusses his attention upon the wise man and his virtue, his spiritual independence of all circumstances, his way of using the material he has at hand both in poverty and wealth. Somewhere Seneca uses the following image: just as Phidias could make the finest statues out of materials of very diverse natures, ivory, bronze, marble, or still humbler matter, 'so the wise man will develop virtue, if he may, in the midst of wealth, or, if not, in poverty'. [4] It is furthermore obvious that Seneca repeatedly bases his remarks upon his own situation which occupies his thoughts even when he does not mention it in so many words. He will frequently have been obliged to defend himself, for we know from other sources as well that he was often attacked on account of his wealth. Tacitus, who records that Seneca was very wealthy and powerful, [5] also informs us that P. Suillius asked most ironically:

> By what philosophy, by the tenets of what sect had he amassed, within four years of royal favour, 300,000,000 sesterces? [6]

and that men of doubtful character had later levelled various accusations at Seneca, 'that he was still increasing his colossal wealth, which already exceeded all bounds for a private person.' [7] Neither does Tacitus make any secret of the fact that Seneca, when he saw the clouds gathering, presented a request to the emperor to be allowed to renounce his fortune and give it to his ruler, because he realized that the possession of a vast fortune in Nero's day was extremely dangerous. [8]

---

[1] *V.B.* 25. 1.
[2] *V.B.* 26. 1.
[3] *V.B.* 26. 4; cf. *Const.* 5. 6.
[4] *Ep.* 85. 40.
[5] Tac. *Ann.* 15. 64; cf. *Dio Cassius* 61. 10. 2, 3; 62. 2. 1.
[6] Tac. *Ann.* 13. 42.
[7] Tac. *Ann.* 14. 52.
[8] Tac. *Ann.* 14. 52-56; 15. 45.

Accordingly it is not to be wondered at that Seneca's writings contain many hidden and unvoiced apologias.

Naturally in this respect Paul's position is a very different one. On several occasions he too refers to his personal situation, but he does so in the first place in connection with the relationship between the Apostle and the Church. An Apostle who preaches the Gospel has the right to be supported by the Church, without being obliged to do other work to sustain himself. In this connection he appeals *inter alia* to the Lord's command: 'that those who proclaim the gospel should get their living by the gospel' (1 Cor. 9 : 14). But because he has not wished to burden some of the churches, he has often not made use of the right (1 Cor. 9 : 1 ff.), instead he has earned his living by the work of his own hands and thus has not encumbered the churches. [1] He may say without boasting that he has in this way been an example to the churches. It goes without saying that this course of action has never brought him any wealth. He can, however, refer to it to prove that he has never aimed to enrich himself at the expense of those for whom he worked.

Consequently Paul's own situation was not such that it gave him any call to discuss wealth in particular. Neither does he ever do so as extensively or in such a wide context as Seneca. His conception of what the Christian attitude towards earthly possessions should be is made clear enough in incidental remarks, which he makes in a different context and not within the framework of an inquiry into the problem of wealth. Here, too, he is dealing with concrete situations which he places in the light of the Gospel of salvation. As far as he himself is concerned, he rejoices greatly in the Lord, when a church sends him alms. He does not say this because he is in want:

> I have learned, in whatever state I am, to be content. I know how to be abased, and I know how to abound; in any and all circumstances I have learned the secret of facing plenty and hunger, abundance and want. I can do all things in him who strengthens me. [2]

If he has sown spiritual good for the sake of a community, is it too much to reap its material benefits? (1 Cor. 9 : 11).

Such an exchange should also take place between churches. It is only natural that contributions should be made to a collection for the poor among the saints at Jerusalem. Gentiles who have received a share in

---

[1] 1 Thess. 2 : 9; 2 Thess. 3 : 8; 1 Cor. 4 : 12; cf. Acts 18 : 3; 20 : 34.
[2] Phil. 4 : 10 ff.

their spiritual blessings should also be of service to them in material blessings (Rom. 15 : 26 f.). Members of a church do not enter into litigation with one another, and certainly not before a temporal judge. They should rather suffer wrong and be defrauded (1 Cor. 6 : 1 ff.). It is most offensive in a church if the well-to-do put the needy to shame with their conduct at the Lord's supper (1 Cor. 11 : 20-22).

Among the works of the flesh which are opposed to the fruit of the Spirit is selfishness, acting from motives of self-interest. [1] Naturally greed and avarice ought not to occur in a church. The greedy are among those who will not inherit the kingdom of God. [2] An avaricious man is an idolater, covetousness is idolatry (Eph. 5 : 5; Col. 3 : 5). Hence this severe judgment of greed and avarice which is reflected in strong attachment to property is placed within the framework of the message of salvation. This is also manifest in the passage in which the Church is reminded of the shortness of time and is therefore exhorted to behave in a particular way. Among Paul's commands is the following: 'let those who deal with the world live as though they had no dealings with it. For the form of this world is passing away' (1 Cor. 7 : 29-31).

Hence although Paul nowhere deliberately discusses wealth, the word-group πλοῦτος, πλούσιος, πλουτέω, πλουτίζω nevertheless occurs fairly frequently, but then in connection with other than earthly riches. It is precisely this use of such words that reveals what constitutes true poverty and true wealth for Paul. It almost automatically implies a judgment upon earthly possessions. If this usage is investigated, it soon becomes quite obvious that here too Paul's estimation is wholly dictated by his proclamation of the Gospel. True wealth is indissolubly linked with God's work of salvation in Christ. It is because of this work of salvation that we may speak of the 'riches of [God's] kindness and forbearance and patience' (Rom. 2 : 4), of the 'riches of his glory' (Rom. 9 : 23), of the 'depth of the riches and wisdom and knowledge of God' (Rom. 11 : 33; cf. 11 : 12). It is this work of salvation which proves that God is 'rich in mercy' (Eph. 2 : 4). In the forgiveness of trespasses the Church knows that God will deal with her 'according to the riches of his grace' (Eph. 1 : 7). The Church may know 'the immeasurable riches of his grace in kindness toward us in Christ Jesus' (Eph. 2 : 7). She may know by the Spirit 'what are the riches of his glorious inheritance in the saints' (Eph.

---

[1] Gal. 5 : 20; cf. Rom. 2 : 8; 2 Cor. 12 : 20; Phil. 1 : 17; 2 : 3.
[2] 1 Cor. 6 : 10; cf. Rom. 1 : 29; 1 Cor. 5 : 10 f.; Eph. 4 : 19; 5 : 3, 5.

1 : 18). On behalf of the Church Paul may pray to God 'that according
to the riches of his glory he may grant you to be strengthened with
might through his Spirit in the inner man' (Eph. 3 : 16).

It goes without saying that this 'being rich' and 'making rich' of
God is not divorced from the 'being rich' and 'making rich' of Christ.
On the contrary, these are one in the good work that God has begun
and that He will bring to completion at the day of Jesus Christ (Phil.
1 : 6). Christ, too, 'bestows his riches upon all who call upon him'
(Rom. 10 : 12). Christ, too, is the one who was rich and yet for our
sake became poor (2 Cor. 8 : 9; cf. Phil. 2 : 7 f.) In Him too are
'unsearchable riches' (Eph. 3 : 8).

Again, it goes without saying that Paul can only speak of true wealth
when it is founded upon the riches of God and of Christ. The Church
has been made rich by the poverty of Christ who in His grace became
poor precisely for the sake of this Church (2 Cor. 8 : 9). Even in
connection with the church of Corinth which is, as is apparent from
the rest of the letter, by no means perfect, Paul is able to thank God
'that in every way you were enriched in him [Christ Jesus] with all
speech and all knowledge' (1 Cor. 1 : 5). For the word of Christ
can dwell in the Church richly (Col. 3 : 16). The Church may know of:

> the mystery hidden for ages and generations but now made manifest
> to his saints. To them God chose to make known how great among the
> Gentiles are the riches of the glory of this mystery, which is Christ in
> you, the hope of glory (Col. 1 : 26, 27).

It is only the fact that all true riches are founded upon the riches
that are embodied in the history of salvation, which enables Paul
to say of himself that although he is poor he makes many rich (2 Cor.
6 : 10), despite the fact that he sometimes has to struggle hard for
the churches and all their members:

> that their hearts may be encouraged as they are knit together in love,
> to have all the riches of assured understanding and the knowledge of
> God's mystery, of Christ, in whom are hid all the treasures of wisdom
> and knowledge (Col. 2 : 1-3).

This has nothing in common with human self-exaltation of which
Paul, with marked irony, accuses the Corinthians who boast of their
riches (1 Cor. 4 : 7 f.), but it is made possible by the life of the
Apostle who, when comparing himself with the other Apostles, ventures to say: 'I worked harder than any of them', but then immediately
adds: 'though it was not I, but the grace of God which is with me'

(1 Cor. 15 : 10). Such an utterance will only be understood by those whose faith has opened their eyes to the nature of true wealth.

This conception of true wealth also places various practical concerns in an entirely new light, not only because it is possible to promise a church that God 'will supply every need of yours according to his riches in glory in Christ Jesus' (Phil. 4 : 19), but also because it automatically dominates mutual relations within the Church. When a collection is held, Paul only needs to remind the Church of its riches in Christ. [1]

All this is far removed from empty moralistic imagery. With this word-group Paul describes what he considers to be true wealth, and thus implicitly expresses his opinion of concrete relations. His estimation of wealth and poverty centres entirely around his proclamation of the Gospel.

The particular way in which Paul uses these words emerges all the more clearly when it is compared with Seneca's occasional figurative use of them. Seneca twice quotes with approval one of Epicurus's sayings in which he maintains that true, spiritual wealth is poverty, adjusted to the law of Nature. [2] While Seneca himself by using these words figuratively also gives expression to the paradoxical situation that whoever is poor and therefore apparently lacking in riches, is in reality rich, because wisdom has made the possession of earthly riches completely superfluous. For it 'offers wealth in ready money'. [3] A wise man knows that it is sometimes hard to say who is rich and who is poor; he knows at all events that the rich do not differ from beggars, or rather that they are even more wretched, 'since the beggar wants little, the rich man much.' [4] After what Seneca has said about wealth, it is plain that he considers spiritual wealth as the only true wealth. He consoles his mother with the reminder that:

> It is the mind that makes us rich; this goes with us into exile, and in the wildest wilderness, having found there all that the body needs for its sustenance, it itself overflows in the enjoyment of its own goods. The mind has no concern with money — no whit more than have the immortal gods. [5]

---

[1] 2 Cor. 8 : 9; 9 : 11; 8 : 2; cf. Rom. 12 : 13; Gal. 6 : 2, 10.
[2] *Ep.* 4 : 10; 27 : 9.
[3] *Ep.* 17 : 10.
[4] *Const.* 13. 3.
[5] *Helv.* 11. 5.

Once again it is clear that what for Paul is bound up with the whole question of salvation in Christ, is for Seneca ultimately linked with the individual human spirit of the strong personality.

It has been seen that wealth is discussed at length in Seneca, while in Paul it is only rarely dealt with deliberately and then usually in connection with some other matter. The reverse is true of *work*. This is by no means fortuitous. It is of course a consequenece of the kind of lives they led. In his relationship to the churches, which were not rich as a rule, Paul had every reason to touch upon the material aspect of this relationship, and to write about work to the members of those churches who probably to a great extent had to earn their living by the work of their own hands. However, the pericopes in which he discusses work are not solely concerned with exhortations appropriate to the occasion. It is plain that they are also bound up with the central theme of his preaching. This has sometimes been denied. Joh. Weiss, for example, writes:

> Für ihn [Paulus] ist die Arbeit nicht eine Herzensbefriedigung, sondern eine nun einmal vorhandene Notwendigkeit — ohne jede Schönmalerei. Diese im letzten Grunde gesunde Lebensauffassung steht mit den höchsten religiösen und ethischen Motiven seiner Ethik kaum in engem Zusammenhang; hier redet nicht der enthusiastische Christ, sondern der bürgerlich tüchtige Mensch. [1]

On closer examination this appears to be incorrect. The fact that Christ's name is expressly mentioned in pericopes in which Paul speaks of work or warns against idleness is evidence that his attitude towards work is an integral part of his preaching (2 Thess. 3 : 6, 11, 12). 'Whatever you do, in word or deed, do everything in the name of the Lord Jesus, giving thanks to God the Father through him' (Col. 3 : 17). The only reason why our work here on earth is not meaningless is to be found in the resurrection of Christ and in the prospect which has thereby been opened. [2]

If it should be thought that Paul is referring to the work of faith, i.e. spiritual work, in the aforementioned texts, Col. 3 : 17 and 1 Cor. 15 : 58, it should be borne in mind that Paul makes no noticeable distinction between physical and spiritual labour. In this respect it is for example striking that he uses κόπος and κοπιᾶν both for the strenuous manual labour with which he earns his living and for his

---

[1] Joh. Weiss, *Das Urchristentum*, 1917, p. 463. To the contrary e.g. Walther Bienert, op. cit. p. 325 f.; A. Juncker, op. cit., p. 159.

[2] 1 Cor. 15 : 58; cf. Alan Richardson, *The Biblical Doctrine of Work.* 1958, p. 57 f.

apostolic work in the service of Christ. Sometimes it is impossible to ascertain with certainty which of the two he is referring to. [1] They are both also on a like footing with regard to the right to rewards. Although Paul did not always lay claim to that right, he is wholly convinced that preaching the Gospel also deserves to be rewarded (1 Cor. 9 : 1-15).

That his attitude towards work is indissolubly linked with the central theme of his preaching is likewise made manifest by what he says to slaves. The slave, although his social relationship to his master remains unchanged, has now become a servant of God and Christ. Therefore, although he may appear to be still doing the same work for his master, it has assumed a different character, because it is no longer an eyeservice, because it is no longer done in order to please men, but in order to comply with the will of God as slaves of Christ. He renders services to the Lord with a good will (Eph. 6 : 6, 7). Even the most arduous and despised work assumes a totally new aspect if it is done in the Lord.

Hence it is not to be wondered at that honest manual labour is mentioned in the description of the 'new' man 'created after the likeness of God in true righteousness and holiness', [2] or that Paul writes about 'faith working through love' (Gal. 5 : 6), about the 'work of faith and labor of love and steadfastness of hope in our Lord Jesus Christ' (1 Thess. 1 : 3). For him all works, regardless of their nature, originate in faith.

Likewise work has a special significance within the Church. As Paul himself has often worked with his hands in order not to be a burden to a particular church, [3] so too should each member of the Church work, so that the Church is in no way burdened with his upkeep (1 Thess. 4 : 12). Such work provides him in addition with the opportunity of earning enough to be able to help his brethren as well. [4] Proof of the churches' actual love may therefore be given in an offertory (2 Cor. 8 : 24); it can be used to test the genuineness of this love (2 Cor. 8 : 8). This love is rooted in the depths of the mysteries of salvation (2 Cor. 8 : 9; Eph. 5 : 1, 2).

---

[1] Manual labour: 1 Cor. 4 : 12; Eph. 4 : 28; apostolic or missionary work done by himself or others: Rom. 16 : 12; 1 Cor. 15 : 10; 16 : 16; Gal. 4 : 11; Phil. 2 : 16; Col. 1 : 29; 1 Thess. 5 : 12.

[2] Eph. 4 : 17-32; v. 28: 'let him labor, doing honest work with his hands.'

[3] 2 Cor. 11 : 9; 12 : 13; 2 Thess. 3 : 8.

[4] Eph. 4 : 28; cf. 1 Thess. 4 : 9-12; Acts 20 : 35.

In Thessalonica Paul came into contact with a heathen way of life which often entailed an apparently accepted idleness, also rife within the church. Therefore in his letters to this church Paul had a specific reason for writing about the significance of work. [1] It is in my opinion doubtful whether the expectation of the closeness of the parousia also played an important part in this. [2] At all events not working is a sign of 'living in idleness' (2 Thess. 3 : 6, 11). Those who err in this way should be chastized. During his sojourn in Thessalonica Paul had already more than once commanded the church not to give food to those who did not wish to work (2 Thess. 3 : 6, 10). The church should not further 'living in idleness' in any way.

Accordingly it may be said that Paul holds very positive views upon work, including manual labour, and that these views are rooted in the Gospel. It is notheworthy that the contempt for manual labour which was current in the ancient world is entirely absent in Paul. Likewise the word βάναυσος which reflects a negative appraisal of a man's work, and which was often used in antiquity to describe an artisan, and frequently also means 'vulgar', does not occur in the Pauline epistles. [3]

It is quite likely that we have a biassed picture of the prevailing attitude towards manual labour, because the writers, in whose works we have become familiar with this attitude, were as is only to be expected intellectuals, who moreover usually belonged to the property-owning classes. It is therefore impossible to say that work was not esteemed among the Greeks or Romans as a whole, since the opinion adhered to by large numbers of the population, who never expressed themselves in writing, may well have been profoundly different. [4] Nevertheless we possess many records which are proof of the more or less deep contempt sometimes felt in antiquity for those who worked with their hands. Such a contempt is the natural consequence of a particular view of life and mankind. As soon as it was realized that manual labour usually prevented a man from occupying himself with 'higher', 'spiritual' matters, and also often almost stifled the

---

[1] 1 Thess. 4 : 10 f.; 2 Thess. 3 : 6 ff.

[2] Cf. on this Bienert, op. cit., p. 370 ff.

[3] Cf. F. Gryglewicz, 'La valeur morale du travail manuel dans la terminologie grecque de la Bible', *Biblica* 37, 1956, p. 329.

[4] This is strongly emphasized by Hendrik Bolkestein, *Wohltätigkeit und Armenpflege im vorchristlichen Altertum,* 1939, pp. 191-9, cf. pp. 23, 332 ff. 411 f.; cf. however Jean Laloup, op. cit., p. 276; Georges Pire, op. cit., 1958, p. 79; Th. Schreiner, op. cit., p. 103.

inclination to do so, manual labour was branded as inferior. If Seneca can display such obvious contempt for the body and such admiration for the mind that he therefore repeatedly contends the undesirability of paying too much attention to the body, [1] then manual labour must have lost much of its value for him, and mental work be correspondingly overrated. Work in service of the state is, for example, highly valued by him, and he wishes on no account to be included among the 'scorners' of magistrates or kings or of those who control the administration of public affairs.' [2] He does not belie the ideal of the Roman aristocracy, that work in service of the state is the only truly important work; it gives the life of a well-born Roman its meaning; the rest is *otium*, idleness. Seneca takes doing 'good service to the state' very broadly. He too has a part in it:

> who admonishes young men, who instils virtue into their minds, supplying the great lack of good teachers, who lays hold upon those that are rushing wildly in pursuit of money and luxury, and draws them back, and, if he accomplishes nothing else, at least retards them — such a man performs a public service even in private life. [3]

Seneca refuses to admit certain professions 'into the list of liberal arts': painting, sculpture, marble-working, and other helps toward luxury, wrestling and all knowledge that is compounded of oil and mud; 'otherwise, I should be compelled to admit perfumers also, and cooks, and all others who lend their wits to the service of our pleasures.' [4] Here his attitude is determined by the fact that these professions are in the service of luxury.

It need hardly be said that Seneca rates the intellectual labour of the philosopher very highly. For the wise man is 'the pedagogue of the human race'. [5] He educates others into men of importance. It is he who creates an intellectual *élite* which is of great spiritual value; that special group of people whose virtue lifts them far above the others. Philosophy is indispensable for the formation of the soul, for

> there is but one thing that brings the soul to perfection — the unalterable knowledge of good and evil. But there is no other art [except philosophy] which investigates good and evil. [6]

---

[1] See above pp. 68 ff.
[2] *Ep.* 73. 1; cf. Seneca's view of the state Th. Schreiner, op. cit., p. 97 ff.
[3] *Tranqu. an.* 3. 3.
[4] *Ep.* 88. 18.
[5] *Ep.* 89. 13.
[6] *Ep.* 88. 28.

Seneca is indeed aware that the 'liberal arts do not bestow virtue, but they prepare the soul for the reception of virtue; .... [they] do not conduct the soul all the way to virtue, but merely set it going in that direction.' But in so doing they are of undeniable importance, while manual labour has nothing in common with virtue. [1] Seneca quotes approvingly Posidonius's division of the arts into four classes, the first of which consists of 'those which are common and low.' He goes on to define these more closely: 'The common sort belong to workmen and are mere hand-work; they are concerned with equipping life; there is in them no pretence to beauty or honour.' [2]

On one occasion Seneca states quite plainly that work must share in the contempt that is due to everything connected with the body. 'Work is not a good. Then what is a good? I say, the scorning of work.' [3] To be sure, he goes on to say that 'work is the sustenance of noble minds,' but this applies to men who automatically change anything into something excellent, because their own excellence is so great. One might almost say that the wise man is enveloped in such an atmosphere of sanctity, that everything he touches is sanctified.

Seneca's estimation of work is partly determined by his evaluation of the various classes of persons. In this his thoughts continually revolve around that small *élite* of wise men who are the only human beings of true significance. Seneca's life and writings are permeated by that aristocratic self-assurance which the tenets of the Stoic school make so inevitable. It manifests itself positively in his idolization of the wise man and negatively in his propensity for looking down on others. Theoretically of course he does not make any distinctions between the various classes of society. It is indeed one of Seneca's favourite themes that wisdom and virtue are to be found everywhere. One of the great qualities of philosophy is that it does not inquire into pedigrees. In this sense we may all be aristocrats. History teaches us that nobility of mind can extend through all classes:

> Socrates was no aristocrat. Cleanthes worked at a well and served as a hired man watering a garden. Philosophy did not find Plato already a nobleman; it made him one. Why then should you despair of becoming able to rank with men like these? They are all your ancestors, if you conduct yourself in a manner worthy of them; and you will do so if you convince yourself at the outset that no man outdoes you in real nobility. [4]

---

[1] *Ep.* 88. 20.
[2] *Ep.* 88. 21.
[3] *Ep.* 31. 4, 5.
[4] *Ep.* 44 : 1-8; cf. *Ep.* 66. 3; *Ben.* iii. 18. 2; *Ira* ii. 10. 6.

It may indeed be said in this respect that Stoicism was not destined for
an intellectual *élite,* but that everyone had the choice of being admitted
into the 'households . . . . of noblest intellects'. [1] But because artisans
lack the opportunity to devote themselves to 'intellectual' matters,
almost all of them are summarily dismissed by Seneca by virtue of his
consciousness of belonging to a new intellectual *élite* and his profound
contempt for the *vulgus, populus, multitudo, plebs, turba, plures.*

Seneca is deeply convinced of the existence of an aristocracy of the
human spirit. In his descriptions of it he frequently becomes quite
lyrical: 'If we had the privilege of looking into a good man's soul, oh
what a fair, holy, magnificent, gracious, and shining face should we
behold'; he goes on to enumerate all the virtues which might be seen
there. [2]

> If you see a man who is unterrified in the midst of dangers, untouched
> by desires, happy in adversity, peaceful amid the storm, who looks down
> upon men from a higher plane, and views the gods on a footing of
> equality, will not a feeling of reverence for him steal over you? [3]

In the midst of the common people the wise man pursues his sovereign
course, 'as the planets make their way against the whirl of heaven'. [4]
A divine inspiration and exaltation, a *sacer instinctus,* enables him to
soar to unprecedented heights. [5] Only a few such men of genius will
be able to hold their heads above water when the floods of time sub-
merge everything. [6]

The other side of this cult of the few upon whom Seneca lavishes
such high praise, is his profound contempt for the common people, the
masses. They consist of those who are enchained by stupidity, foolishness, who are swayed by all kinds of passions, who surrender to the
lower pleasure of life and know nothing of the higher life of the spirit.
To defend their own iniquity, they pit themselves against reason. Therefore, Seneca urges repeatedly, those who desire spiritual health must
retire from the world. [7] It is useless to say: "This side seems to be in
a majority", when the happy life is under discussion:

---

[1] *Brev.* 15. 3; cf. R. Bakker, *Lot en daad, geluk en rede in het Griekse denken,*
1957, p. 144 f.; Pohlenz, *Stoa* I, p. 367.
[2] *Ep.* 115. 3.
[3] *Ep.* 41. 4; cf. *Ep.* 45. 9.
[4] *Const.* 14. 4.
[5] *Tranqu.* an. 17. 11.
[6] *Ep.* 21. 5.
[7] *V.B.* 1. 4, 5; *Brev.* 18. 1; *Ep.* 10. 1; 25. 6.

For that is just the reason it is the worse side. Human affairs are not so happily ordered that the majority prefer the better things; a proof of the worst choice is the crowd. Therefore let us find out what is best to do, not what is most commonly done — what will establish our claim to lasting happiness, not what finds favour with the rabble, who are the worst posible exponents of the truth. But by the rabble I mean no less the servants of the court than the servants of the kitchen. 1

The *vulgus* never judges rightly. 2 It is for instance mistaken in its judgment of true happiness. 3 Those things desired or feared by the common man are really neither goods nor evils. 4 'We ought to bring ourselves to believe that all the vices of the crowd are, not hateful, but ridiculous'. 5 The intellectual *élite* should lead a better life than the vulgus, but not completely contrary to it, for then it will lose its pedagogic influence upon the common people. 6

One must avoid contact with the masses as much as is possible, for one is always contaminated by them:

To consort with the crowd is harmful; there is no person who does not make some vice attractive to us, or stamp it upon us, or taint us unconsciously therewith. Certainly, the greater the mob with which we mingle, the greater the danger.

This is why all public amusements are so damaging to the morals. 7 The populace has always been a *honesti dissuasor* (a discourager of honourable things). 8 A weak judgment is easily undermined still further with the aid of the crowd. 9 Therefore in all one's conduct one must remove oneself from the common herd and tower above it. 10 Therefore one should never strive to win the acclaim of the crowd. That should be left to actors. Philosophy should make a man completely independent of the praise of the masses: 'It will make you prefer to please yourself rather than the populace, it will make you weigh, and not merely count, men's judgments'. 11 The philosopher must be especially on his guard against applause: 'These outcries should be left

---

1 *V.B.* 2. 1, 2; elsewhere too he warns against attaching value to the opinion of the majority, *Ep.* 7. 12; 8. 3; 102. 17; 99. 17; *Helv.* 6. 1.
2 *V.B.* 14. 2; cf. *Ira* iii. 41. 2.
3 *Ep.* 45. 9; cf. *Ep.* 94. 73; 98. 13; 94. 60.
4 *Prov.* 5. 1.
5 *Tranqu. an.* 15. 2.
6 *Ep.* 5. 3.
7 *Ep.* 7. 1-3; cf. *Ep.* 8. 1.
8 *Ep.* 108. 7.
9 *De Otio* 1. 1.
10 *Ira* iii. 25. 3; cf. *Ep.* 18. 3.
11 *Ep.* 29. 12.

for the arts which aim to please the crowd; let philosophy be wor-shipped in silence.' [1]

However much the Stoic school proclaimed and was obliged to pro-claim the equality of all human beings, since it took reason, which after all breaks down all barriers between men, as its major premise; however much this principle sometimes influences the Stoic attitude towards others (e.g. slaves); however successful it was in overcoming all social distinctions among its adherents (M. Aurelius and Epictetus!), in practice ancient culture was and remained in the hands of an *élite*. The very social conditions excluded the masses from it. In addition, the Stoic school, including Seneca, greatly encouraged and cultivated an aristocratic consciousness. Although his fundamental principles will have led him to give his own interpretation to Horace's words: *Odi profanum vulgus et arceo*, 'I hate the common people and keep them at bay', it is obvious that the philosopher's consciousness of his own aristocracy could easily nurture and strengthen a sense of social super-iority. Hence although Seneca too theoretically considered a man's value to be wholly independent of his social status, and although he theoretically acknowledged the equality of all men, his deeply rooted consciousness of his own intellectual aristocracy made him in practice despise the masses even more profoundly than he probably would otherwise have done as a prominent Roman, belonging to the oligar-chical *élite*. [2]

It need scarcely be said that Paul's conception of human equality is founded upon very different premises and consequently in practice exerts a very different influence upon human relations; for Paul considers that men are equal in that they are all by nature sinners before the holy God, all are spoken to by God, all may hear the offer of salvation, all who have put on Christ may be one in Him (Gal. 3 : 27 f.).

---

[1] *Ep.* 52. 13.
[2] Cf. Baur, p. 209; W. Nestle, *Griechische Studien*, 1948, pp. 626, 655; H. Gree-ven, op. cit., pp. 141, 153.

CHAPTER SIX

ESCHATOLOGY

We have chosen to reserve the discussion of the significance of eschatology in the writings of Paul and Seneca until now. Paul's eschatology should not by rights be dealt with in a separate chapter at the end of a book. It will be obvious from what has gone before that his whole theology is steeped in eschatology, and that within this eschatological framework the past, present and future are most closely linked with one another. Together they form one great history of salvation, in which although the expectation of the salvation to come can of course be mentioned and described to a certain extent independently, it can never be wholly separated from the salvation which has already taken place. Accordingly Paul is never solely concerned with the expectations of the individual, instead everything he has to say about the death and future of the individual is indissolubly linked with the history of salvation as a whole.

In Seneca the only thing comparable with this is what he writes about cyclic destruction and return. [1] Although such an expectation is of course entirely different in content from Paul's expectation of the salvation to come, it is at least an expectation which concerns the whole of things and is not restricted to the individual. Nevertheless the fate of the individual in and after death remains of prime importance for Seneca. Hence it is far more in keeping with Seneca's outlook than with Paul's if eschatology is placed last here. Almost the entire range of subjects Paul deals with in his letters throws light upon his eschatology. This is only to be expected, since Paul considers the history of salvation as one vast unity. However, we are scarcely doing Seneca an injustice by leaving the discussion of his 'eschatology' until last.

It may, it is true, be said that for Seneca too all kinds of human actions and relationships are overshadowed by the knowledge of man's mortality. Seneca frequently reminds his readers of the transitoriness of their lives. He writes a great deal about death and continually

---

[1] See above p. 32 ff.

exclaims how foolish it is not to look the reality of death in the face. In his *De Brevitate Vitae* Seneca says: 'You have been engrossed, life hastens by; meanwhile death will be at hand, for which, willy nilly, you must find leisure.' [1] And elsewhere in the same work he cautions: 'Life is divided into three periods — that which has been, that which is, that which will be. Of these the present time is short, the future is doubtful, the past is certain.' [2] Towards the end of his essay on anger he states his belief that the most powerful means of quelling anger is reflection upon our mortality, *cogitatio mortalitatis*. Those enmities we bear with such relentlessness may rapidly and suddenly be brought to an end by an attack of fever or some other disorder: 'Soon death will step in and part the fiercest pair of fighters.' None of us is exempted from the fact that 'fate looms above our heads' and therefore it may well be so that: 'That hour which you appoint for the death of another is perchance near your own.' Why, Seneca asks, do men not rather gather up their brief lives and make them peaceful for themselves and others? For death, which makes us all equal, may come at any moment. [3]

Not only the old, but also the young should bear in mind that they may die at any moment:

> Hence, every day ought to be regulated as if it closed the series, as if it rounded out and completed our existence. [4] You do not know where death awaits you; so be ready for it everywhere. [5]

Therefore:

> the mortal heart is never more divine than when it reflects upon its mortality, and understands that man was born for the purpose of fulfilling his life, and that the body is not a permanent dwelling, but a sort of inn (with a brief sojourn at that) which is to be left behind when one perceives that one is a burden to the host. [6]

Death threatens us all everywhere, not only in obviously dangerous situations. Seneca never tires of repeating this. How foolish is the man who will not look reality in the face. All that lives grows for death. Death is a law of nature. We should therefore contemplate it with

---

[1] *Brev.* 8. 5.

[2] *Brev.* 10. 2.

[3] *Ira* iii. 42. 2, 3, 4; 43. 1, 2; cf. *N.Q.* vi. 1. 8; *Ep.* 30. 11; 123. 16; see also above p. 180 f.

[4] *Ep.* 12. 6, 8.

[5] *Ep.* 26. 7.

[6] *Ep.* 120, 14; Kreyher (p. 89) compares this with 2 Cor. 5 : 1.

equanimity, and not fear the word but make ourselves so familiar with it that we can go to meet it when necessary. [1]

In one sense death is not only a moment that still lies before us. Death is, for instance, already master of the years that lie behind us. Every man should understand that he is dying daily, *se cotidie mori*. [2]

> We die every day. For every day a little of our life is taken from us; even when we are growing, our life is on the wane. We lose our childhood, then our boyhood, and then our youth. Counting even yesterday, all past time is lost time; the very day which we are now spending is shared between ourselves and death.

It is not the last drop that empties the water-clock, but all that which previously flowed out; 'similarly, the final hour when we cease to exist does not of itself bring death; it merely of itself completes the death-process'. [3] How great is:

> our madness in cleaving with great affection to such a fleeting thing as the body, and in fearing lest some day we may die, when every instant means the death of our previous condition. [4]

Accordingly Seneca is filled with the realization of the transitoriness of all human life. Nevertheless death need not be feared. Again and again he claims that death is not an evil. [5] Death, he writes, is sometimes rated as the worst of evils. Yet there is nothing evil in it except the fear which is not in death, but which precedes it. [6] The actual moment of death is so brief and fleeting that it cannot be realized. Is it not shameful, Seneca asks, to fear so long that which happens so quickly? [7] Dying is easy; our fear of it is hard. [8]

Death is neither a good nor an evil. It could only be one or the other if it were anything, but it is nothing. [9] Seneca therefore considers death as one of the ἀδιάφορα, the *indifferentia*. [10]

---

[1] Such lamentations are to be found in e.g. *Ep.* 70. 2; 93. 12; *Tranqu. an.* 11. 7; *Pol.* 11. 4; *N.Q.* vi. 2. 6; 32. 8, 9; *Ep.* 49. 11; *Hercules Furens* 870: *tibi crescit omne*; *N.Q.* vi. 32. 12: *Mors naturae lex est.*

[2] *Ep.* 1. 2.

[3] *Ep.* 24. 19, 20.

[4] *Ep.* 58. 23; the death of the soul of those who surrender entirely to a life of lust is also a favorite theme of Seneca's, cf. E. Benz, op. cit., p. 98 ff.; Kreyher (p. 90) compares in this respect *Brev.* 12. 9 and *Ep.* 122. 3, 4 with Eph. 2 : 1; 5 : 14 and 1 Tim. 5 : 6.

[5] *Ep.* 75. 17; 123. 16; *Const.* 8. 3.

[6] *Ep.* 104. 10.

[7] *Prov.* 6. 9.

[8] *N.Q.* vi. 32. 7.

[9] *Marc.* 19. 5.

[10] *Ep.* 82. 10.

Consequently death may be despised. Seneca repeatedly recommends such an attitude. Contempt of death is effective against every weapon and all enemies. [1] In times of sickness Seneca's counsel is "Despise death", [2] a remedy which will not only cure the complaint of the moment, but which will act as a cure for life. Any complaint may be borne, if the sufferer despises its final threat. [3] Death ought to be despised more than it is in reality, [4] although at all times, even in Seneca's own times, there have been men who despised death, *contemptores mortis*. [5] But it is not so easy to lay aside our fear of death, for

> we are ignorant of the future into which we shall transfer ourselves, and we shrink from the unknown. Moreover, it is natural to fear the world of shades, whither death is supposed to lead. Therefore, although death is something indifferent, it is nevertheless not a thing which we can easily ignore. The soul must be hardened by long practice, so that it may learn to endure the sight and the approach of death. [6]

It cannot be denied that death is in bad odour. Yet it is foolhardy to condemn what one does not know. Death is, it must be conceded, helpful to many, because it frees them from all kinds of miseries. Let us always remember: 'We are in the power of nothing when once we have death in our own power!' [7] While 'He who fears death will never do anything worthy of a man who is alive.' [8]

Difficult though it may sometimes be to have to die, it can be *learnt*. A worthy death is then possible. 'It takes the whole of life to learn how to live, and — what will perhaps make you wonder more — it takes the whole of life to learn how to die.' [9] In this the 'highpriests of liberal studies' can be of assistance. They teach a man how to die. [10] Learning to die is so important that preparation for death should really precede preparation for life. [11] The only one to go to meet death cheerfully is the man who has long since prepared for it. [12] A worthy death sets a seal of nobility upon life. [13]

---

[1] *Ep.* 36. 8.
[2] *Ep.* 78. 5.
[3] *Ep.* 78. 12; cf. *N.Q.* ii. 59. 3; *Ira* iii. 15. 3.
[4] *Ep.* 82. 16.
[5] *Ep.* 24. 11; cf. *Ep.* 30. 6.
[6] *Ep.* 82. 15, 16.
[7] *Ep.* 91. 21.
[8] *Tranqu. an.* 11. 6; cf. *Ep.* 78. 25; *N.Q.* vi. 32. 9, 12.
[9] *Brev.* 7. 3.
[10] *Brev.* 14. 5; 15. 1; cf. *Ep.* 4. 5; 49. 9, 10.
[11] *Ep.* 61. 4.
[12] *Ep.* 30. 12.
[13] *Ep.* 13. 14.

A man's attitude towards death is naturally determined to a considerable degree by what he understands death to be, and by what he believes will happen after death. For Seneca, with his dualistic anthropology, death is primarily the separation of the spirit from the body. If we recall how contemptuously Seneca refers to the body and how lyrically he alludes to the spirit, the soul, it is understandable that he looks upon death which frees the soul from the body as a blessing. Death is the fleeting moment 'when the breath forsakes the body', *quo anima discedit a corpore,* [1] 'when the soul has escaped from this present prison', [2] when the divine soul issues from the mortal man, [3] 'when the souls are freed from their chains'. [4] Seneca lets the soul say:

> When the day comes to separate the heavenly from its earthly blend, I shall leave the body here where I found it, and shall of my own volition betake myself to the gods. [5]

Therefore he is able to comfort Marcia on the death of her son by saying:

> Only the image of your son — and a very imperfect likeness it was — has perished; he himself is eternal and has reached now a far better state, stripped of all outward encumbrances and left simply himself.

For he has now left existence in this earthly body, 'the chains and darkness to our souls.' And now eternal peace, *aeterna requies,* awaits his soul, 'when it has passed from earth's dull motley to the vision of all that is pure and bright.' He counsels Marcia not to visit her son's grave; for what lies there is only:

> his basest part and a part that in life was the source of much trouble — bones and ashes are no more parts of him than were his clothes and the other protections of the body. He is complete — leaving nothing of himself behind, he has fled away and wholly departed from earth. [6]

In exile Seneca comforts his mother with the thought that the spirit can easily relinquish all earthly things, for if the spirit is conscious of its own nature, it cannot possibly love such things, 'since it is itself light and uncumbered, waiting only to be released from the body before is soars to highest heaven.' [7]

---

[1] *Prov.* 6. 9.
[2] *Ep.* 88. 34.
[3] *Ep.* 92. 34.
[4] *Pol.* 9. 8.
[5] *Ep.* 102. 22.
[6] *Marc.* 24. 5; 25. 1.
[7] *Helv.* 11. 6.

So death is the moment in which the soul is separated from the body. But it is not so easy to ascertain what Seneca thinks of the life after death. His works contain all kinds of irreconcilable ideas upon this subject. It would seem that Seneca expresses his personal conviction when he leaves the question of what occurs after death undecided, when he adopts an attitude of sceptical uncertainty towards the life after death, declaring that he at any rate has made his peace with death:

> What is death? It is either the end, or a process of change. I have no fear of ceasing to exist; it is the same as not having begun. Nor do I shrink from changing into another state, because I shall, under no conditions, be as cramped as I am now. [1]

This *aut finis aut transitus* is a favourite theme of Seneca's, which recurs time and again in his writings in all kinds of variations:

> Death either annihilates us or strips us bare. If we are then released, there remains the better part, after the burden has been withdrawn; if we are annihilated, nothing remains; good and bad are alike removed. [2]
> Scorn death, which either ends you or transfers you. [3]
> Let great souls comply with God's wishes, and suffer unhesitatingly whatever fate the law of the universe ordains; for the soul at death is either sent forth into a better life, or else, at least, without suffering any harm to itself, it will be mingled with nature again, and will return to the universe. [4]

In this notion there is great comfort. Polybius, who has lost his brother, may console himself with the thought of these two possibilities, both of which really preclude all grief:

> If the dead retain no feeling whatever, my brother has escaped from all the ills of life, and has been restored to that state in which he had been before he was born, and, exempt from every ill, he fears nothing, desires nothing, suffers nothing. What madness this is — that I should never cease to grieve for one who will never grieve any more! If, however, the dead do retain some feeling, at this moment my brother's soul, released, as it were, from its long imprisonment, exults to be at last its own lord and master, enjoys the spectacle of Nature, and from its higher place looks down upon all human things, while upon things divine, the explanation of which it had so long sought in vain, it gazes with a nearer vision. And so why should I pine away in yearning for him who either is happy or does not exist? But to weep for one who is happy is envy; for one who does not exist, madness. [5]

---

[1] *Ep.* 65. 24.
[2] *Ep.* 24. 18.
[3] *Prov.* 6. 6.
[4] *Ep.* 71. 16; cf. *Ep.* 99. 30.
[5] *Pol.* 9. 2, 3.

A man should be able to bear bravely the fact that what happens after death remains uncertain until the end. In this respect he can take a lesson from Canus who, when condemned to death by Caligula, continued to search for truth until the very end 'and to make his own death a subject for debate', *ex morte sua quaestionem habere.* 1 In my belief Seneca too considered death as a *quaestio.* Nothing can be said about it with certainty. But whatever the outcome may be, whether there is a life after death or not, death is not a cause for grief.

Sometimes, however, Seneca does not leave this question undecided. It is noteworthy that he sometimes chooses the first possibility and at other times the second. For he declares repeatedly that death is non-existence, that the state after death is the same as before birth. Not only does he present this as a possibility, but he also states it as his own conviction. He has already had long experience of death:

> "When?" you ask. Before I was born. Death is non-existence [*non esse*], and I know already what that means. What was before me will happen again after me. If there is any suffering in this state, there must have been such suffering also in the past, before we entered the light of day. 2
> It is all the same; you will not be, and you were not. 3
> Nothing can hurt him who is as naught ... no torment can come to him from the fact that he is no more — for what feeling can belong to one who does not exist? 4

Then, too, death is of course the end of al trouble:

> Death is a release from all suffering, a boundary beyond which our ills cannot pass — it restores us to that peaceful state in which we lay before we were born.

If death 'is itself nothing and reduces all things to nothingness', then: 'Fortune cannot maintain a hold upon that which Nature has let go, nor can he be wretched who is non-existent.' 5

So while Seneca is in some places very definite about death being non-existence, a return to the pre-natal state, in others — sometimes even in the same work — he attests to a firm belief in a life after death, the glorious life that awaits the souls:

> The souls that are quickly released from intercourse with men find the journey to the gods above most easy; for they carry less weight of earthly

---

1 *Tranqu. an.* 14. 7, 8.
2 *Ep.* 54. 4.
3 *Ep.* 77. 11.
4 *Ep.* 99. 30; cf. *Troades* 392-408.
5 *Marc.* 19. 5.

dross ... And souls that are great find no joy in lingering in the body; they yearn to go forth and burst their bonds, and they chafe against these narrow bounds, accustomed as they are to range far aloft throughout the universe, and from on high to look down in scorn upon the affairs of men. 1

On the death of her son Seneca consoles Marcia with the thought that his soul is now at last released from his body:

It ever strives to rise to that place from which it once descended. There eternal peace [*aeterna requies*] awaits it when it has passed from earth's dull motley to the vision of all that is pure and bright. 2

Her son, freed from his body, 'soared aloft and sped away to join the souls of the blessed.' There he was welcomed by 'a saintly band', *coetus sacer,* among whom was Marcia's father who would instruct his grandson in the movement of the stars, 'not by guesswork, but by experience having true knowledge of them all.' Marcia should no longer think of her father and her son as they were here on earth, but as:

far loftier beings, dwelling in the highest heaven .... [They] have changed for the better! Throughout the free and boundless spaces of eternity they wander; .... there every way is level, and, being swift and unencumbered, they easily are pervious to the matter of the stars and, in turn, are mingled with it. 3

It is with similar lyrical effusions that Seneca comforts Polybius on the death of his brother: death is like entering a safe harbour after being tossed around for a long time on a stormy sea:

There is no harbour save death .... At last he is free, at last safe, at last immortal .... He delights now in the open and boundless sky, from a low and sunken region he has darted aloft to that place (whatever it be) which receives in its happy embrace souls that are freed from their chains; and he now roams there, and explores with supreme delight all the blessings of Nature. You are mistaken — your brother has not lost the light of day, but he has gained a purer light. 4

It is plain that such eulogies on the glory of the life after death may be expected first and foremost in those writings in which Seneca wishes to console someone upon the death of a friend or relation. After all it is only human to be most positive when trying to give comfort to the bereaved; then we go as far as possible in camouflaging

---

1 *Marc.* 23. 1, 2.
2 *Marc.* 24. 5; cf. *Marc.* 19. 6: *aeterna pax.*
3 *Marc.* 25. 1-3.
4 *Pol.* 9. 6, 7, 8; cf. *Ep.* 70. 3.

the seriousness, the decisiveness of death, if necessary laying a smoke-screen of comforting words which at least have a heartening sound in the ears of the grieved.

It cannot be said, however, that statements of this nature occur only in the *Consolationes*. In his letters too Seneca does not merely restrict himself to questions; occasionally he makes very positive pronouncements upon the survival of the soul after death, as for example in *Epistle* 102 where he makes the soul say *inter alia* (102. 23):

> "When the day comes to separate the heavenly from its earthly blend, I shall leave the body here where I found it, and shall of my own volition betake myself to the gods. I am not apart from them now, but am merely detained in a heavy and earthly prison."

This is followed by:

> These delays of mortal existence are a prelude to the longer and better life. As the mother's womb holds us for ten months, making us ready, not for the womb itself, but for the existence into which we seem to be sent forth when at last we are fitted to draw breath and live in the open; just so, throughout the years extending between infancy and old age, we are making ourselves ready for another birth. A different beginning, a different condition, await us. We cannot yet, except at rare intervals, endure the light of heaven; therefore, look forward without fearing to that appointed hour, — the last hour of the body but not of the soul . . . . That day, which you fear as being the end of al things, is the birthday of your eternity [*aeterni natalis*].

When a human being lays aside the body he has inhabited for so long, he is drawn into noble communion with the stars: 'Then you will say that you have lived in darkness, after you have seen, in your perfect state, the perfect light'. [1] With respect to Scipio Africanus Seneca is convinced that 'his soul has indeed returned to the skies whence it came'. [2]

For Seneca, however, immortality is — even when he states his certain belief in it — bounded by the cyclic return of all things. When one cycle is replaced by another and everything is renewed, the soul too participates in that temporary destruction and in the renewal. At the end of the *Consolatio ad Marciam* Seneca makes Marcia's father, who is in heaven, say:

> "Then also the souls of the blest, who have partaken of immortality, when it shall seem best to God to create the universe anew — we, too,

---

[1] *Ep.* 102. 22-24, 26, 28.
[2] *Ep.* 86. 1.

amid the falling universe, shall be added as a tiny fraction to this mighty destruction, and shall be changed again into our former elements." 1

Elsewhere too it is apparent that Seneca adheres to the Stoic belief in the rebirth of all things. None of the things which we see disappear and which are re-absorbed by nature, is permanently destroyed:

> they merely end their course and do not perish. And death, which we fear and shrink from, merely interrupts life, but does not steal it away; the time will return when we shall be restored to the light of day. 2

Hence although immortality is circumscribed it is clear from what has been said above that there are places in Seneca's writings where he thinks in terms of the survival of the soul after death. But despite this he nowhere makes any attempt to justify this belief in immortality. It can of course be said that it is a natural outcome of Seneca's anthropology: if the soul is the divine part of man, then it may be expected to survive death. Accordingly it is not to be wondered at that Seneca quotes from Plato's *Phaedo* 64 A in the *Consolatio ad Marciam,* in which his belief in the life after death is expressed more positively and explicitly than anywhere else. But it would seem that even his anthropology did not lead him to an unwavering belief in immortality. This may be concluded from the number of statements testifying to his disbelief, or to say the least, doubt on this point. It would seem that Seneca himself is highly sceptical of the possibility of life after death, and that the passages in which he apparently writes with confidence about such a life are either inspired by a desire to give comfort or are a concession to a fairly widespread opinion. He sometimes concedes the latter possibility himself:

> when we discuss the immortality of the soul, we are influenced in no small degree by the general opinion of mankind [*consensus hominum*], who either fear or worship the spirits of the lower world. 3

But his trust in the correctness of the 'general opinion of mankind' is by no means absolute:

> perhaps, if only the tale told by wise men is true and there is a bourne to welcome us, then he whom we think we have lost has only been sent on ahead. 4

His objection to the opinions of great men, who with respect to the immortality of souls, *aeternitas animarum,* hold up visions of all kinds

---

1 *Marc.* 26. 7.
2 *Ep.* 36. 10.
3 *Ep.* 117. 6.
4 *Ep.* 63. 16.

of delights before men's eyes, is that they promise more than they prove. He has, he writes, sometimes momentarily succumbed to them but a letter from Lucilius was sufficient to arouse him from that 'pleasant dream', that 'lovely dream'. Not until he has dealt with this, will he be able to recapture his dream. [1] True proof of the life after death is not to be found in the *consensus hominum* either. [2] At best this can temporarily lull Seneca into pleasant dreams. However the slightest down-to-earth criticism awakens him with a start. Even in the *Consolationes* in which he frequently tenders comfort with lyrical eulogies upon the glories of the life after death, what would seem to be his personal view, i.e. that death may be equated with non-existence, often breaks through. It is as if, whenever he forgets that he is supposed to be consoling someone, he suddenly awakes from a pleasant dream and falls back upon not pronouncing judgment on that which can never be known with absolute certainty. [3]

Like Seneca, Paul too has a very personal conception of the shadow of mortality which hangs over humanity, because he has been threatened by death many times. This may be concluded not only from Acts but also from his own letters. He can say of himself that he is 'in peril every hour' — 'I die every day.' While immediately after this he alludes to a personal experience: 'humanly speaking, I fought with beasts at Ephesus.' [4] Whatever the precise meaning of this may be, it is plain that Paul was in mortal danger in Ephesus, one of the apparently many times that he was 'often near death' (2 Cor. 11 : 23). Was it on this occasion that Priscilla and Aquila 'risked their necks' for Paul's sake, a sacrifice which he later recalls with gratitude (Rom. 16 : 3, 4)? We do not know for sure, and probably we will never know. It is once again evident that Paul never writes about such things from motives of self-preoccupation, but always in connection with other matters that are for him of essential importance. Time and again we have to be

---

[1] *Ep.* 102. 1, 2; *iucundum somnium, bellum somnium.*

[2] Cf. C. C. Grollios, op. cit., p. 38 f.

[3] Many scholars have pointed out Seneca's uncertainty and inconsistency in this respect; cf. e.g. J. B. Lightfoot, op. cit., p. 323; Ludwig Friedlaender, *Sittengeschichte Roms,* 1934, p. 1025; Pohlenz, *Stoa* I, p. 322 f.; K. Deissner, *Paulus und Seneca,* 1917, p. 10; id., *Auferstehungshoffnung und Pneumagedanke bei Paulus,* 1912, p. 131 f.; Erwin Rohde, *Psyche,* [4]1907, II, p. 328; Franz Cumont, *After Life in Roman Paganism,* 1923, p. 14; G. A. van den Bergh van Eysinga, *Voorchristelijk Christendom,* 1918, pp. 6, 85; H. Wagenvoort, *Varia Vita,* 1927, p. 101 f.; E. Vernon Arnold, op. cit., p. 268 ff.; P. Faider, op. cit., p. 178; Th. Schreiner, op. cit., p. 65.

[4] 1 Cor. 15 : 30-32.

content with brief hints which nevertheless make it clear enough in what mortal danger he was often placed. We know of the affliction he had to bear in Asia, where he felt as if he had already received the death-sentence (2 Cor. 1 : 9). We know that when he wrote to the Philippians he seriously took into account the possibility of dying (Phil. 1 : 20). And even when he does not speak of the threat of death in so many words, it may frequently be inferred from passages in his letters that he was in danger of his life more often than his direct admissions in this respect would lead us to believe. He was surely faced with death when he was shipwrecked — a disaster which happened at least four times (2 Cor. 11 : 25; Acts 27) —, when his ship was adrift for a full twenty-four hours (2 Cor. 11 : 25); probably also on a number of occasions during his journeys when he was beset by all possible dangers (2 Cor. 11 : 26), perhaps also when he just managed to slip through king Aretas's fingers (2 Cor. 11 : 32 f.; Acts 9 : 23-25).

Such scanty and often incidental remarks and allusions are at all events sufficient for us to understand that Paul was justified in regarding himself as in constant danger of death, and that such comments as 'in peril every hour' (1 Cor. 15 : 30); 'I die every day' (1 Cor. 15 : 31); 'we are afflicted in every way' (2 Cor. 4 : 8); 'always carrying in the body the death of Jesus' (2 Cor. 4 : 10); 'while we live we are always being given up to death' (2 Cor. 4 : 11), 'like men sentenced to death' (1 Cor. 4 : 9), are inspired by the stern reality of his life.

Paul does not, however, write about these matters within the framework of a description of man's mortality in general. But when he speaks of his sufferings and of being in mortal danger he is almost always referring to the suffering and death which he voluntarily takes upon himself as a servant of Christ and in fellowship with Christ. These sufferings and afflictions, threats and perilous situations are the result of his preaching the Gospel. When he writes: 'while we live we are always being given up to death', he is not alluding to the transience of man's life in general, but to the dangers in the life of an Apostle who is always being threatened by 'death for Jesus' sake' (2 Cor. 4 : 11). It is the 'death of Jesus' which he always carries in his body (2 Cor. 4 : 10).

Accordingly the threat of death referred to by Paul is very different from anything mentioned in Seneca. 'I die every day' (1 Cor. 15 : 31) superficially bears a close resemblance to Seneca's 'daily dying'. However, whereas the latter wishes to say that death is not only a moment that lies before us, but that it really dominates our lives (i.e. he thus wants to remind man of his mortality in general), [1] Paul is expressing the fact that he always carries the death of Jesus in his body. [2]

Hence here too superficial verbal coincidences are by no means indicative of more profound resemblances. A further example also brings us, with regard to Paul, into the field of eschatological expectation. It has sometimes been thought that a striking parallel was to be found in Seneca to what is said in one of the Pauline epistles about the shortness of time. Seneca counsels Marcia always to remember that all we own is only temporarily our property: 'All these fortuitous things, that glitter about us — children, honours, wealth — are not our own but borrowed trappings; not one of them is given to us outright.' We never know when they will all be taken from us, which is all the more reason why we should enjoy them as much as possible while we may:

> Snatch the pleasures your children bring, let your children in turn find delight in you, and drain joy to the dregs without delay; no promise has been given you for this night — nay, I have offered too long a respite! — no promise has been given even for this hour. We must hurry .... [3]

It is particularly these last words 'we must hurry', *festinandum est,* which remind some scholars, who believe Stoic doctrines to be one of the sources of the Gospel, of what Paul writes to the church of Corinth:

> I mean, brethren, the appointed time has grown very short; from now on, let those who have wives live as though they had none, and those who mourn as though they were not mourning, and those who rejoice as though they were not rejoicing, and those who buy as though they had no goods, and those who deal with the world as though they had no dealings with it. For the form of this world is passing away (1 Cor. 7 : 29-31).

Is this really the same as the notion to be found in Seneca? This has sometimes been argued. [4] At first sight it may certainly seem to be so. But on closer examination it becomes obvious that the two writers mean entirely different things. When Seneca counsels Marcia to enjoy all her possessions as much as possible and as soon as possible, he is thinking of the transience of human life. We soon have to die, we do

---

[1] *Ep.* 1. 2; 24. 20, cf. above p. 221.
[2] 1 Cor. 15 : 31; 2 Cor. 4 : 10; cf. 2 Cor. 6 : 9; *Th. W.* III, p. 21.
[3] *Marc.* 10. 1, 4.
[4] E.g. Bruno Bauer, *Christus und die Caesaren,* ²1879, p. 47 f.

not know when. This should remind us how little opportunity we may have of finding delight in each other. When Paul writes that time is short, that 'the form of this world is passing away', then he does not intend to indicate the transience of all earthly things, of human life in general, but the fact that this world passes away when seen in the light of the course of the salvation-occurrence. This world, however, is followed by the world to come. God's salvation has already been revealed in Christ, but this work of salvation, which God has begun and which has become clearly visible in Christ, still awaits its completion in the world to come. Christ's advent upon earth, His life, His death and His resurrection have already taken place, His second coming lies in the future. So life on earth is provisional in character; it is an interim which passes, and no one knows how quickly. This expectation also irradiates the personal lives and communal lives of those who expect the second coming of Christ, the resurrection of the dead and the last judgment. In Seneca all attention converges upon the life and death of the individual, the transience of mankind in general; in Paul everything revolves around the history of salvation, which is moving from the already clearly visible beginning to the completion which Paul cannot perceive, but in which he believes.

Accordingly Paul's expectations are entirely centred around the history of salvation. Everything he has to say about death and the future of the individual is indissolubly linked with this. He makes the inseparability of these two things abundantly clear. When he hears that some members of the church of Corinth are saying that there is no resurrection of the dead, Paul writes as bluntly as possible:

> if there is no resurrection of the dead, then Christ has not been raised; if Christ has not been raised, then our preaching is in vain and your faith is in vain .... if the dead are not raised, then Christ has not been raised. If Christ has not been raised, your faith is futile and you are still in your sins. Then those also who have died in Christ have perished. If in this life we who are in Christ have only hope, we are of all men most to be pitied (1 Cor. 15 : 12-14, 17-19).

An entirely new situation has arisen as a result of Christ's resurrection. It has ushered in a new era. Now an end can come to the irrevocable death of all who are descended from Adam. In Christ all shall be made alive. Christ, who has been raised from the dead proclaims the coming of a new world (1 Cor. 15 : 20-22). He is the beginning, the firstborn of the dead, He is the first to give certainty to the expectation of the great harvest. The resurrection of the dead rests upon the resurrection of Christ (1 Cor. 15 : 20).

Hence Paul by no means only speaks of the resurrection of Christ in a single chapter in answer to a question which gives rise to this subject. The extent to which all his preaching is pervaded by the creed of the resurrection becomes clear, if we take stock both of the number of times he mentions the resurrection when giving a brief outline of his message, and of the hold the reality of the resurrection already has upon his life and upon that of the Church. He addresses himself to the unfaithful Galatians as 'Paul an apostle — not from men nor through man, but through Jesus Christ and God the Father, who raised him from the dead' (Gal. 1 : 1). When informing the Romans of the tenor of his preachings, he refers to these at the beginning of his letter as 'the gospel concerning his Son, who was descended from David according to the flesh and designated son of God in power according to the Spirit of holiness by his resurrection from the dead, Jesus Christ our Lord' (Rom. 1 : 3, 4). Further on in the same epistle he is able to define himself and the Church of Christ thus: 'us who believe in him that raised from the dead Jesus our Lord, who was put to death for our trespasses and raised for our justification' (Rom. 4 : 24, 25). This belief in the resurrection is no mere lip service, it springs from the heart (Rom. 10 : 9) as is witnessed by the Apostle's own life. If Christ had not been raised, then there would be no resurrection of the dead either, and all Paul's struggles with the threat of death before him would have been in vain (1 Cor. 15 : 32). After having been in such great peril in Asia that he despaired of his life and felt as if he had already received his death sentence, he realizes that all this was 'to make us rely not on ourselves but on God who raises the dead' (2 Cor. 1 : 9).

It is true that what we may already know in faith is not yet the whole of salvation. The Spirit which already assures us of these things, and is therefore a guarantee for the Church, the first fruits, [1] points towards the time of fulfilment. Despite the fact that the resurrection of Jesus Christ gives complete certainty that the powers of evil and of death have in principle already been overcome, and hence despite the fact that the outcome of the tremendous struggle which is taking place throughout the cosmos is not uncertain for an instant, the ultimate redemption from the power of death is not yet operative, and can never be so in this world. As yet all men die, even those who are by faith one with Christ who has been raised, and who know the

---

[1] 2 Cor. 1 : 22; 5 : 5; Eph. 1 : 14; Rom. 8 : 23.

power of His resurrection and thereby eternal life. As yet the whole
of creation groans in travail together, so that it awaits with eager
longing the revealing of the sons of God. As yet creation is subjected
to transiency and consequently its hopes go out towards being set free
from its bondage and obtaining the glorious liberty of the children
of God (Rom. 8 : 22, 19, 21). A beginning has been made, visible
to those who believe, but this beginning cries out for fulfilment, the
first fruits augur the full harvest, the pledge anticipates the principal.
The reality, the revelation of which has begun in the resurrection of
Christ, instantaneously invokes the hope for the fulfilment of the
salvation-occurrence at the second coming of Christ, when He will
finally surrender up all dominion and power to God:

> Then comes the end, when he delivers the kingdom to God the Father
> after destroying every rule and every authority and power. For he must
> reign until he has put all his enemies under his feet. The last enemy
> to be destroyed is death. "For God has put all things in subjection under
> his feet." But when it says, "All things are put in subjection under him,"
> it is plain that he is excepted who put all things under him. When all
> things are subjected to him, then the Son himself will also be subjected
> to him who put all things under him, that God may be everything to
> every one (1 Cor. 15 : 24-28).

No wonder Paul automatically mentions the resurrection of Christ
and His second coming in one and the same breath, when giving
briefly the substance of the faith of a church of Gentile origin, which
has embraced the Gospel. He can address this church thus:

> you turned to God from idols, to serve a living and true God, and to wait
> for his Son from heaven, whom he raised from the dead, Jesus who
> delivers us from the wrath to come (1 Thess. 1 : 9, 10).

This great work of salvation, the climax of which is the second
coming of Christ, the resurrection of the dead, the last judgment, the
end of all things, when God will be all in all, is the moving force
behind Paul's life and expectations of what will happen after death.
He never wavered in his expectations. He never admitted thoughts of
an entirely different nature into his central kerygma. There are, however, those who believe that here and there in his letters the contrary
is the case; that in this respect a great variety of ideas are to be found
in Paul. It has been suggested that 2 Cor. 5 : 1-10 and Phil. 1 : 23
in particular diverge profoundly from Paul's customary trend of
thought and are even in direct contradiction to it. In connection with
the first pericope Windisch, for example, argues that Paul's eschatology

keine Einheit, sondern eine Summe von teils selbständigen Konzeptionen, teils einander ergänzenden Fragmenten ist. Paulus greift bald in dies, bald in jenes Fach der Stimmung; so kommt es, dass er gleichzeitig einander ausschliessende Gedankenreihen reproduziert und entwickelt, dass er fundamentale Vorstellungen gelegentlich völlig ausschaltet, dass er aber neue Anschauungen ergreift (mit oder ohne einen für uns erkennbaren Anlass), den Widerspruch mit früher Gelehrtem dabei nicht bemerkt oder nicht aufzuheben sucht, weil er kein Dogmatiker, sondern ein Mann der Traditionen und ein Mann der Intuition und der Impulse ist. [1]

While Bultmann too is of the opinion that Paul deviates greatly from his usual anthropology in 2 Cor. 5 : 1 ff. and comes very close to Hellenistic-Gnostic dualism, and that he is here influenced by the Hellenistic-dualistic depreciation of the body. In Phil 1 : 23, according to Bultmann, Paul comes into conflict with his own doctrine of resurrection, which would go to show how little importance he attributes to notions expressing the belief that the life to come surpasses the life in the flesh in desirability. [2] Hatch also concludes that what Paul writes in 2 Cor. 5 : 1 ff. and Phil. 1 : 23 cannot be reconciled with the notion of the resurrection of the dead, and he infers from this that, like great rivers such as the Nile, Paul's pattern of ideas are a confluence of two streams:

> One of those streams was Judaism, and the other was Hellenism. Judaism and Hellenistic religion were fundamentally different from each other, and the influence of each of them can be seen in St. Paul's view of the future life. [3]

According to some writers the change, which they maintain is to be observed in Paul's expectations, took place between the writing of the first and second epistle to the Corinthians. [4] If this be so, it is of course of the utmost significance to a comparison between Paul and Seneca. Hence it is not surprising that those who adhere to such a belief quote statements of Seneca's, in particular from *Epistle* 102, in

---

[1] H. Windisch, *Der zweite Korintherbrief*, 1924, p. 174.

[2] R. Bultmann, *Theologie des Neuen Testaments*, 1948, pp. 198 f., 342.

[3] W. H. P. Hatch in an article 'St Paul's View of the Future Life' in *Paulus-Hellas-Oikumene*, 1951, p. 96; cf. Dupont op. cit., p. 190; R. de Langhe, 'Judaïsme ou Hellénisme' in *L'attente du Messie*, 1954, p. 179 f.; Fritz Husner, op. cit., p. 71.

[4] According to Holtzmann Paul then moves from a 'populäre Eschatologie' to a 'pneumatische Eschatologie', H. J. Holtzmann, *Lehrbuch der neutestamentlichen Theologie*, II, 1897, pp. 188, 195; cf. W. L. Knox, *St. Paul and the Church of the Gentiles*, 1939, p. 128: 'The Second Epistle to the Corinthians is largely devoted to a complete revision of Pauline eschatology in a Hellenistic sense'. Schoeps also attaches great importance to the change which he believes to have taken place before the writing of 2 Corinthians, H. J. Schoeps, *Paulus*, 1959, p. 102.

connection with a pericope like 2 Cor. 5 : 1-10. [1] However, it is my belief that the history of salvation, which will find fulfilment in the second coming, the resurrection of the dead, and the last judgment, was and always remained the centre of Paul's eschatological expectations, and that Hellenistic ideas never infiltrated his belief in the last things. In this connection it is most significant that even in the allegedly Hellenistically influenced letters Paul apparently held firmly to his belief in the resurrection and the last judgment. He himself declares that his experiences, whereby he has been closely confronted with the possibility of dying, have obliged him to 'rely not on [himself] but on God who raises the dead' (2 Cor. 1 : 9). Accordingly there is nothing to prove that the threat of death has brought about any alteration in his expectations. In this letter, too, as in all his letters, he refers to the coming day of the Lord (2 Cor. 1 : 14). Even in the pericope in which Hellenistic notions have often been claimed to be present, he writes in complete agreement with what has always formed the centre of his expectations: 'We must all appear before the judgment seat of Christ, so that each one may receive good or evil, according to what he has done in the body' (2 Cor. 5 : 10). In the same letter he affirms: 'he who raised the Lord Jesus will raise us also with Jesus and bring us with you into his presence' (2 Cor. 4 : 14). All four chapters of his letter to the Philippians also contain clear references to his expectation that God 'will bring to completion at the day of Jesus Christ' the good work that He has begun (Phil. 1 : 6; cf. 1 : 10; 2 : 16), that there will be a resurrection of the dead (3 : 11), that Jesus 'who will change our lowly body to be like his glorious body' will return from heaven. [2]

It is this unshakable hope which Paul regards as being radically new in the lives of the members of the Church who were formerly Gentiles. When they were still Gentiles and did not yet know Christ they could be considered as 'having no hope and without God in the world' (Eph. 2 : 12). But now Paul can address them saying that their attitude towards the problem of death is no longer that of others 'who have no hope' (1 Thess. 4 : 13).

---

[1] C. F. G. Heinrici, Der zweite Brief an die Korinther, 1900, p. 191; H. Windisch, op. cit., p. 166; A. Plummer, Second Epistle of St. Paul to the Corinthians, 1951, p. 153; C. Clemen, op. cit., p. 335; cf. Kreyher, p. 89; Dupont, op. cit., p. 162.
[2] Phil. 3 : 20 f.; cf. 1 : 28; 3 : 14, 19; 4 : 5, 19; see my articles 'Some Remarks on the γυμνός in 2 Cor. 5 : 3' in Studia Paulina in honorem Johannis de Zwaan, 1953, p. 202 ff., and 'Einige Bemerkungen über den "Zwischenstand" bei Paulus' in New Testament Studies, May 1955, p. 291 ff.

If Paul did not have this hope and faith, he would be helpless, powerless, and desperate in the face of death. For it is not in him to speak kindly of death as if it were really a good friend. For Paul death is not the moment when the spirit is released from the fetters of the body; it is not the natural transition to another state, which takes place so spontaneously and gradually that it should arouse no fear whatsoever; it is not the natural consequence of a law of nature. [1] Paul would not contemplate saying that death has nothing terrifying in itself, or that life is made dear to us by the boon and mercy of death, [2] that death might be called 'the most precious discovery of Nature', *optimum inventum naturae*. [3] On the contrary, for him death without Christ, 'the hope of glory' (Col. 1 : 27), is an enemy which has been able to force its way into God's universe. It is the wages of the sin which dominates the human race: 'As sin came into the world through one man and death through sin, so death spread to all men because all men sinned' (Rom. 6 : 23; 5 : 12). 'By a man came death .... in Adam all die' (1 Cor. 15 : 21, 22). Since the first man sinned, death has, as it were, swept over the human race, swallowing up even 'those whose sins were not like the transgression of Adam, who was a type of the one who was to come.' [4] Mankind groans under its domination (Rom. 6 : 9, 16). Death is not natural, but unnatural in God's universe. It really has no place therein. [5] Hence it can never become a kind and merciful friend; it would always have remained a feared enemy if Jesus Christ had not risen, if this had not deprived death of all hope of an ultimate victory, and removed death's sting, if Christ had not dethroned the last enemy, death, once and for all (1 Cor. 15 : 55, 26).

It is only because he knows this that Paul ventures to speak of dying as a gain (Phil. 1 : 21). The word Paul uses here for 'gain' (κέρδος), is used twice by Socrates in the *Apology,* in the belief that

---

[1] Cf. Seneca N.Q. vi. 32. 12; cf. W. Nestle, *Griechische Studien,* 1948, p. 653: 'Der Tod ist für ihn [ancient man] ein notwendiger, gottgewollter Naturvorgang, für den Christen dagegen der Sünde Sold.'

[2] *Marc.* 20. 3.

[3] *Marc.* 20. 1; *Marc.* 20. 1-3 has been called 'the most passionate eulogy to death ever written by a Roman', H. H. Janssen, *Gedachten over het lijden in klassieke oudheid en Christendom,* 1949, p. 16.

[4] Rom. 5 : 14; cf. Rom. 8 : 13; Gal. 6 : 8; Rom. 6 : 21; 7 : 5; 8 : 6.

[5] Cf. John A. T. Robinson, op. cit., 'For animals to die is natural; for man to die is unnatural' (p. 34). 'Death is an intruder in God's universe: it entered upon its reign over man from outside' (p. 35).

he can deprive death of its fearfulness by representing it as a probably dreamless sleep (*Apol.* 40, d, e). Paul knows of no other reason for calling death a gain than the fact of the victory over death which has already taken place, and which will in time lead to a complete conquest. Without this victory death would not be a good, an adiaphoron: it would be impossible to imagine a worse evil than death. That Paul now and then expresses the desire to depart this world arises from his knowledge that he would then be with Christ, which is preferable by far (Phil. 1 : 23). Death is dominated by the idea of 'being with the Lord':

> So we are always of good courage; we know that while we are at home in the body we are away from the Lord, for we walk by faith, not by sight. We are of good courage, and we would rather be away from the body and at home with the Lord (2 Cor. 5 : 6-8).

This notion also dominates the prospect of the ultimate glory: 'and so we shall always be with the Lord' (1 Thess. 4 : 17).

Hence it is out of the question that Paul should consider death as such as a deliverance, because it is the separation of body and soul. It cannot even be established with certainty from his letters whether he visualized death as the detachment of the soul from the body, and it is most noteworthy that Paul never even mentions the word 'soul' in those passages in which he speaks of his expectations. He probably believed that after death the soul would continue to live on separately for a time, namely for the period that elapses between the death of the individual and the resurrection of the dead and the last judgment. For it is plain that he does not expect the immediate resurrection of the individual. His answer to the question put to him by the church at Thessalonica is proof of this (1 Thess. 4 : 15-18). In the intervening time man preserves his identity in nakedness (2 Cor. 5 : 3), which probably means in the soul detached from the body. However, it is not surprising that Paul throws no light upon this intervening period. For his faith enables him to look beyond this period as it were, and to focus his attention upon what is truly essential, the coming of Christ, the resurrection of the dead and the last judgment. And this resurrection means resurrection in the body; not, it is true, of man as he is on earth — 'flesh and blood cannot inherit the kingdom of God' (1 Cor. 15 : 50) — but nevertheless in the body (1 Cor. 15 : 35 ff.), in 'a spiritual body' (1 Cor. 15 : 44). For then Christ will 'change our lowly body to be like his glorious body, by the power which enables him even to subject all things to himself'

(Phil. 3 : 21). And because Paul longs for the ultimate glory, he hopes that the period between death and resurrection will be brief. He desires to be covered as soon as possible in the body of the resurrection, in order that the nakedness may be of short duration (2 Cor. 5 : 2-4). [1] The contrast between Paul and Seneca once again emerges most strikingly here. For Seneca the separation of the glorious soul from the contemptible body is precisely what makes death so desirable, and for him, as for Celsus [2] and Porphyry, [3] it would have been unthinkable that anyone could after death, which liberates the soul from the body, wish to be covered again by a body. The final liberation of the soul from the body, [4] so that the soul is at last no longer burdened by the body and can enjoy heavenly things without inpediment, which is what Seneca finds so desirable in death, is for Paul the temporary state of 'nakedness', which he wishes to be as brief as possible and from which he apparently recoils. [5] While what Paul longs for with all the ardour of his faith, the resurrection of the dead in a new spiritual, transfigured body, would strike Seneca as a relapse into a state which death had finally superseded. Here too it is clear that 'der Eschatologe muss fast alle seine theologischen Geheimnisse verraten.' [6] In expressing their views on the after-life, both Paul and Seneca disclose the mysteries of their doctrine concerning God and man, and in so doing also reveal their soteriology.

---

[1] This contrast would cease to exist if we were to accept the theory of Earle Ellis who interprets the 'nakedness' of 2 Cor. 5 : 3 on the basis of Old Testament eschatology: 'In the O.T. nakedness (or being stripped) and shame often denote the guilty under the glaring light of God's judgment.' A drawback to this interpretation is, in my opinion, the fact that Paul would then in the two words οὐ γυμνοὶ be broaching a theme that is dealt with nowhere else in this pericope, unless one takes v. 1 to refer not to the body of the resurrection but to 'the righteous Body of Christ'. At all events this interpretation proves once more that much will always remain uncertain in the exegesis of this pericope, E. Earle Ellis, 'ii Cor. 5. 1-10 in Pauline eschatology', N.T.S. Apr. 1960, pp. 211-24; cf. also A. Feuillet, 'La demeure céleste et la destinée des chrétiens (ii Cor. 5. 1-10)' in Recherches de Science Religieuse, 1956, pp. 161-92, 360-402 and R. F. Hettlinger, '2 Cor. 5. 1-10' in The Scottish Journal of Theology, 1957, p. 174 ff.; W. D. Stacey, op. cit., p. 189 f.

[2] See e.g. Origen, Contra Celsum 5. 14.

[3] See e.g. Frag. 94.

[4] Seneca uses the same image as Paul when he says of death: Mors nos aut consumit aut exuit (strips us bare). Emissis meliora restant onere detracto ...., Ep. 24. 18, or counsels Marcia not to visit her son's grave, for: pessima eius et ipsi molestissima istic iacent, ossa cineresque, non magis illius partes quam vestes aliaque tegimenta corporum, Marc. 25. 1; cf. Ep. 92. 13; 102. 25; Fritz Husner, op. cit., pp. 85-89.

[5] Cf. Th. Schreiner, op. cit., pp. 82[1], 123.

[6] P. Althaus, Die letzten Dinge, [4]1933, p. viii.

So we see that there is a profound and lasting contrast between Paul and Seneca. Paul may occasionally have derived terms and expressions from the Hellenistic world around him and even from the Stoic school,[1] he may now and then use phrases which are at first sight reminiscent of Seneca, but he always makes them instrumental to the particular purpose of his own preachings. Seneca's language would sometimes seem to have an affinity with that of the Apostle, while certain of his notions would also seem to coincide with Paul's, but on looking deeper we find that he even then pursues his own particular line of thought.

This study has, it is hoped, shown that great care must be taken when drawing parallels. Naturally it is not always without value to assemble, as is done in many commentaries, quotations from ancient writers, including Seneca, which correspond with texts in the Pauline epistles. However, in order to determine the true significance of such statements, both Paul's words and those of the writer quoted must be read in their context. The same words do not always mean the same thing. On the contrary, in this study the fact has time and again emerged that superficial resemblances are precisely what, on closer examination, reveal the underlying difference most clearly.

There was to come a time when the resemblance between Christianity and Stoic philosophy was no longer restricted to a few words and expressions, but also extended to notions and trends of thought, sometimes even of a very fundamental nature. The earliest stage in this process may already be observed in the writings of some of the apostolic fathers and apologists; it is even more noticeable in certain of the ancient Fathers of the Church, [2] and it has continued up to the present day, sometimes openly, sometimes more concealed. It need scarcely be said that it can be of great importance to ascertain by means of a comparison between Paul and Seneca that this process was not ushered in by Paul.

---

[1] συνείδησις, φύσις, τὰ μὴ καθήκοντα (Rom. 1 : 28), αὐτάρκης (Phil. 4 : 11), συμφέρειν, τὸ σύμφορον (1 Cor. 6 : 12; 10 : 23; 2 Cor. 8 : 10; 12 : 1; 1 Cor. 7 : 35; 10 : 33); cf. Joh. Weiss, Das Urchristentum, 1917, p. 134; W. D. Stacey, op. cit., p. 36, 39.

[2] The influence of Stoic thought upon the writings of the ancient Fathers of the Church is dealt with at length in e.g. J. Stelzenberger, Die Beziehungen der frühchristlichen Sittenlehre zur Ethik der Stoa, 1933. This study is, however, restricted, as the title indicates, to the field of ethics; cf. also Spanneut, op. cit.

INDEX LOCORUM

PAUL

SENECA
EPISTULAE MORALES

DE PROVIDENTIA

DE CONSTANTIA

DE IRA

DE CLEMENTIA

DE CONSOLATIONE AD MARCIAM

DE VITA BEATA

DE OTIO

DE TRANQUILLITATE ANIMI

DE BREVITATE VITAE

DE CONSOLATIONE AD POLYBIUM

DE CONSOLATIONE AD HELVIAM

DE BENEFICIIS

NATURALES QUAESTIONES

INDEX AUCTORUM